D1150225

A TRAVELLER'S HISTORY OF SCOTLAND

A TRAVELLER'S HISTORY OF
SCOTLAND

JOHN BURKE

JOHN MURRAY

© John Burke 1990
First published in 1990
by John Murray (Publishers) Ltd
50 Albemarle Street, London W1X 4BD

All rights reserved.
Unauthorized duplication
contravenes applicable laws

British Library Cataloguing in Publication Data
Burke, John, *1922–*
A traveller's history of Scotland.
1. Scotland – Visitors' guides
I. Title
914.11'04858

ISBN 0–7195–4776–8   (cased)
ISBN 0 7195–4840–3   (limp)

Printed and bound in Great Britain by
Butler & Tanner Ltd, Frome and London

Contents

Illustrations

Acknowledgements

The author and publisher wish to thank the following for permission to reproduce photographs:

Plates 1, 2, 7 and 8, Crown copyright; 3, Dumfries and Galloway Tourist Board; 4, reproduced with permission from John Slezer, *Theatrum Scotiae* (1693) in the Aberdeen University Library; 5, Guildhall Library; 6, 9, 10 and 11, Mansell Collection; 12, United Distillers.

Preface

THE MAIN aim of this book is not to provide yet another tourist guide to picturesque scenes with a few brief background notes on castles, cathedrals and battlefields encountered along the way. Nor is it simply a potted history of Scotland. Rather, it attempts to relate that history to its natural and man-made setting, showing how the landscapes and townscapes we see today have influenced and been influenced by human needs and human conflicts. In order to enjoy a region, or indeed a whole country, the responsive traveller will soon become aware that history and topography are indivisible, best appreciated not in piecemeal snippets but in a slow, interweaving growth. Generations of ghosts still walk through glens and over hills whose contours fashioned their destiny. They themselves refashioned fields and settlements, built walls and dug ditches, and left their names on monuments, streets and fortresses. Each aspect enhances the flavour of another.

A strictly chronological history of Scotland is, despite its complexities, a not impossible task. Many such have been written, from many conflicting viewpoints. Equally, a reasonably logical guided tour of the countryside can be devised, touching on prehistoric and historic sites and on scenic splendours. Combining the two is far from simple. Important events were not all tidily confined within any one region at any one time. Men and women who coloured history had an exasperating habit of moving from one part of the country to another; and both history and countryside can at times overlap, or diverge, or slip perversely out of sequence.

Robert the Bruce may have been born in Ayrshire; but he was a lord of Annandale in Dumfriesshire. He appears at different times in Galloway, in Perthshire, and outside Stirling. A map of the travels of Mary, Queen of Scots, within her realm, or of the wanderings of Prince Charles Edward would involve a fine confusion of dates and places interspersed with awkward gaps. Nevertheless I have tried in the following pages to weave a coherent historical thread through a not too awkwardly distorted framework of regions, with inevitable cross-references to another time or region when the logic of the story demands it. Major themes are dealt with, wherever possible, in one appropriate chapter even though there are relevant events or traditions in other parts of the land. For instance, religious conflicts, especially the story of the Covenanters, are concentrated in the section devoted to Dumfries and Galloway; but the basic story affects other regions, and the theme has to be picked up again in the Grampian chapter. Similarly, rather than scatter fragmentary references to the fishing industry throughout a succession of coastal regions, I have chosen to focus on this subject in the Grampian chapter, but with cross-references also to the harbours of East Fife and elsewhere.

Many splendid sights which the traveller will find standing close together are often divided by considerable stretches of time. For example, a first-century broch may be within a few hundred yards of a medieval castle, or be incorporated within the earthworks of a settlement some 2,000 years older. To avoid squeezing them arbitrarily together in some contrived paragraph, a select list of sites, buildings and museums has been added at the end of each chapter. These contain additional, complementary material to that already dealt with in the specific chapter, and are not merely a summary of what has gone before. In some cases they refer, historically or geographically, to subjects covered in another chapter but related also to this particular region.

In explorations over the years I have met, and been helpfully directed in many a rewarding direction by, too many people to list here. In particular, though, I must for one reason and another – or a hundred others – thank David and Rosemary Bythell; Michael Davison; Jean Elliot; Martin Heller; Brian Innes; Macallan-Glenlivet Distillery; Peter and Shirley Massey; Grant McIntyre (without whom the book would never have been started); Dr Michael Robson; the Border Library and Middle March Centre in Hexham; a number of patient librarians in Edinburgh, Langholm, Norwich and London; and my wife Jean for her research, note-taking on bumpy roads, rainswept moors and breezy street corners, and so many other contributions during all our travels.

At proof stage I must also add a last-minute tribute to Gail Pirkis, whose editing has been of a standard I have hitherto not encountered: observant, creative, good-humoured in the face of indignant argument and, it has to be confessed, all too often right.

'To travel hopefully', said that admirable Scottish writer Robert Louis Stevenson, 'is a better thing than to arrive.' I can only hope that readers of these pages will be encouraged to travel widely through Scotland and will be happy with what they find on arrival at each destination. If on the journey they are tempted to stray down some alluring byway, historical or scenic, which has not been mentioned in these pages, it is a temptation on no account to be resisted. The book has been designed as a stimulus and not a route map to be rigidly observed. It is too late to alter the facts of history; not too late to find some fresh light cast upon them in the landscape, all the more stimulating because of the way in which each facet reflects upon another..

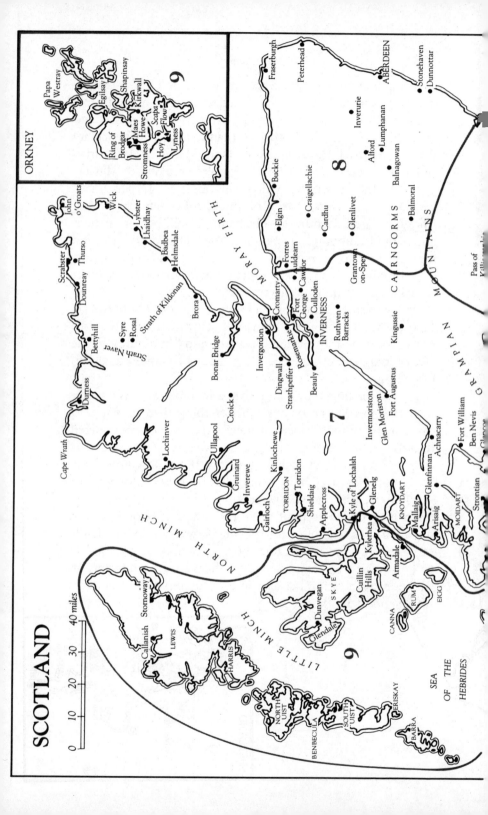

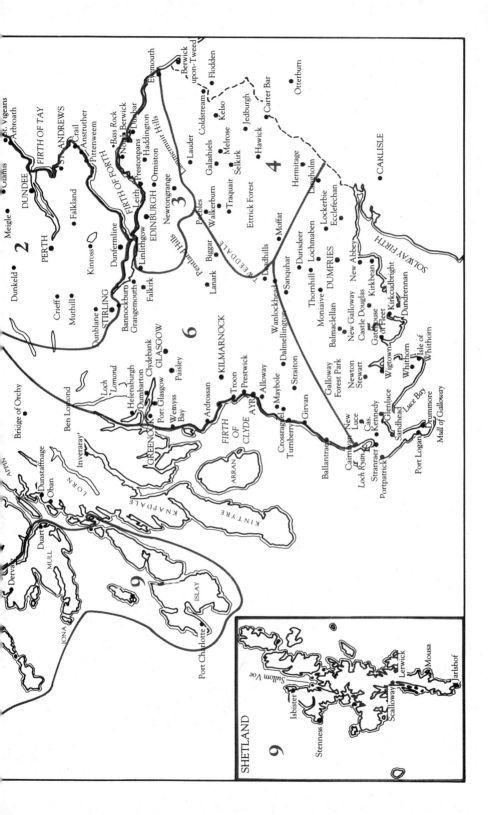

1

Incomers and Settlers

APPROACHING SOME of the more forbidding coasts of
Scotland in a modern vessel, one must surely marvel at
the temerity of those prehistoric voyagers who crossed the sea
in flimsy boats and refused to be deterred by lowering cliffs or
storm-lashed, perilous rocks. Some may have regretted the
excursion and eventually turned back for home. But once
ashore, others seem to have had little difficulty in establishing
new homes.

Many of the first traces of human habitation in what we
now call Scotland have been identified from bones and stone
implements found in caves along the approaches to the eastern
firths of Forth and Tay. These and remnants of temporary
nomadic camps date from between 8000 and 6000 BC. In the
west, hunter-gatherers from Ireland have left plentiful flint
knives and arrowheads, deer antlers and whalebones, around
the shores of Luce Bay in Galloway. Others found their way
into the western reaches of Argyll, also using shore caves as a
base from which they went out seasonally fishing, hunting and
gathering fruit, nuts and birds' eggs. A whole warren of such
caves was rediscovered in the cliffs during the nineteenth-
century expansion of Oban.

This peripatetic life gave way to the more settled communities of Neolithic farmers, and by the time of the Bronze
Age their hut circles had become substantial enough for the
foundations, post-holes and fragments of stone wall to survive
into our own time. In the Tayside uplands alone there are

around 200 recognizable agricultural settlements from 1500 BC onwards. Both hunters and farmers fished in the rivers, lochs or sea from skin-boats and log-boats, and further incomers braved the waters between Ireland and Britain in similar small craft.

Much low-lying land which today is fertile was in the past an exasperating jigsaw of bog, burn and loch, difficult to negotiate, let alone exploit. Mountainsides and glens with their rocks only sparsely coated with acidic, unproductive soil offered different problems. Incomers had to combine harsh subsistence farming with hunting in forest and stream. The marshy lands around Stirling and Bannockburn must have been inhospitable to these early settlers, but were to prove of incalculable worth to fourteenth-century patriots determined to assert their independence from southern predators.

As successive batches of immigrants strove to carve out their own territories and perhaps take over existing farm and hunting lands by force, the already established settlers built impressive hill-forts to watch over their possessions and shelter people and livestock in time of emergency. But their earliest important memorials gave priority to honouring the dead and to their religious practices.

The most ancient burial chambers consisted of huge stone slabs forming a chamber with entrances through which further corpses might be introduced. These passage-graves were covered with cairns of stone, frequently mixed with shells in coastal districts. There were also gallery-graves, sometimes called Clyde cairns because of their prevalence around the Clyde estuary, and very much resembling Irish burial chambers in their rectangular construction and internal division into separate compartments. Simpler interments took place in smaller round cairns, common in the Western Isles. Later the practice of cremation led to tidier storage of ashy remains in cinerary urns, though still ritually accompanied by pottery beakers and food bowls, animals and birds, and even helpings of fish to succour the departed on their way.

Examples of all types are plentiful in different regions: the long cairn of Balnagowan in Aberdeenshire, fragmented into heaps of stones lined up over some 230 feet; the well-preserved Clyde cairn of Brackley in Kintyre, excavated in 1952 to reveal both inhumation and cremation procedures, with food vessels and jet necklace beads; and the protracted cemetery of Nether Largie tombs below Kilmartin village in Argyll. On a slope high above Wigtown Bay in Dumfries and Galloway, nearly always fretted by a breeze or whistling more stridently in the wind, is an especially fine duo of 5,000-year-old tombs called Cairnholy.

A circular type known as Clava tombs can be found at the northern end of the Great Glen, many without an entrance, which would seem to signify that each was used only once and then sealed. The most beautifully situated group of these is at Balnuaren of Clava, off a byroad below Culloden. Under sheltering trees stand three cairns and stone circles, worn yet awesomely dignified after more than 5,000 years. They are believed to have been family shrines rather than communal burial places.

Quite apart from the sturdiness of their burial mounds, the settlers made sure of leaving solid, lasting tributes to their deities and their belief in certain seasonal rhythms. Standing stones on their own, in groups, or in circular henge patterns often seem an integral part of the rocky landscape, growing out of the earth itself or lying at ease upon it; but the work of human hands can be detected in the cup-and-ring decorations on some, the geometrical arrangement of others. The three standing stones of Lundin Links in Fife now watch over play on a golf course, though without providing any additional hazard. Like many such groups, they have acquired a patina of legend: during the nineteenth century there were those who referred to them as Druid stones, others who thought they were of Roman origin, and yet others who asserted they must be the gravestones of Danish invaders vanquished by Banquo and Macbeth. Inevitably there is also speculation, as with Stonehenge and with the Ring of Brodgar on Orkney, about a possible astronomical significance.

In Caithness there are many upright monoliths from the Bronze Age, some standing alone, others in patterns suffused with some ancient significance. Most bewildering of all are the parallel ranks of 200 small slabs on the 'Hill o' Many Stanes' at Mid Clyth. At Raigmore, near Inverness, a stone circle almost 60 feet in diameter was raised around 1600 BC over a much earlier Stone Age settlement.

A later use of stone can be found in everyday rather than religious or funerary building. The souterrains so plentiful in Angus settlements were tunnel-like underground chambers lined with slabs and probably roofed with timber, supporting further slabs. Archaeologists who first came across them assumed that since these 'earth houses' were so small, their inhabitants must have been midgets. Later research showed that they were in fact storehouses and workshops, attached to hut-dwelling communities during the first and second centuries AD: quernstones were found in such a cellar at Barns of Airlie, and a chamber in a Carlungie souterrain seems to have been used for both stone and metal working. In cases where the souterrain was too large for storage of one village's produce, it may have been used by the chief of an area as a sort of tithe barn for goods paid to him as tax.

During the first century AD a number of homesteads on islands and in coastal regions were fortified, possibly against Roman slave traders. These brochs (a word derived from the Old Norse *borg* – a citadel – later transmuted into *borough*) nearly all followed one basic pattern: that of a large circular dwelling with drystone walls up to 15 feet thick, and some of them as much as 50 feet high. Chambers were built into the walls, and remnants of ledges suggest support for wooden floors. Some incorporated timber-framed lean-to houses, and the central open space could accommodate livestock. Among better preserved examples is the almost complete broch on the island of Mousa, in Shetland. One at Edinshall in Lothian is part of a whole complex of settlement and hill-fort, the broch itself suggesting a military role with a guardroom to either side of the entrance. This hillside defence system was probably set up by the Votadini, a tribe whose continual harassment by the neighbouring Selgovae led it to seek alliance with Rome at a very early stage.

Such hill-forts of successive races or groups living uneasily side by side continued to dominate the landscape during recurrent tribal and racial struggles for power. A healthy number still survive in spite of the activities of farmers, planners and roadbuilders in search of cheap metal. In Lothian, for example, there are Castlelaw Hill near Glencorse, and the superb example of Chesters Hill a mile from Drem; Barry Hill in Perthshire and the two forts of Brown Caterthun and White Caterthun in Angus; and the grass-covered expanse of Knock Farril above Strathpeffer. The main *oppidum* or tribal centre of the Votadini was excavated in the early years of this century on Traprain Law, a steep volcanic upthrust from the East Lothian plain. The presence of a rich hoard of Roman silver and Roman pottery of the Flavian period shows the strength of the tribe's alliance with and compliance with the dictates of Rome.

The Romans left fewer substantial marks on what they called Caledonia than they did on southern Britain, largely because so many of their attempts to establish regional centres collapsed when they were recalled to deal with unrest in southern Britain, or even back to Continental Europe and to Rome itself. Resources had to be overstretched to maintain even a foothold north of the Tay, in wild mountainous regions inhabited by 'half-naked savages with reddish hair and large limbs', as Tacitus put it.

The first major campaigns into the unknown were led in AD 79 by Gnaeus Julius Agricola, whose son-in-law, Tacitus, wrote a hagiographical account of the proceedings which is infuriatingly vague about the actual geography. The culmination of the invasion was a mighty battle against an alliance of Caledonian tribes under Calgacus at a place the historian called Mons Graupius. He implies that it was close to the sea in the far north: but what, to Romans venturing into uncharted territory, was the *far* north? Some scholars have suggested a site near Inverness; others the junction of the rivers Tay and Isla. Recent theories favour identification of the mountain with Bennachie, close to a Roman marching camp revealed in the late 1970s by aerial photography at Durno, 15 miles north-east of Aberdeen. Tacitus records that just before his death the defeated Calgacus denounced the Romans as 'Pillagers of the world . . . to robbery, butchery and rapine they give the lying name of "government"; they create desolation and call it peace.' His descendants were to have good reason for echoing such sentiments in relation to the behaviour of Henry VIII's troops in Scotland.

After Agricola's recall to Rome, the will to hold on to large parts of the north seems to have ebbed. Tacitus lamented that Britain had been 'completely conquered and immediately thrown away'. Excavations have shown that the extensive legionary fortress near Inchtuthil, north of Perth, had had to be evacuated as early as AD 87 before construction had been completed. Buildings were hastily demolished, and ironwork likely to be of use to the natives was buried in a deep pit. Although the Romans maintained a number of marching camps across the Lowlands such as those at Pennymuir, Roxburgh, and Glenlochar in Kirkudbrightshire, signal stations on heights such as the Eildon Hills, and sentinel forts substantially reinforced at one time and another, these were subjected to repeated tribal attacks and occasionally a combined assault.

Two major constructions were the forts at Dalswinton north of Dumfries and Newstead near Melrose, close beside the major Roman thoroughfare of Dere Street across the Border. Newstead, known to the Romans as Trimontium, has in the present century yielded up wonderful finds including shoes, sandals, jewellery and the iron helmet of a cavalryman. But no Romanized townships sprang up; there were no farmstead villas of the type found in southern Britain; and the sheer cost in fortification, roadworks and supplies required to maintain a presence in such bleak and unrewarding country finally defeated even the most assiduous empire-builders.

As if to seal off the barbarians and leave them to their own

devices, Hadrian's Wall was built from Solway to Tyne between
AD 122 and 127. This, too, was so frequently overrun that by
AD 143 it was decided to attempt another defence further
north, across the narrower neck of land between Forth and
Clyde. This Antonine Wall, named after Antoninus Pius, was
mainly a turf rampart on stone foundations behind a ditch,
with barracks and forts at two-mile intervals. It proved of little
value, and had to be abandoned within twenty years. Examples
of centurial stones or distance slabs with which different legionary detachments marked sections they had constructed are to
be seen in the National Museum of Antiquities in Edinburgh
and the Hunterian Museum in Glasgow. It is interesting to
note a shortening of the working distances at the Clyde end
of the rampart: the menace from attackers over the Kilpatrick
Hills was such that working parties had to keep protectively
closer together.

Not merely the Antonine Wall but Hadrian's Wall fell to
hostile tribes. In AD 208 the Emperor Severus took personal
charge of a fleet into the Firth of Forth and from it led an
expedition across Fife, over the Tay valley, and on into the
ever inhospitable north to put an end to these depredations.
The enemy cunningly avoided direct confrontation and concentrated on guerrilla warfare. Severus managed to get as
far as the Montrose region and perhaps briefly beyond that:
tantalizingly, in 1869 labourers on the Duke of Sutherland's
railway extension to Helmsdale and ultimately to Thurso in
distant Caithness unearthed a collection of Roman bronze
coins in a region never held and supposedly never reached by
imperial forces. In any case, after Severus's death at York in
AD 211 the momentum was lost, and again the legions
withdrew, after making a number of treaties which were not
observed for long.

Towards the end of the third century a new name appeared
in Roman records, though the people to whom it was applied
had established themselves in the country much earlier. The
significant factor was that a number of racial groups incorporating pre-Celtic and Celtic influences from France and

Ireland were now showing signs of working together and establishing not merely tribal *oppida* but a virtual kingdom to pit against their rivals, Roman or otherwise. Because of their habit of painting and tattooing themselves, these people were dubbed *Picti* ('painted men').

They were notoriously warlike, subduing or assimilating lesser tribes and raiding sketchy Roman settlements to loot silver and make it into ornaments to add to their warpaint. Their federation was probably governed by a number of minor rulers, but these gradually came to offer tribute to a paramount king. This kingdom spread itself over Scotland north of the Forth and Clyde and for a time seems to have included Orkney.

As the Roman hold on Britain slackened, Picts joined with other Gaelic-speaking incomers from Ireland known as *Scotti* – a word meaning simply pirates. Although for a time they were merely raiders, these Celtic cousins had ambitions to acquire land and permanent residence, and were as ready to fight the Picts as to co-operate with them. Originating from the northern part of County Antrim in Ireland, anciently known as Dalriada, they set about establishing another Dalriada in Argyll and the nearer islands, including Iona. In the sixth century AD they fortified what was to become one of the most symbolic sites in national rather than regional history.

Dunadd fort clings to an isolated rocky hillock near Kilmartin, starkly visible from the road between Lochgilphead and Oban, above what must once have been a naturally protective boggy valley. There are remains of four levels of wall, the lowest of which would have had wooden gates to protect its main entrance. But ruined walls are, at best, just ruined walls. What Dunadd has most provocatively to offer is a hollowed-out bowl in one slab of rock, accompanied by carvings of a boar, the outline of a footprint, and several lines of ogam inscription.

The ogam script, using clusters of strokes at angles above, below and across a base line to shape its 20 basic characters, was commonest in its pure form in Ireland. On the Isle of Man it was mixed with runic characters, and with Latin in

Wales. Slight variations found in the Isles are usually known as Pictish ogams. At Dunadd the carvers made use of fissures in the rock itself as their base line. No reliable interpretation of these scripts has yet been established, but in the Dunadd fort the wording must surely, along with the bowl and footprint, be related to coronation rituals of the Dalriadic kings rather than to the Picts.

Distinctions of tribes and languages become very blurred when we try to catch their echoes from far across the centuries. Very roughly it would seem that the predominant tongues in what came to be called Scotland were, from 600 BC to 300 BC, Early Celtic; from then until AD 800, Pictish Celtic; from AD 800 to 1200, Gaelic Celtic; and thereafter, English. From the sixth century AD onwards the country fell, with frequent incursions from varying directions, into five main spheres of influence. In the north and east were the Picts, their realm divided into seven main provinces or sub-kingdoms. In Argyll the Dalriadic Scots were building up their strength. The region of Strathclyde, spreading south from the Clyde to encompass Cumberland and Westmorland, was in the hands of Britons speaking Cumbric, a Welsh form of Gaelic which gave Cumbria its name. In the south-west corner, Galloway was a land of Gaelic-speaking Picts.

A constant threat from the east was the Anglo-Saxon kingdom of Bernicia, reaching from the Tyne to the Forth and amalgamating in the early seventh century with Deira to form Northumbria. In AD 685 King Ecgfrith decided to expand his realm still further by a large-scale attack on the Pictish lands. At Nechtansmere, near Forfar in Angus, he and his troops were trapped in a narrow pass, Ecgfrith himself was killed, and thereafter Northumbria abandoned any attempts at invasion. It was not, however, until the battle of Carham in 1016 on Northumbrian territory that the Scots made their own effective inroads and claimed Lothian for themselves. By then its established language had become a form of English referred to by Gaelic speakers as 'Inglis', then 'Scots'. The dialect which inspired much Scottish literature came to be known, sometimes admiringly and sometimes mockingly, as 'Lallans' (Lowlands). Yet it is the 'capital of the Highlands', Inverness, whose inhabitants boast of speaking the purest English in the British Isles; and in the Black Isle fishing village of Avoch (pronounced 'Ouch') a unique local patois is variously ascribed to an influx of Cornishmen long ago or to seamen from Spanish Armada wrecks.

Although languages or local inflections may have been disguised or distorted, the traveller can often catch a resonance of the most influential peoples in a region through its place names. It is now generally accepted that words prefixed by *pett* or *pit* (similar to the Welsh and Cornish *peth* for 'thing' or 'piece') are of Pictish origin, as in places such as Pitlochry ('stony share') and Pittenweem ('share of the cave'). The greatest incidence of such names is in the region between the Forth and Inverness, known to be the main Pictish area. Cumbric produced a prefix as familiar in Strathclyde as in Wales: *caer*, meaning a fort or, more generally, a dwelling-place. Caerlanrig signifies a settlement in a glade; the embattled frontier city of Carlisle, fought over so often by Scots and English, is a blend of *caer* with the Roman name for the old tribal centre of Luguvalium (Luguvalos's town), which the natives adapted as *luel*.

Three of the commonest Gaelic elements are *baile, achadh* and *cill*. *Baile*, signifying a farmstead, is still in common use as the description for small crofting communities. The most familiar corruption of it appears in Balgowan ('the smith's steading'), Balmalcolm ('Malcolm's steading' – personal ownership was frequently declared), and Balnab (probably 'the abbot's place' because of its proximity to the early Christian settlement at Whithorn). *Achadh*, a field, generally takes the form of *Auch, Auchen* or *Auchin* : Auchtermuchty ('pig-breeding field'); Auchenbegg ('small field'); and Auchintoul ('field of the barn'). *Cill* is more common in its *Kil* form, meaning a church, often attached to the name of a saint or bishop, as in Kilpatrick or Kilmartin. Later such formations had to share honours with those designated *Kirk*, of Norse origin, as in Kirkpatrick (dedicated to the same saint as Kilpatrick) and Kirkcudbright, the church of St Cuthbert. Norse and Gaelic combine in Kirkintilloch, derived from *tulach*, meaning a low hill or ridge.

Other place-name ingredients which the traveller and map-reader will frequently encounter are:

Aber	a river mouth
Ban	white
Dhu	black
Eccle	a church
Eilean	an island
Haugh	alluvial land beside a river
Holm	a small island
Inch	an island
Inver	a river mouth
Kin	a head or headland
Mor	great
Ross	a forest
Strath	a wide valley

During the eighth and early ninth centuries the Vikings pillaged the coasts, sacking the monasteries of Lindisfarne and Iona. They had already acquired bases in Orkney and Shetland, and began settling there and along the north and west of Scotland. Places associated with them are identifiable in the adaptation of *stathr* or *bolstadr*, a farm, into the suffix 'ster', as in Camster and Shebster in Caithness, and 'bister' as in Fladdabister in Shetland. Wick, on its own or as a suffix, comes from *vik*, a bay or sheltered inlet.

In spite of the pagan savagery of the Vikings, Celtic Christianity kept a hold on the country. St Ninian and St Columba had converted Picts and Dalriadic Scots during the fifth and sixth centuries. It was still, however, dynastic and political considerations rather than religion which began drawing Picts and Scots into a closer relationship.

For some time after the battle of Nechtansmere the Picts had remained the more powerful of the two. Then, because of their geographical position, they were seriously weakened by the Viking onslaught down the east coast. Leadership also presented problems because of complicated rules of inheritance. The Pictish succession was not by primogeniture but by tanistry, a system in which the senior and fittest member of the same blood was appointed heir, frequently from the matrilineal side. This had the advantage of assuring leadership by a strong adult rather than the possibility of a child inheriting – a hazard which was so frequently to affect the later Stuart dynasty. On the other hand it raised the danger of an ambitious cousin, too impatient to wait for the present ruler's death, committing regicide; and there were many instances of this.

In 844 Kenneth MacAlpin, a Dalriadic Scot on his father's side but with a mother of Pictish royal blood, became king of both the Picts and the Scots. Distinctions were soon lost, and after a spell of being known as Alba the country became once and for all Scotland, though some of its boundaries were still in a state of flux. What has most puzzled students of the period is the complete disappearance of the Picts as a distinct entity within a very short time. Their administrators ceased to hold any sway. Their language has survived only in fragments of place names, and many of those are arguable. No written records exist. What they did incontestably leave were remarkable examples of those hard-wearing memorials which we have already observed from prehistoric times: stones.

Pictish symbol stones are not merely raw chunks of rock standing upright or propped across burial mounds. The carvings on many of them are skilled, sophisticated and often breathtaking in their beauty of line. Many carry intricate designs incorporating discs, crescents, arches and horseshoes; others are alive with grotesque or naturalistic beasts and human figures. A number have ogam inscriptions. The placing of such stones often suggests they may have served as boundary markers between tribes, and the linking of different symbols could signify intermarriage between families. At some stage Christian symbols, especially in the form of crosses adorned with elaborate convolutions, began to find their way into the carvings, with a striking similarity to designs known in the Anglo-Saxon monasteries of Northumbria. The Maiden Stone near Chapel of Garioch, about 5 miles north-west of Inverurie, carries interlaced panels with the figure of a man standing between two contorted fish, and designs on the back include the characteristic 'Z-rod' and mirror and comb symbols. There is a fine cross-slab by the roadside at Aberlemno in Angus, and an ornate one in the actual churchyard of the village. A stone by another roadside, on the isle of Skye, served for years as a door jamb in the Tote shoemaker's house until rescued in about 1880.

Although there are major collections in the National Museums of Scotland in Queen Street, Edinburgh, and the museums at Meigle, near Coupar Angus, and St Andrew's cathedral, one of the most attractive settings in which to study such stones is the row of cottages below the church at St Vigeans, just outside Arbroath. The examples here were originally memorial slabs from a church existing on the site before the Norman and medieval buildings. Used as part of the walls in the later fabric, a number are badly mutilated as a result. Some display robed and seated clerics. One must have served as a recumbent tombstone, since it has a slot at one end to hold a vertical cross. The most tantalizing is known as the Drosten Stone because of the remains of a Roman inscription:

DROSTEN
IREUORET
(E)TTFOR
CUS

It seems most likely that three personal names are commemorated here – Drosten, Uoret and Forcus – but one would dearly love to know the significance, on the back, of a hooded archer holding what appears to be a crossbow.

At Rosemarkie in the Black Isle, north-east of Inverness, a remarkable number of stones were found within a few hundred yards of the present Groam House museum, indicating past importance as a tribal and then a religious centre. In the early twelfth century this was in fact the cathedral town of the Ross diocese, superseded in the following century by Fortrose. The museum houses an informative display of stones, with some of the engraved patterns picked out in colour by the American artist Marianna Lines, who has tried to achieve authentic hues by using natural pigment dyes. The gem of the collection is the 7-foot high pink sandstone Rosemarkie cross-slab, a riot of abstract patterns, interlace, and animal heads, with a cross sunk into panels near the top.

Of all symbolic stones, one has laid an overpowering weight upon Scottish history and Scottish sentiment. Its legend goes back to the book of Genesis. While Jacob was dreaming of Jacob's Ladder at Beth-El, his head was pillowed on a rock which upon waking he set up as a holy monument. This was taken by him and his sons as a sacred treasure when they went into Egypt. During the Exodus it was left behind, and became an equally revered treasure of the Pharaohs, one of whom gave it as part of his daughter's dowry when she married a Celtic prince. There is even a fanciful tale that the young couple, Prince Gaythelus and Princess Scota, gave their name to the Gaels and Scots as they progressed through Europe to an eventual home in Ireland, taking the Stone of Destiny with them.

For some considerable time the stone provided a ceremonial seat for the inauguration of High Kings of Ireland until one of them, Fergus MacErc, became ruler of the new kingdom of Dalriada in Argyll, and took the stone with him to the fortress of Dunadd. Here it played the same role. Scottish kings were crowned on the sacred stone, and at their death were buried on the holy island of Iona. Later the stone was transferred to the new stronghold of Dunstaffnage on a crag above the mouth of Loch Etive.

Then came the population and administrative drift from west to east. A number of factors were involved in this. Norse raids down the west coast had already made it necessary to move sacred relics from St Columba's isle of Iona to relative safety at Dunkeld in Perthshire, which became the ecclesiastical centre of the Scottish realm, though kings continued to be buried on Iona, as did several Viking chieftains. Agriculture and stock-rearing fared better in the drier and more fertile east than in the western mixture of peat lands and thinly coated, often precipitous rocks. Trade with Europe, which alternated with aggressive incursions from Europe, was easier to handle through the eastern firths. It was inevitable that the seat of government should be moved to the region where the growing population was most prosperous and royal control easiest to exercise.

When Kenneth MacAlpin decreed that his capital should be moved to Scone he also ensured that the Stone of Destiny went with him. From now on the coronations of Scottish kings took place on the Moot Hill in the grounds of Scone Palace, on the outskirts of modern Perth. The original abbey there was destroyed by John Knox's followers during the Reformation, and the present neo-Gothic mansion is an early nineteenth-century reconstruction of earlier palaces. Worst of all for Scottish pride, what has come to be called the Stone of Scone is no longer in its honoured place.

A prophecy concerning the stone declared that wherever it was held, a Scot would be king. This could be interpreted in different ways, as later patriots were to find to their cost. In 1296 it was seized by King Edward I of England in the apparent belief that mere possession of the stone validated his claim to be King of Scots. Not until James VI of Scotland became James I of England at a ceremony in Westminster Abbey could it be said that a truly Scottish monarch had once more been ritually crowned upon the Stone of Destiny.

2

Fife, Tayside and Central

THE BOUNDARY changes of 1974 gave the name of Tayside to what had been the counties of Perthshire, Kinross-shire and Angus (which itself had once been known as Forfarshire), while Clackmannanshire and Stirlingshire became rather drably Central. Such an unimaginative word blurs the historical resonances which the mere name of Stirling surely evokes; while the ancient royal burgh of Forfar, whose castle was a residence of several early Scottish kings, is quite an appreciable distance from the side of the Tay.

Much of the region is truly Lowland. Along the northern bank of the firth lies the fertile Carse of Gowrie, the word *carse* meaning much the same as *haugh* – a stretch of alluvial levels beside a river. Following the northward curve of the coast is a rich corn-growing belt which from early times profited from ample supplies of seaweed as fertilizer. Sea and river ports simplified trade with Continental markets. In one of them, Dundee, advantage was most shrewdly taken of the fruit-growing capabilities of local soil and climate when the Keillers set up their jam and marmalade manufactory in 1797. Between the Sidlaw Hills and the Braes of Angus, the red loam of Strathmore has provided healthy cropping and stock-rearing since the twelfth century in spite of disruptive wars and civil strife.

South of the firth are gentle hills such as the Lomonds, attractively breaking the otherwise unremarkable skyline and not harsh enough to impede farming up their shallow slopes.

Many of the small, trim villages owe their neatness to the desire of eighteenth-century landowners to add picturesque touches to their estates, moving employees tidily into settlements which would enhance the lordly view, or establishing small industrial and 'tradesman' villages. One feature which recurrently catches the traveller's attention in such communities is the local doocot, or dovecot. There is a greater concentration of these in Fife than in any other region of Scotland. Some were built by lairds for their own estates, or by burghs for the benefit of their citizens, to provide fresh meat during winter when, before the introduction of turnips as winter fodder, cattle had to be slaughtered and salted down in wooden tubs. There is one in the shape of a beehive beside the terraces of Aberdour castle, with some 600 nesting-boxes formed of stone slabs. Another, again like a beehive but with a flattened top and a pillbox entry on it, belonged to the priory and collegiate church at the medieval fishing port of Crail.

Fish provided a harvest from earliest times. In the seaward wedge of Fife known as the East Neuk – *neuk* being an old Scots word meaning a corner – there was busy medieval trade with the Continent, still remembered in the crow-stepped gables of many Flemish-style houses, and a wide-ranging herring fishery. Crail's activities declined long ago and now there are only a few shellfish boats, but its seventeenth-century Customs House is still an attractive feature of the harbour. Anstruther, which until the outbreak of World War II was the major East Coast herring fishing base, now houses the Scottish Fisheries Museum in period buildings near the water's edge. The main centre of today's dwindling East Neuk fleet is at Pittenweem. St Andrews still has an attractive, if not overworked, little harbour below the gaunt shapes of ruined castle and cathedral. On the northern bank of the Tay, Dundee grew as a result of the whaling industry, which among other things supplied plentiful fuel for the town's oil lamps. Importing jute from India, its merchants found that this could be mixed with whale oil to provide hard-wearing coarse fabric. In due course Dundee's shipyards were to build Shackleton's

Terra Nova and another exploration vessel which, after years moored in the Thames, is now back home on display – Scott's *Discovery*.

The coastline, even when assaulted by North Sea storms, is less rugged and inhospitable than that of the west. Inland, the whole landscape is essentially a domesticated one until on its northern and western fringes the Highlands begin to lift their stern shoulders; yet it was in these desirable lowlands that many of the most violent deeds in Scottish history were planned or carried out.

The move of Kenneth MacAlpin's capital to Scone must have meant a great deal more physical comfort for kings and their retainers after the rocks and raw rain of Argyll, but the heads wearing the crown were offered little chance of lying easy. It is difficult to sum up the succession of kings and sub-kings who schemed and killed their way to brief spells of power – eight of them in one century – or to keep in steady perspective the shifting boundaries and aspirations of petty earldoms and self-proclaimed kingdoms. Only two strands appear consistent throughout; and both of them meant lasting complications. Firstly, it was accepted by all Scots that the coronation of their king was valid only if carried out upon the Stone of Destiny, and in spite of the Christian ceremony accompanying it the right to place the crown on the new monarch's head belonged irrevocably to the Earl of Fife, premier layman of the realm. Secondly, it was accepted by all English rulers that, whatever her own misapprehensions on this score, Scotland was basically an English colony.

We know how Edward I of England chose to misinterpret the meaning of the Stone of Destiny. But even before Edward's time, seeds of dissension had been sown. In 945 Malcolm I had signed a treaty with Edmund of England agreeing that in respect of lands held by himself in Strathclyde, which included Cumberland, he owed fealty to Edmund. This and a similar arrangement by Kenneth II for lands in Lothian came to be regarded by the English as an admission that Scottish rulers were not equals but vassals in relation not merely to a few specific regions but to the whole of Scotland – which had never been contemplated by the Scottish signatories. Whatever nominal agreements might be contrived, only to be misread, there were repeated raids by one side upon the other in contravention of treaty terms. Internecine feuds between Scottish aspirants to the throne did little to strengthen the national cause. Kenneth II, mysteriously murdered, was followed by Kenneth III, but he in turn was killed by Kenneth II's son Malcolm. As Malcolm II, the assassin wrested northern Northumbria from the English, but then was himself murdered in Glamis castle by some of his disaffected nobles. The room where the deed was done is still shown to visitors. His rightful heir, according to the tradition of tanistry, should have been Kenneth III's grandson, but Malcolm had already disposed of him and other possible candidates while laying plans for his own grandson Duncan to succeed. This leads us directly to one of the most wantonly falsified stories in Scottish history.

Five or six miles north-east of Scone stands the hill of Dunsinane. As well as an old fort on its summit, the climber will be presented with a view of Birnam Wood about twelve miles away. Echoes of Shakespearian declamation hang inevitably in the air. The fort, however, is unlikely to have belonged to the much denounced Macbeth: the ramparts are those of a prehistoric tribal fortification. Furthermore, Macbeth did not murder Duncan in his palace of Cawdor in Nairn, since the castle there was not built until the fourteenth century; and Duncan was not the pitiable old greybeard portrayed in the play but a ruthless and ambitious man regarded by many as a usurper.

Macbeth, *mormaor* or high steward of Moray, had a stronger lineal claim to the throne than Duncan but, so far from being a self-seeking assassin, was acting on behalf of his stepson Lulach, Lady Macbeth's son by her first marriage and, through her, direct descendant of the legitimate royal line. Lulach was unfortunately simple-minded – probably the only reason he had been allowed to survive, when two other claimants contesting Duncan's pretensions happened to be murdered just before and after the investiture. Having killed Duncan, not in any ghost-ridden Shakespearian castle but on a battlefield near Elgin, Macbeth reigned conscientiously in Lulach's stead for seventeen years. Then Duncan's son Malcolm, who had been sheltering in England all this time, joined forces with the Earl of Northumbria and, with Edward the Confessor's approval, invaded Scotland in 1057. Macbeth was brought to battle and death at Lumphanan in Aberdeenshire: a long way from Birnam Wood or Dunsinane. Malcolm was briefly opposed by forces still loyal to 'Lulach the Fool', but they and their lord were also soon disposed of. The bodies of Macbeth and his stepson were taken for burial to Iona, already the graveyard of many kings.

Surviving vicious family feuds and a number of humiliations at the hands of the English, Malcolm III established a line which was to last for over two centuries. It is generally referred to as the House of Canmore, though Canmore was originally only a nickname – Malcolm 'the Great Head' – not bestowed in any complimentary sense by those who suffered under his notorious rages and lust for war.

In spite of his own savage appetites, Malcolm took as his second wife a remarkably pious woman. English by birth, Margaret fled to Scotland in 1068 with her brother Edgar Atheling, claimant to the English throne after the death of Harold at the battle of Hastings. When she became queen she encouraged English refugees from William the Conqueror's tyranny to settle in her husband's country, though in due course he was forced to reach an agreement with the Norman invader. In 1072 William led a large army up to Stirling, forded the river there, and rode on to join up with his fleet entering the Tay. He and Malcolm met at Abernethy, a place of import-ance from prehistoric times through its days of glory as a major Pictish centre. A ruined Iron Age hill-fort still overlooks the little Perthshire town, and close to its tall eleventh-century round tower is a Pictish stone etched with mysterious designs. In this tower Malcolm Canmore is reported to have done homage to William. The Scots claim that Malcolm offered homage only in respect of his holdings in Cumbria and the largely anglicized Lothian; William and his successors chose to interpret the acknowledgement as embracing all Scotland. Certainly there can be no denying the fact that at Abernethy the King of Scotland gave his son Duncan as hostage to the King of England.

In a way this was, or ought to have been, supererogatory. The devout and cultured Margaret had been brought up in Anglo-Norman ways, and persuaded her husband to speak English rather than Gaelic. He is said to have shown his adoration for her by kissing her holy manuscripts and having them richly bound for her. Where conflicts between the Roman and Celtic branches of Christianity continued to erupt, she favoured the Roman rite. She settled Benedictine monks from Canterbury in a priory at Dunfermline. The third son of her marriage to Malcolm to become king, David I, shared her religious views and elevated Dunfermline to the status of an abbey, with rich endowments. The massive pillars of its nave are very reminiscent of the Norman splendours of Durham cathedral. In 1916 remains of St Margaret's earlier foundation were rediscovered under the nave, and the lines of its walls are now marked out on the floor.

Royal patronage continued throughout the centuries, and the abbey guest-house became a royal residence for monarchs seeking temporary respite from cares of state. Even after the iconoclasm of the Reformation, when much of the abbey church survived only because of its adaptation as parish church, James VI fell under its spell, granted it to his queen, Anne of Denmark, and set about refashioning it into a sumptuous palace. The window of the room in which his son, Charles I, was born can still be seen; and after Charles's execution, Charles II stayed here following his coronation at Scone on New Year's Day 1651.

Among other foundations, Queen Margaret (whose efforts on behalf of the Church were duly recognized in her canonization) set up her own private chapel on the Castle Rock in Edinburgh, now the oldest surviving building in the city. She

helped monks to resettle Iona in the west, and in the east
contributed lavishly towards the religious houses of St Andrews
on their breezy promontory above the North Sea.

This settlement had grown in importance since the day
when, according to legend, the bones of Scotland's patron
saint, the apostle St Andrew, were brought here by the Greek
monk St Regulus or St Rule under the aegis of Nechtan, late
seventh-century king of the Picts. A church set on the rocky
bluff by the Celtic sect of the Culdees ('Companions of God')
later submitted to Roman usage and to the transformation of
its survivors into Austin canons. A patchy stone outline on
Kirkhill is all that remains of St Mary-on-the-Rock, close to
the massive wall surrounding the later church of St Rule, itself
to be overshadowed in 1160 by the cathedral of Our Lady and
St Andrew. The internal length of this 'new cathedral', 357
feet, made it one of the longest churches in Britain and certainly
the greatest in Scotland. Battered by enemies, most fiercely
after the Reformation, it is now a gaunt ruin with seabirds
swooping in and out of the gaping socket of its east window.
Relics have been housed in the neighbouring priory ruins,
including a huge stone chest decorated in high relief with
scenes from the biblical tale of David and known as St Andrew's
Sarcophagus, although there is no reason to suppose that it
ever served as a coffin.

The town also became the home of Scotland's first university, founded in 1410 and formally recognized by the Pope at
Avignon three years later. Its first building, the College of St
Salvator, was not completed until 1450. Above the arch of its
clock tower is an eroded stone said to be miraculously
imprinted with the features of Patrick Hamilton as he was
burnt at the stake before it in 1528. A member of the university
who had taught Lutheran doctrines, Hamilton became the first
martyr of the Scottish Reformation. His initials are set in the
cobbles in front of the tower.

In South Street is St Mary's College, founded in 1537 on
the site of the 'Old Pedagogy'. Its quadrangle is graced by two
historic trees: one a huge holm oak planted in 1728, the other

a thorn tree said to have been planted by Mary, Queen of Scots.

Poor students at the university were long known as 'mealie students' because they took a sack of meal and salt lumps with them and had to make it last all term.

In spite of his wife's gentleness and her liking for Anglo-Norman culture, Malcolm Canmore continued to terrorize northern England, especially after the death of William I. He met his end at Alnwick when facing the troops of William Rufus. Three days after the news had been brought to Margaret in Edinburgh she died, and her body was taken to the church she had endowed at Dunfermline. Malcolm's brother Donald Bane declared his right to the throne, and in violent tirades against English influence in the country rallied forces to drive out most of Margaret's entourage. Her son Edmund hastily swore loyalty to him, and was rewarded with the lordship of Lothian.

Duncan, the son presented to the English king as hostage some twenty years earlier, now appealed for William II's help in return for a promise of fealty. With an Anglo-French army he invaded Scotland and deposed Donald, but allowed him to live. Then Duncan sent his allies away, proudly declaring that he would allow no English or Norman troops to continue military service in his homeland. As a reward for this patriotism he was murdered as soon as they had left, probably with the connivance of his half-brother Edmund. Donald Bane returned, lent his support to a misguided Northumbrian rebellion against William Rufus, and in the ensuing turmoil was deposed again, this time by his nephew Edgar, second son of Malcolm and Margaret. Edgar put out the ageing Donald's eyes and consigned him to prison. Edmund was allowed to enter a monastery, where after his death he was buried in chains at his own request.

Edgar and two brothers who succeeded him, Alexander and David, achieved something quite unusual: all three died peacefully. During his reign Edgar made one decision which was to have great significance later. Abandoning the family residence of Dunfermline, he established his own home near his mother's chapel on the Castle Rock of Edinburgh. His successor, Alexander I, was known as 'the Fierce', and there were legends of his suppressing an uprising by rebels from Moray so brutally that nobody survived to explain the reasons for their disaffection. Yet at the same time, perhaps on his own fierce insistence, he was spoken of as 'a lettered and godly man'.

This pious strain was much more apparent in the third brother, David I. Although he contributed lavishly to the Dunfermline foundation, David continued to favour the Edinburgh residence. He also continued his mother's religious benefactions, and was largely responsible for the splendour of the great Border abbeys at Melrose, Kelso, Jedburgh and Dryburgh. Again like his mother, he favoured Anglo-Norman laws and institutions. Marrying the widowed sister of Henry I, he was created Earl of Huntingdon, and before becoming king spent a great deal of time in the land and company of his brother-in-law. It was probably as a result of this that the Anglo-Norman chronicler William of Malmesbury was impelled to describe his manners as being 'thus polished from the rust of Scottish barbarity'. Upon his accession he set about the introduction of the Norman feudal system by dividing his realm up into feus or fiefs, and gave monopolistic trade charters to many towns on whose loyalty he henceforth hoped to rely. He established the concept of the King's Peace, whereby the king was not merely a war leader but a representative of God on earth, with the duty of ensuring safe conduct and good behaviour throughout his realm. In return his subjects owed him the duty of honouring that peace. Breaches of the peace were punished with large fines or imprisonment.

David also imported Anglo-Norman acquaintances on whom he bestowed land and privileges. Among these were a number of scions of William the Conqueror's knights whose descendants were to wield great influence in Scotland's tumultuous history: Bernard de Bailleul (later Balliol); Robert de Brus (Bruce or 'the Bruce'); and Walter FitzAlan, who

became hereditary Steward of Scotland, a title leading ultimately to the name and royal family of Stewart.

During the conflict between the factions of Stephen and
Matilda, David invaded England in the hope of seizing Northumberland and even Durham for himself. The defence
against him was supervised by the Archbishop of York, and
three holy banners of St Peter of York, St John of Beverley
and St Wilfrid of Ripon were flown from a standard in a cart,
giving the subsequent engagement near Northallerton the
name of 'Battle of the Standard'. The Scots were defeated, but
a year later King Stephen could achieve a peace treaty only by
ceding the earldom of Northumberland to David's son Henry.

In 1153 David died, to be succeeded by his grandson
Malcolm 'the Maiden', so called because of his youth and
celibacy: he was only 23 when he died in 1165, unmarried.
Malcolm was followed by his red-haired brother William 'the
Lion' (from the beast on his standard as much as from his
personal courage), instigator of the first of so many attempts
over the centuries to form a binding union with France against
the English. With French help he invaded England as an ally
of Henry II's rebellious son Henry, but while besieging
Alnwick in Northumberland was 'surprised in a mist' and
captured. Mortifyingly he had to swear vassalage to Henry II
for the whole of Scotland. Fortunately within a short time
Richard I was compelled to sell back these rights in order to
finance his Crusades, and the Scottish king reverted to being
a vassal of the English king only in respect of English lands
which he possessed. There was now a spell of peace until
William died in 1214 and was buried at the abbey of Arbroath.
He himself had founded this in honour of St Thomas of
Canterbury, at whose tomb Henry II was doing penance just
at the time of William's capture at Alnwick.

When Edward I succeeded to the throne of England in
1272, the king of Scotland was Alexander III. He did homage
to Edward explicitly for the land held by him of the English
king, but is reputed to have added 'saving my kingdom of
Scotland'. This was denied by all succeeding rapacious English

kings, on the basis of a blatant forgery concocted by Edward or his minions.

In 1285 Alexander died in a riding accident. His children had predeceased him, and the only lawful successor was his granddaughter Margaret, 'the Maid of Norway'. She was recognized by a grand national assembly at Scone as heiress to the throne. In view of her absence in Norway at the time, and the need for regents during her minority, six guardians of the kingdom were appointed. Edward I, with his eye on a complete subjugation of Scotland on the lines of his conquest of Wales, pressed for the marriage of the child to his son Edward, later installed as the first Prince of Wales. A marriage treaty was signed, including in its provisions an agreement that the independence of Scotland should be recognized. The Maid of Norway died (it is said from seasickness) on her way from her homeland in 1290, bad weather having forced her ship to seek shelter on Orkney.

The young Margaret's claims and the authority of her guardians had never been too highly regarded by the powerful Bruces, lords of Annandale and Carrick. Now that she was dead they boldly advanced their own claim to the throne. They were not the only ones. Black John Comyn, lord of Badenoch, asserted his right as direct descendant of Duncan I. Five others were remote descendants of Malcolm IV. But the only really close dynastic rival to Robert Bruce was John Balliol, like himself a great-grandson of William the Lion's younger brother. Supporters of Bruce were prepared to testify that Alexander III had appointed Bruce of Annandale as his successor; but Balliol's backers and some less committed nobles and clerics, fearful of civil war, invited Edward I of England to come and arbitrate. He was delighted to do so, with the implication of being regarded as overall ruler of the kingdom. He decided in favour of Balliol, but made it clear that this was only the appointment of a figurehead: he himself was the true monarch. On St Andrew's Day 1292 Balliol was crowned at Scone according to the ancient ritual.

Edward, who had probably shrewdly observed that this

pretentious lordling, though haughty in manner, was a vacil-
lating and easily manipulated nonentity, did not trouble even
to be civil to his puppet or to Scottish laws and traditions. He
encouraged Scots to appeal direct to himself against their
own king's judgements. Planning a campaign against Philip
of France, he demanded men and money from Scotland. A
committee of clerics and nobles meeting at Scone in 1295
persuaded the so-called King John that enough was enough,
and that instead of pandering to the King of England he should
seek an alliance with the King of France. This was the first
formal treaty in the continuing saga which later generations
were to refer to wistfully as 'the Auld Alliance'. John Balliol,
though opposed by nature to any activities whatsoever which
might threaten war, summoned up the courage to tell Edward
that promises of fealty extracted under threats of violence were
not valid.

Edward immediately seized all Balliol's English estates.
Balliol retaliated by banishing all English property owners and
any others he or his advisers suspected of being pro-English.
Among these were the Bruces, whose lands he handed to their
old rivals, the Comyns. The Bruce claimant to the throne had
just died, but his son and grandson were determined to assert
family rights, even if it meant offering their services to Edward
I for as long as it might take to drive the Comyns from the
seized lands in Annandale. After that the Bruces could renew
their struggle for the throne.

In 1296 Edward invaded Scotland to subdue the ineffectual
Balliol, massacring the inhabitants of Berwick and marching
on to defeat the Scots at Dunbar. At Brechin, the ancient red
sandstone cathedral town in Angus with its tall watch-tower,
Balliol hastened to surrender himself and his crown. All heraldic
insignia were shamingly torn from his coat, signifying that he
was unfitted to be a knight. Mocked as Toom Tabard, the
'empty coat', he was taken as prisoner to England along with
other loot: the Black Rood of St Margaret, and the coronation
Stone of Destiny from Scone. The stone was placed within a
specially designed chair in Westminster Abbey to make it

symbolically clear that all coronations of English kings henceforth should be regarded as simultaneous coronations of the
kings of Scotland. Before leaving a cowed Scotland, Edward
rode about demanding oaths of submission from all the magnates in the land.

The discredited Balliol was eventually released from his
comfortable English captivity after an appeal from the Pope,
and passed the rest of his days on his ancestral estate at Bailleul
in France. He died in 1315, but during his lifetime was still
regarded as rightful king by many of his one-time subjects.
Among these was a tall firebrand of a patriot in his middle
twenties. William Wallace of Elderslie, son of a Renfrewshire
landowner, was one of the lesser gentry who had not put his
name to the document of submissions, known as the Ragman's
Roll because of the ribbons dangling from its seals. Having
impetuously killed the English sheriff at Lanark – perhaps,
according to a fifteenth-century minstrel, in revenge for the
killing of his own wife by the English – and been proclaimed
an outlaw, he fled into Ettrick forest to assemble a force
of rebels against the domination of English governors and
garrisons.

The Bruces, whose currying of favour with Edward had
resulted in the restoration of their estates, stirred up minor
troubles but seemed glad to yield for the time being to their
benefactors and express disapproval of Wallace's wild conduct.
Many other Scottish nobles preferred subservience to English
gentlemen of their own rank rather than alliance with upstarts
and peasants of their own race. Another young patriot, Andrew
of Moray, however, assembled further dissidents and joined
forces with Wallace after a mutually enthusiastic meeting at
Perth. Neither sought superiority for himself. Between them
they claimed to act for the wrongly deposed King John Balliol
(another reason for the Bruces' disfavour) and between them,
in the absence of Edward on one of his French campaigns,
systematically mopped up English defences across central and
south-east Scotland. On one occasion Wallace rode daringly
down upon Scone and put to flight an English justiciar who

was busily pronouncing outlawry upon anyone who refused to swear loyalty to Edward.

In September 1297 Wallace and Moray faced their sternest test.

During John Balliol's imprisonment Edward had appointed John de Warenne, Earl of Surrey, as Guardian of Scotland. He seems to have been a somewhat slipshod caretaker, complacently assuming that ill-coordinated groups of rebels could pose no significant threat to seasoned English troops. Neither he nor his associates really took alarm when Scottish forces began to assemble on Abbey Craig, a hill beside the Forth near Stirling.

To this day the strategic importance of Stirling is obvious to anyone approaching from the south. On a rocky eminence commanding what was for centuries the lowest point at which the Forth could be bridged, the castle – on the site of a Roman fort – and its steeply pitched town stand between what was once a marshy plain and the shadowy beginnings of the Highlands beyond, with the Ochils and Trossachs already edging in. Possession of Stirling meant control of a crucial gateway between north and south. Wallace's men, rushing into position from the siege of Dundee, formed up into schiltrons – tightly packed, bristling clusters of spears and a number of home-made weapons within a shield carapace – to face the skilled archers, cavalry and well-equipped foot soldiers of the English army.

There was some argument on the English side as to the best way of crossing the river and finishing the whole business as swiftly as possible. De Warenne was recommended to use a ford some distance below the narrow bridge, but opted instead for a quicker, decisive attack over the bridge. Mounted knights struggled across two abreast, and plunged immediately into a marsh. As those behind came piling into the snarl-up, the Scottish schiltrons launched themselves downhill and cut the stumbling knights to pieces. The bridge was soon blocked with the dead and dying, so that survivors could not retreat and reinforcements could not be sent in to help. When English resolution faltered and they turned to flee, the Scots pursued them down the Lowlands and across the Border, laying waste to Northumberland and Cumberland.

Andrew of Moray died of wounds received during the battle, but Wallace went on to be proclaimed Guardian of Scotland, and was given the accolade of knighthood by dignitaries still claiming, like himself, to represent the absent Balliol. This displeased not only Edward of England but also Robert the Bruce, who could offer no support to any faction standing between him and the crown. After a brief spell of backing the rebel cause, wavering between patriotism and expediency, Bruce once more allied himself with the English.

Edward returned from France determined to put an end to the rebellion. He had trouble feeding his 40,000-strong army as they reached the north, largely because of Wallace's scorched earth policy, and was considering a temporary period of recuperation in Edinburgh when two treacherous Scottish lords betrayed Wallace's whereabouts. Edward was able to take his enemy by surprise near Falkirk. Although hopelessly outnumbered, the schiltron hedgehogs held the English cavalry at bay until the remorseless fire of archers thinned their ranks and they were defeated.

Fleeing from the carnage, Wallace resigned his Guardianship and made his way to France, seeking aid there and from Norway, and ultimately from the Pope. Refused by all, he doggedly returned to Scotland and carried on guerrilla warfare until, captured by further treachery, he was handed over to the English by the sheriff of Dumbarton. After a mockery of a trial in London, at which he proudly denied that he was a traitor, 'since I never swore fealty to the English king', he was hanged, drawn and quartered. His heart was tossed into a fire, his head stuck on a pike on London Bridge, and the four quarters of his body displayed at Newcastle, Berwick, Perth and Aberdeen.

On Abbey Craig, overlooking Stirling's fifteenth-century Old Bridge, now stands a tall monument designed by a local mason and completed in 1869. A statue of Sir William Wallace flourishes a sword from the outside of the tower. Within, vaulted chambers include a Hall of Heroes from the nation's past, and the Wallace Sword Room in which is housed his actual sword. For some reason which has never been explained, in September 1936 four men broke in and stole the sword. It was missing for three years, until recovered unharmed from Bothwell Brig in Lanarkshire. There is another tower at Ayr, with a statue by a local self-taught sculptor, which in fact pre-dates the Stirling monument by some forty years. On the probable site of Wallace's birthplace at Elderslie a modern memorial bears inscriptions in Gaelic (*Bas agus Buaiad* – Death and Victory), English, and Latin, a translation of which reads

> I tell you the truth. Freedom is what is best.
> Son, never live a life like a slave.

Important as the victory at Stirling Bridge had been for Scottish pride, there was, after a period of despondency and subjugation, to be an even more significant battlefield above the Bannock Burn two miles south of the town.

In an attempt to establish a national administration in the absence of John Balliol, Scottish nobles and clerics had in 1299 appointed a triumvirate of Guardians: Bishop William Lamberton of St Andrews; John, the Red Comyn of Badenoch; and a member of the Comyns' long-standing rival family, young Robert Bruce of Carrick. Their approaches to Pope Boniface VIII and the resulting admonitions from the Pope condemning English invasions of the Papal fief of Scotland had incensed Edward and driven him to some of his more savage oppressions. Bruce, forever wavering, had muted his criticisms and been allowed by Edward to continue as joint Guardian after Wallace's execution; but old ambitions began to stir once more.

If Scotland was ever again to have a free, strong ruler, there had to be consistent support from the nobles. The most powerful of these magnates were the Bruces themselves and the Comyns. Whatever personal designs Robert the Bruce might have on the throne, he was unlikely to achieve them without some mutual agreement. He and John, the Red

Comyn, had come to blows before. On a February day in 1306 Bruce arranged what was apparently meant to be a conciliatory meeting at the Greyfriars' monastery church in Dumfries. Exactly what happened in that building will never be known. It seems that the two men had yet another quarrel, though there is no way of knowing who started it. Bruce was a short, stocky man with red hair and a burning ambition. Comyn had a reputation, even in that violent day and age, for his uncontrollable temper. From whichever side the provocation came, it is certain that Bruce stabbed his rival before the altar. He himself admitted so when he emerged, telling his followers that he thought he had killed Comyn, whereupon one of them rushed in 'to mak siccar' (make sure): the Kirkpatricks of Dumfries have ever since carried the emblem of a bloody hand with dagger and the motto 'I mak siccar' on their coat of arms.

The sacrilege of committing a murder on holy ground would obviously lose any Papal support Bruce might have hoped for, and alienate other European monarchs. As soon as the news reached Edward in England he was only too happy to appeal to the Pope for the murderer's excommunication. This the Pope did; but Bruce was granted absolution by the Bishop of Glasgow, who joined his cause. The only possible course now was to gamble everything on becoming king.

Bruce and his four brothers threw the English out of Dumfries castle and set off to capture other fortresses. Before Edward could retaliate, Bruce headed for Scone. The Stone of Destiny was in alien hands, but in other respects the coronation ceremony on 25 March 1306 was carried out according to tradition. Bishop Wishart of Glasgow was in attendance; Bishop Lamberton of St Andrews conducted the ceremony. One essential person was missing, however. The Earl of Fife, who had the hereditary right to place the crown on the king's head, was in captivity in England. His sister Isabel, although the wife of the Red Comyn's kinsman, the Earl of Buchan, asserted her family right by appropriating her husband's horses and riding to Scone. She arrived too late for the actual ceremony, so another took place two days later, on Palm Sunday, when she placed a gold circlet on the head of King Robert I.

Although old and ill by now, Edward was still determined not to let Scotland slip from his grasp. His armies poured north over the Border, slaughtering men, women and children indiscriminately. Many Scots magnates, related to or on good terms with the Comyns, took the English part. Bruce's forces were defeated first in Methven wood by the English, and then beside Loch Tay by Comyn's uncle, the Lord of Lorn. The king's sister and the Countess of Buchan who had crowned him were dragged out of sanctuary where they had been sent for safety, and exhibited in cages hanging from castle walls at Roxburgh and Berwick. Robert himself disappeared, and it seemed that Scottish attempts at independence had yet again been humbled.

Many romantic tales are told of the king's subsequent wanderings. He spent some months hiding in the Western Isles and perhaps in Ireland. The cave in which, close to despair, he is said to have won fresh heart after seeing a spider succeed in securing a thread of its web after several failed attempts, is claimed by several localities. Rathlin island is one. Another 'Bruce's Cave' is signposted for tourists above the Kirtle Water near Kirkpatrick Fleming in Dumfriesshire, near the old family terrain of Annandale.

Early in 1307 Bruce returned to the mainland near his estate and possible birthplace at Turnberry. So weakened by his privations that at first he had to be carried in a litter, he soon forced himself to re-establish his authority by donning armour and leading crucial assaults himself. Edward I, heading yet again for Scotland, died in July of that year, leaving the continuing conflict to his feeble son Edward II. From early surprise victories in the wild hills around Loch Trool, Bruce and his reinvigorated followers went on with growing confidence during the next seven years to capture one castle after another from the English. At Perth in January 1313 Bruce himself was second to scale the castle wall after wading neck-high through icy cold water. By the spring of the following year only two major strongholds remained in English hands, but one of them was crucial: Stirling.

Edward Bruce, Robert's brother, was laying siege to the castle, but there was a stalemate. In the end it was agreed under a chivalric code that if no English forces came to relieve the beleaguered garrison by Midsummer Day 1314, the governor would honourably surrender it to the Scots. Such an outcome would have been so great a blow to Edward II's prestige that he decided to throw all his resources into reaching the garrison and destroying the besiegers. Levies of heavy cavalry, archers and foot soldiers were summoned from the English shires and from Wales and Ireland. Some 17,000 in all assembled at Wark in Northumberland, and on their way into Scotland were joined by contingents supporting the Comyns or for other reasons opposed to the rule of Bruce.

King Robert himself came to his brother's aid, though with few more than 5,500 trained fighters. These were organized into four divisions of foot soldiers and about 500 light cavalry. A supply depot was established at Cambuskenneth, within a protective loop of the river. At Cambuskenneth Abbey twelve years later the Scots Parliament was to swear allegiance to King Robert's chosen successor; and a later king, James III, was to be buried here after his murder in 1488. Today its Gothic bell-tower, much restored in the nineteenth century, is the only substantial survivor.

The battlefield itself survives, thanks to the National Trust for Scotland and a National Committee formed to fight another kind of battle – against the threat of a housing development obliterating the site. The rise of the hill is dominated by a statue of Robert the Bruce on horseback, and within a swirl of concrete rotunda is the Borestone, at which the first blow of the battle was struck and by which Bruce set up his standard. Making a preparatory tour of his advanced troops on a pony, he was spotted by an English patrol. Sir Henry de Bohun levelled his lance and charged at the unarmoured king; but Bruce rose in his stirrups, and with his battleaxe cleft right through the English knight's helmet and skull.

This was not, however, the scene of the major confrontation. Bruce had disposed his men along the Bannock Burn and its succession of bogs, and had dug camouflaged pits between the treacherous marshy patches. He also sowed clusters of caltraps, spikes projecting upwards to bring down the cavalry. But rather than wait for the English to be lured on to these snares, he decided to launch the first attack himself. Advancing on a narrow front, the bristling schiltrons threw their opponents into confusion on such unfamiliar, unstable ground. English reinforcements approaching along the edge of the Carse were intercepted by the Earl of Moray and driven off in disorder, leaving heavy casualties. Resisting all temptations to pursue, Bruce and his men regrouped and rested, in a strong position and in good heart.

King Edward was still sure that the sheer weight of his mounted knights must prevail. He decided to move his forces across the Bannock Burn by fords closer to Stirling, so that he could personally relieve the castle next day. It proved an exhausting process, and even when accomplished there were fears that the Scots might attack during the night. Bruce had in fact been contemplating a withdrawal to the hills rather than risk a head-on clash with forces which so visibly outnumbered his own. But when a Scottish defector from Edward's army arrived with reports of the miserable morale of the English and exhorted him with the words 'Now's the time and now's the hour', he again decided to take the initiative.

During the night the Earl of Atholl, jealous of Bruce and foreseeing a probable English victory, descended on Cambuskenneth and killed the depot commander and his men. But it was too late to hinder the Scots. On the morning of Midsummer Day, after a blessing accompanied by a holy relic of St Columba carried in the Monymusk Reliquary, Bruce threw all his forces down upon Edward's. The tightly packed schiltrons might have been in some danger if the enemy's Welsh archers had been used at once; but Edward or his advisers thought they could settle things swiftly by an all-out cavalry charge. In fact the broken ground made it impossible for the English knights to manoeuvre easily. Bruce's far lighter cavalry cut them off in a flanking movement. Men and horses were jammed into one awkward mass, into which the Scottish spearmen slowly and murderously thrust their way. As the English were forced back, their archers belatedly came into action, but showered more arrows into the backs of their own troops than into Bruce's.

The end came when Edward's royal standard was seen to be leaving the field. Edward himself sought refuge in Stirling castle, but was refused entry by the governor on the understandable grounds that he would certainly be captured. He fled via Linlithgow to Dunbar and ignominiously took a rowing-boat back to the English border at Berwick. Behind him he left, according to a contemporary chronicler, the Bannock Burn so dammed by the dead 'that men might pass dry over it upon drowned horses and men'. England had lost 2 earls, more than 60 barons and bannerets, 268 knights, and at least 10,000 foot soldiers.

Scotland had re-established itself as an independent nation. This was not, however, accepted either by the English or by the Pope, to whom Edward repeatedly appealed for help. On 6 April 1320 the clergy, barons and community of Scotland made their own appeal, asserting Scotland's right to freedom from alien domination. In the Declaration of Arbroath they made their principles splendidly clear:

> For as long as one hundred of us shall remain alive we shall never in any wise submit to the rule of the English, for it is not for glory alone we fight, for riches, or for honours, but for freedom, which no good man loses but with his life.

Arbroath abbey was to provide the setting for another nationalistic upsurge in our own century. On Christmas morning 1950 the Stone of Scone was removed from Westminster Abbey by a group of young Scots led by a law student, Ian Hamilton. When police investigations began to point towards the culprits, they addressed a petition to King

George VI appealing for the stone's formal return to Scotland, and fastened this to the door of St Giles's cathedral in Edinburgh. Then, on 11 April 1951, they drove the stone to Arbroath and laid it on the altar of the ruined abbey, draped in the saltire flag of St Andrew. No proceedings were taken against them; but nor was any attention paid to their appeal, and the stone was hurried back to Westminster.

Another important declaration was made in 1328, when the Treaty of Northampton temporarily ended Scottish invasions of northern England in the time of Edward III. Its chief clause read:

> Scotland shall remain to Robert, King of Scots, and his heirs, free and undivided from England, without any subjection, servitude, claim or demand whatsoever.

For a time there had been grave apprehensions on that question of inheritance. Late in life, King Robert had still fathered no male heir. Marjory, his daughter by his first wife, was persuaded to agree that if the king died without a son the crown should pass to his brother Edward; but to be on the safe side a marriage was arranged between Marjory and Walter, the hereditary High Steward, who in spite of his youth had distinguished himself at Bannockburn and become one of Bruce's most trusted lieutenants. If all else failed they at any rate ought to produce children. This proved a wise precaution. Edward Bruce, crowned High King of Ireland under dubious circumstances, died at the battle of Dundalk in Ireland in 1318. Marjory had been killed in a fall from a horse two years earlier; but a boy child, Robert, was born from her dead body. Her widower, Sir Walter, rose in power and influence. By the time of the Declaration of Arbroath he had attained sufficient eminence to be included as a principal signatory along with five earls. Then in 1324 something unexpected happened. After twenty-two years of married life King Robert's second wife, Elizabeth de Burgh, gave birth to a son. At the age of 5 this child, David, was married to Joan, 7-year-old sister of Edward III.

Robert himself, afflicted by leprosy, spent the last two years of his life in Cardross castle beside the Clyde, dying before he could learn that the Pope had lifted his excommunication and acknowledged him and his successors as rulers of Scotland. His embalmed body was carried to Dunfermline for burial, but at his own request his heart had been removed by a trusted comrade-in-arms, Sir James Douglas, to be taken on Crusade. After Douglas's death in battle with the Moors in Spain, the embalmed heart was brought back to Scotland for a final resting-place in Melrose abbey.

David II was crowned at Scone in 1331, though effective administration of the land during his minority was entrusted to Robert Stewart, son of Walter the Steward. In spite of David's childhood marriage to the sister of the English king, Edward did not hesitate to help a Balliol descendant make a bid for the Scottish throne, driving David and Joan into exile in France after the battle of Halidon Hill near Berwick. An attempted return led David to disastrous defeat at Neville's Cross, after which he was a prisoner in English hands for eleven years until bought back for what could truly be called a king's ransom. There was a further period of tussles for power until the ageing grandson of Bruce and son of Walter and Marjory at last reached the throne in his own right as Robert II, and gave to the royal house the name which would remain as Stewart until Mary, Queen of Scots, altered its spelling to Stuart.

Although his son Robert III was lame, sickly, and also elderly at the time of his succession, a royal dynasty had now been established. A settled administrative capital did not yet exist. Until well into the sixteenth century the royal court and its functionaries were peripatetic. The only place with an inalterable role was Scone. Nearby Perth was a favourite venue for general councils. Five days after his coronation in 1424, James I called his first parliament there, and later his third one. He personally favoured Perth as a national capital, but it was unhappily to become the scene of his assassination.

Scotland's first truly constitutional monarch, James, made

many enemies among the nobility. Given too free a hand during years when he, like David II earlier, had fallen into English captivity, they resented the disciplines which their returning king was determined to impose on them in the cause of national unification. He executed, imprisoned or dispossessed many of his own relatives to ensure the containment of their territorial ambitions and safeguard against any attempted seizure of the throne. Sir Robert Graham, angered by a spell of imprisonment from which he had escaped into the Highlands, set up a conspiracy with two Stewarts, one of them James's uncle and the other his own domestic chamberlain. Pretending that they desired only to rid the country of a tyrant, on 21 February 1437 they burst into the Blackfriars monastery in Perth in spite of the attempt by Catherine Douglas, one of the queen's attendants, to bar the door by using her arm as a bolt, earning herself the name of Kate-Bar-the-Door. Unarmed and half dressed, the king was slaughtered in a frenzy of dagger thrusts. In due course the conspirators were taken to Edinburgh, subjected to protracted torture, and finally beheaded. All that remains on the site of the monastic gatehouse in modern Perth is the stone house associated with Walter Scott's novel *The Fair Maid of Perth*.

Although vengeance had been wreaked on the assassins in Edinburgh, that was still by no means the main administrative centre. Kings and their councils sat in judgement in different towns, and were accommodated in different palaces. Stirling remained a favourite with several monarchs: James II was born there, James III preferred it to other residences, James IV added to it, and James V transformed the interior into a Renaissance palace after his marriage to Mary of Guise. Their daughter Mary was born at Linlithgow, of which her father was also fond and to which he fled after defeat by the English at Solway Moss, before going on to Falkland in the wooded heartland of Fife. It was on his deathbed in this French-style palace, an exquisite architectural tribute to the shared tastes of the Auld Alliance, that James heard of his daughter's birth and predicted of his realm 'It cam' wi' a lass, and it'll gang wi' a lass.'

Mary's own child, James VI, though born in Edinburgh, was baptized in Stirling castle while the father, Darnley, sulked in a house in the town. The infant James himself was, breaking with all tradition, given a hurried coronation in Stirling's medieval Church of the Holy Rude after his mother's forced abdication. He continued to live in Stirling with guardians and tutors, on his way to becoming the best educated of all Scottish monarchs.

Not until kings grew weary of perambulating in bad weather over rough countryside from one provincial centre to another were judges appointed to branch out from the royal court on circuits known as eyres, listening to pleas and sorting out local problems. The need for centralization of the royal court and parliament led at last to the choice and subsequent development of Edinburgh as Scotland's capital city.

SELECTED SITES OF INTEREST

Antiquities

ABERLEMNO   Sculptured Pictish stones beside the B9134 between Brechin and Forfar, and cross-slab in churchyard.

ARDESTIE   Souterrain signposted north-west of Mains of Ardestie from the A92 Dundee to Arbroath road. Huge boulders and slabs enclose a long chamber with a central drainage gully. Nearby at Carlungie is another souterrain discovered during ploughing in 1949, 120 feet long and 6 feet deep.

ANTONINE WALL   Substantial remains of fort at Rough Castle, 6 miles west of Falkirk; military bath-house at Bearsden outside Glasgow; and stretches of wall at Watling Lodge, the Kinneil estate in Bo'ness, and cutting across New Kilpatrick cemetery and golf course.

ARDOCH   Signposted north of Braco village. One of the best preserved Roman fortified camps in Britain, set on the edge of the Highland Fault, with subsidiary camps nearby testifying to the importance of the situation for the occupying forces.

FOULIS WESTER Standing stones, cairn, and stone circles on Ardoch moor, north of the A85 east of Crieff.

MEIGLE Collection of cross-slabs, vertical and recumbent carved tombstones (one hog-backed and decorated with roof-tiles) and fragments, on the B954 south of the village square.

(*For a general study of the foregoing see also Chapter 1.*)

Historic Buildings

AUCHTERARDER Glenruthven Weaving Mill and Heritage Centre have fabric displays and the only working steam textile engine in Scotland.

BRECHIN Round tower of Irish type from eleventh or twelfth century, originally free-standing but now linked to restored cathedral by an aisle. Within the cathedral is a collection of early and medieval carved stones, some belonging to a previous monastery.

DOUNE Off the A84 8 miles north-west of Stirling, castle built by the Regent Albany in late fourteenth or early fifteenth century, later the home of the 'Bonnie Earl o' Moray'. The present Earl of Moray displays a collection of vintage and other automobiles in his Doune Motor Museum.

DUNKELD Cathedral attractively set beside the Tay. Main character established between twelfth and fifteenth centuries, with the choir later restored for use as parish church. Dunkeld Bridge is one of Telford's finest achievements, overlooking path to Birnam Oak, reputedly the last remaining tree of the Birnam Wood which Macbeth was sure would not come to Dunsinane.

GLAMIS Off the A94 5 miles south-west of Forfar, a largely seventeenth-century castle with earlier remains including Dun-can's Hall, associated with Macbeth. Childhood home of

Queen Elizabeth, the Queen Mother, and birthplace of her younger daughter Princess Margaret.

HUNTINGTOWER   Once known as Ruthven castle, created from two tower houses linked together, with fine painted ceilings. The setting for the 'Raid of Ruthven' *(see Chapter 4)*.

ST ANDREWS   Castle clinging to rocky headland, much eroded. Served not merely as a defence but as palace for bishops and archbishops of St Andrews. Mine and countermine driven through foundations during siege of 1546–7 still accessible.

STIRLING   Castle and Visitor Centre. The King's Knot, lavish early seventeenth-century landscaped gardens below castle. Mar's Work, remains of a Renaissance mansion built for the Earl of Mar, Regent of Scotland, with a heraldic panel above the gateway incorporating his coat of arms and those of James VI.

Museums

ANSTRUTHER   North Carr Light Vessel moored at East Pier. Also Scottish Fisheries Museum.

ARBROATH   Abbey. Also Signal Tower Museum, with a history of the hazardous building of Robert Stevenson's Bell (or Inchcape) Rock lighthouse 12 miles out to sea. The tower provided shore accommodation for keepers and kept in communication with the lighthouse by means of flagstaff signals and carrier pigeons.

CERES   Fife Folk Museum in old weigh-house and adjoining buildings in the centre of the burgh.

CULROSS   Largely administered by the National Trust for Scotland, a town still essentially sixteenth- and seventeenth-century in building and layout, with cobbled streets for the poor, 'planestane' strips for the gentry, a dignified Town House, preserved 'Little Houses', and a shipping merchant's white-harled, pantiled mansion which he chose to designate a 'palace'.

DUNDEE   Maritime survivors include the frigate *Unicorn*, the oldest British-built ship still afloat; Scott's *Discovery*, and mementoes of whaling industry and local lifeboats in castle at Broughty Ferry. McManus Galleries have extensive local history displays, including valuable material from Roman fort at Carpow.

DUNFERMLINE   Abbey with many royal burials. Also Andrew Carnegie Museum in tiny weaver's cottage, birthplace of the tycoon who endowed his home town with a magnificent public park and other amenities.

FALKIRK   Local history museum with material on the Antonine Wall.

GLAMIS   Angus Folk Museum, in six estate cottages in the village near Glamis castle, with displays of agricultural tools and methods, local spinning and weaving (regular demonstrations of handloom production), development of domestic lighting, laundry, and a completely equipped country schoolroom.

INVERKEITHING   Museum of local history in fourteenth-century friary, with particular emphasis on the story of Rosyth dockyard.

PERTH   Balhousie castle beside the North Inch houses HQ and museum of the Black Watch (Royal Highland Regiment), covering its history from 1740 to the present *(see also Chapter 8)*.

ST ANDREWS   Preservation Trust museum in seventeenth-century fishermen's cottages in North Street has re-creations of old grocer's and chemist's shop interiors.

3

Edinburgh and Lothian

THE COUNTY now known simply as Lothian is an amalgamation of what used to be East Lothian, Midlothian, and West Lothian, with a few bits chipped off the edges here and there: for example, the little settlement of Stow with its packhorse bridge over the Gala Water was once in East Lothian but has now been lured into the Borders region.

Like a gentler shadow of the Cheviot borderline separating much of England and Scotland, the ranges of the Lammermuir, Moorfoot and Pentland Hills link into a parallel barrier closer to the Firth of Forth. Between it and the water lies a plain fragmented by rivers and burns, interspersed with spectacular upsurges of rock left behind by volcanic upheaval and the crushing grip of glaciers. These volcanic plugs, from North Berwick Law on the Forth estuary and the Bass Rock in the firth itself to Castle Rock in Edinburgh, provided early tribes with natural defensive sites. An Iron Age fortification on North Berwick Law is still visible despite the damage done to it by a quarry which provided stone for many of the town buildings. Traprain Law was a tribal centre until well into the Roman age, and has yielded up over a hundred pieces of fine Roman silverware. On the peak of Edinburgh's rock, with a tail of ground sloping sharply away down the Royal Mile, the Picts had a stronghold around AD 450. Even mightier in the background is the extinct volcano of Arthur's Seat.

Farming began to flourish in the Lothian plains once the bogs had been cleared and fords or bridges provided over the network of rivers and streams. Under the feudal system, landowners owing service to the king imposed their own service demands on their tenants, usually involving a cash rent in return for the lease of farmlands. In their turn, the stronger and financially sounder tenant farmers, or lairds, would extract money and labour from those a step lower down the scale. A few sturdily independent types might save up enough cash to buy their own patch outright and farm it independently, becoming known as 'bonnet lairds'.

The use of resources was a piecemeal affair. Open fields without hedges or other divisions were awkwardly split up in a system known as 'run-rig' between joint small tenants living in a small village or 'fermetoun', each annually allocated strips or 'rigs' of from a quarter to half an acre, with a rough-and-ready attempt to balance the better and poorer land between the respective individuals. The ground was cropped until it was exhausted and had to be left for a few years to recuperate. On his travels through the region early in the eighteenth century, Daniel Defoe noted the disparity between its natural fertility and the inadequacy of its farming methods. His opinion was confirmed by John Cockburn of Ormiston: 'Excuses for putting off is the highest pleasure in our Indolent Country.'

Cockburn himself was one of those whose reappraisal led to East Lothian becoming a notable region for agricultural reformers, ploughing their profits back into the improvement of the earth. There was a more carefully calculated rotation of crops. New breeds of livestock were introduced. Among the attractive little villages and market-places snuggling under the foothills, Ormiston became the centre of Cockburn's model estates during the first experimental enclosures. As a Scottish member of the Parliament in London for more than thirty years after its inception in 1707, he had the opportunity to make direct contrasts between what he saw of improved English farming methods and those still prevailing in his own country. At home he decided to go in for wholesale enclosures, encouraged his tenants to take long leases by reducing their rents, and instructed them in modern scientific methods. Ormiston

village was redeveloped with the aid of the inhabitants themselves, for whom he provided timber from his estates, stipu-
lating only that no houses should be built 'but what are two
storeys high'. He also introduced a bleachfield to supplement
the local cloth trade, and built up a local mining and coal-
selling business.

Not all sub-tenants found themselves incorporated into such
an idealistic new system. Many in the Lowlands were simply
discarded, and in their place the landlords engaged labourers
or 'hinds' on a yearly basis. Taken on around Whitsuntide,
such men were provided with a cottage for the period of the
hire, and in return were expected to supply from their own
meagre resources a 'bondager' – a woman who would perform
field-work or any other menial farm duty required of her. This
would usually be the wife, sister or daughter of the hind.
During much of the nineteenth century almost half of the
Lothian agricultural force consisted of women, though some
of these were seasonal workers imported from Ireland and the
Highlands. Short-term employees lived cramped together in
shabby, draughty one-room huts or 'bothies'. Although hinds
and their bondagers occupied more substantial cottages, their
own tenancy was comparatively brief, so there was little incentive for either them or their employer to undertake any
improvements to the accommodation.

The hind was supposed to be able to cope with all tasks on
the farm; but an ambitious worker might endeavour to become
an indispensable expert. A ploughman with a knack for handling horses could establish himself as a virtual NCO above the
lower ranks on the land. For a long time there were few
specialized tradesmen: most farm workers made their own
tools and carried out their own running repairs, until the spread
of cheaply manufactured iron began to displace wood, and
more sophisticated craftsmanship was called for.

In line with Cockburn's experiments, other villages in the
region began to develop industries for local craftsmen, such
as Andrew Fletcher's attempted factory at Saltoun. A bale-
weighing tron or steelyard preserved at Stenton recalls the

importance of the woollen trade. The historic site of Athel-staneford was developed as an estate village by Sir David Kinloch, leasing out smallholdings on which his tenants could build their own harled (rough-cast) and pantiled cottages; and here, too, many of them wove cloth. The church which Kinloch also provided has in its churchyard a flagstaff from which permanently flies the saltire or St Andrew's cross, floodlit at night, recalling the vision of a white cross against blue sky which supposedly inspired combined Pictish and Scottish forces to victory against the invading King Athelstan and later became the national flag.

Around Preston and East Linton there were by the middle of the nineteenth century seven watermills: in the whole of East Lothian the total in 1854 was recorded as 73. Preston Mill at East Linton is admirably preserved in working order. On nearby Phantassie Farm, birthplace of the engineer John Rennie, a wind-powered threshing machine was introduced in 1799. The farm still has its beehive doocot with 600 nesting boxes, between three and four hundred years old. There are other substantial ones at Athelstaneford and the village of Dirleton with its attractive houses around wide greens, preserving the medieval shape of the community if not its original buildings, other than the imposing baronial castle.

Before the belated awareness of the plain's potential fertility, the growing importance of the region owed at least as much to trade and communications. Edinburgh's growth as an administrative centre went hand in hand with this. Tracks and, later, roads converged on the city from every strategic direction. Like Stirling, it commanded a vital dividing line. More closely linked than Stirling with the sea, it could do business with other maritime centres in England (during times of truce) or Continental Europe. Leith developed as both a trading and fishing port. Quays were extended at the beginning of the nineteenth century by John Rennie, coal docks and graving docks followed, while fishing harbours and piers continued to prosper from one century to another. Today the intermingled

old streets and waterfront are almost suffocated by grain ware-
houses.

When granting the abbey of Holyrood a foundation charter,
David I had given its canons the right to build and profit from
a burgh of their own, in what has since become the Canongate.
Above this, climbing towards the castle, was the burgh of
Edinburgh, to which Robert the Bruce granted a royal charter
including, among other privileges, jurisdiction over the port of
Leith. Nevertheless it took many centuries for Edinburgh to
become unequivocally the royal and national capital. It was the
Stewart dynasty which most markedly set its seal on the place;
and which ultimately abandoned it when James VI achieved
his goal of becoming King of England and thereafter neglected
his Scottish capital.

The Stewarts suffered a sequence of disasters which would
almost suggest that some evil magician had set a curse upon
the entire house. Several inherited the throne in childhood,
even in early infancy – 'Woe to the kingdom whose king is a
child' – and were oppressed or imprisoned by their regents
and guardians, kidnapped by the English, or bandied to and
fro between powerful nobles. They created further complications by the rarity of their legitimate male heirs surviving
into manhood, though they littered the landscape with a surfeit
of illegitimate children. Yet each in his own way sincerely
struggled to impose order on a country where Lowlander
and Highlander rarely met in friendship, and could rarely
communicate in the same tongue; where there was the continual threat of another English excuse for invasion, often
abetted by self-seeking elements within the kingdom itself; and
where arrogant noblemen prolonged family feuds disruptive
not merely to the families concerned but to the governance of
the kingdom itself.

James I, son of Robert III, was born at Dunfermline in
1394. Sent by his father to France at the age of 12, he was
captured at sea by the English and kept in their custody for
eighteen years. His uncle, the Duke of Albany, was content to
act as Regent after Robert III's death without making too

strenuous an effort to liberate the rightful king. He issued proclamations and charters in his own name, and promoted his relatives to high office. Serious negotiations for James's return began only after the deaths of Albany and of Henry V of England, and after he had married the Duke of Somerset's daughter, Joan Beaufort, for whom he wrote the moving love poem *The King's Quair*. Almost 30 when he was finally crowned at Scone, and with his naturally introspective, melancholy temperament soured by long, enforced idleness, he drove himself to become a man of action and set about destroying those who had grown rich and powerful in his absence, especially the Albany faction. The second Duke's eldest son, Sir Walter Stewart, who had been Keeper of Dumbarton castle, was imprisoned on the bleak Bass Rock, and others were summarily tried and executed for treason and conspiracy. The result was James's own assassination at Perth, just when he was planning to make it his capital and the new home of St Andrew's University.

His son, with a face blemished by a large red birthmark which led to his being known as James of the Fiery Face, was only 6 at the time of the assassination. Crowned in Holyrood abbey rather than Scone because of the rebellious atmosphere around Perth and the southern Highlands, James II was left nominally in the care of his mother. The Three Estates of parliamentary lords, prelates and burgesses, however, had given effective control to the Guardian, the fifth Earl of Douglas. The widowed queen was granted Stirling castle as a residence, but when she tried to take her son there the Keeper of Edinburgh Castle held on to him until she contrived to smuggle him out. Intrigues between various factions striving to make the king their puppet continued throughout his minority. The queen mother remarried but her new husband, Sir James Stewart, the Black Knight of Lorne, was soon seized by her enemies and 'put in a pit and bollit' (presumably boiled in a pit or pot) until she agreed to relinquish her son to one scheming clique. Carried back to Edinburgh, James witnessed the fate of two Douglas brothers who, scorning to collaborate with the intriguers, had been treacherously invited to a feast known to posterity as the 'Black Dinner' and there beheaded before his eyes. Yet other Douglas robber barons continued to indulge in their own intrigues against king and country, in the 'almost aimless treachery', as Andrew Lang describes it, which 'endured for centuries from the reign of David II to that of James VI'.

When he reached the age of 19 and married Mary of Gueldres in Holyrood abbey, James could no longer be denied the full authority of kingship. It is hardly surprising that, after what he had witnessed, he should set about some slaughter of his own. Past persecutors were convicted of treason and hanged; the scheming eighth Earl of Douglas was summoned to Stirling and, when he had refused to give up his association with his own particular clique of conspirators, was stabbed to death by James himself. The king then decided to move his court to Perth, so long favoured by his father. It was unfortunate that, just when he had quelled a great deal of internal disorder and was aiming at a profitable alliance with the Lancastrians during the Wars of the Roses, he chose as a grand gesture to drive out the English garrison still holding Roxburgh castle, only to be killed when one of his own bombards exploded. His son and heir was 8 years old.

Again there was a break with tradition for strategic reasons. Rather than make the risky journey to Scone, James III was crowned in Kelso abbey near Roxburgh. His mother and a council of nobles were appointed to act as Regents, but in a short time the queen had fallen out with her colleagues, not least because she was an avowed supporter of the house of York, while several of them stood for Lancaster. Even those uncommitted to either side in the English dispute made clear their disapproval of any procedure 'that gave the keeping of the kingdom to a woman'. When James III assumed full kingship, there were several elements pitted against him. After murdering some of his art-loving favourites in 1482, one group imprisoned him in reasonable comfort in Edinburgh castle and formed a provisional government. His own brother, with an eye on the throne, allied himself with Richard, Duke of Gloucester (later Richard III), and accompanied a Yorkist army headed for Edinburgh; but, in the face of a compromise suggested by the provisional government, changed his mind. Gloucester thereupon went off to capture Berwick-upon-Tweed and, after thirteen changes of ownership over the centuries, made it once and for all English.

James was released from captivity but not from his nobles' displeasure, incited largely by the scheming Red Douglas family. His eldest son James, who had been living in Stirling castle, was persuaded to join the malcontents. They mustered an army at Linlithgow and marched on Edinburgh. The king escaped to Perth to rally his own forces, and the two sides met at Sauchieburn, near the immortal field of Bannockburn. James had armed himself with the sword of Robert the Bruce, but it stood him in poor stead. Persuaded by advisers to leave the battlefield, he fell from his horse and was carried, injured, into a nearby mill. A man claiming to be a priest was admitted to his presence, drew a sword, and killed him.

During his reign, despite constant intrigue and the treacherous attempts of the Douglases and others to do shabby deals with England, living standards had notably improved. Parliaments met regularly, trade blossomed. Over fifty small burghs were granted privileges for buying and selling specific goods, making and selling cloth, or acquiring a monopoly in other crafts. These were known as burghs of barony and regality. Of higher standing were the royal burghs, which alone were entitled to handle foreign trade, now expanding with exports of wool, hides and salted fish.

James III was buried in Cambuskenneth abbey. His son, aged 17, became James IV at a coronation ceremony at Scone on 24 June 1488.

It was this Stewart who really stimulated the growth and pride of Edinburgh. A great dandy, he loved fine clothes, opulent surroundings and good company. Well educated in Latin, French, German, Flemish, Spanish and Italian as well as in the Gaelic which enabled him to talk to the most suspicious and recalcitrant Highlanders, he gathered about him scholars and artists to add distinction to what soon became not merely the constitutional but also the cultural capital of the north. Proud of his own appearance and punctilious in all his social and religious observances, he was praised by the Spanish ambassador of the time as being

> as handsome in complexion and shape as a man may be
> ... He never cuts his hair or his beard. It becomes him
> well ... He says all his prayers. Before transacting any
> business he hears two masses. After mass he has a cantata
> sung, during which he sometimes dispatches very urgent
> business.

The poet William Dunbar, born in East Lothian and educated at St Andrews, celebrated James's marriage to Margaret Tudor of England – a liaison which led in the fullness of time to the Stewart succession to the throne of England – with a poem, *The Thistle and the Rose*, and summed up his entourage thus:

> Kirkmen, courtmen and craftsmen fyne
> Astrologis, artists and oratouris
> Musicianis, menstralis and mirrie singaris
> Glasing wrichtis, goldsmyths and lapidaris
> Printouris, payntouris and potingaris.

James granted two Edinburgh businessmen a patent to set up a printing press and produce books at reasonable prices: a comfortable monopoly, since at the same time he proscribed the import into Scotland of any books printed abroad. His infant son's personal companion, Sir David Lindsay, was made Lyon King of Arms and carried out major diplomatic missions, but is best remembered today for his wry attacks on the corrupt and greedy nobles in *Ane Satyre of the Thrie Estates*.

Around 1500 James set about building a suitable royal palace beside David I's Holyrood abbey and under the mighty presence of Arthur's Seat. Holyroodhouse incorporates the Chapel Royal, where some Scottish monarchs were married and some were buried in the royal vault. Here James's own marriage of convenience to Margaret Tudor took place in 1503, after he had sired a number of children on various mistresses. Unashamed nepotism ensured that one of the boys became Archbishop of St Andrews while still a minor. Some eight years after that wedding James was less happily responsible for another major work in the city: the Flodden Wall, of which only a battlemented tower now remains in the Vennel between Lauriston Place and the Grassmarket.

Despite the designedly conciliatory Anglo-Scottish marriage, James had not remained long at peace with his wife's brother. Unlike his predecessors, he seems to have got his nobles more or less under control, and had pacified the Highlands; but, like those predecessors, he found that England was rarely in a mood to be pacified. His own conduct does seem provocative. In the time of Henry VII he had stripped the whole of Fife of oak and fir trees in order to build a huge man-of-war, the *Great St Michael*, and had given hospitality to the impostor Perkin Warbeck as son of Edward IV and therefore rightful king of England. He strengthened old castles and built new ones. When Henry VIII acceded to the throne, James let himself be drawn into a dubious alliance with the French king Louis XII, and after Henry had invaded France wrote him a brash letter demanding a cessation of hostilities. When it was clear that Henry was outraged and in a mood for immediate retaliatory action, James decided on what in current jargon would be called a pre-emptive strike. He set out with an army across the Border. Dragging with them seventeen unwieldy brass cannon from Edinburgh castle, they took Norham castle on the south bank of the Tweed, and pressed on a few miles to Flodden in Northumberland.

The battle there lasted less than two hours. The Scots were routed. James, his son and most of his knights were slain. At Scottish military funerals ever since the eighteenth century, when the poem inspiring it was written, the bagpipe lament of *The Flowers o' the Forest* is played in memory of that dreadful day. A tall stone cross on the site bears the following dedication:

To the Brave of Both Nations.

The inhabitants of Edinburgh, fearing imminent invasion, hastened to build the Flodden Wall as a defence.

Again a child was crowned. As James V was not yet 18 months old, his mother was appointed Guardian, threatening a re-run of old melodramas. The sensual Margaret Tudor very quickly stirred up trouble by taking a second husband, the sixth Earl of Angus – a Red Douglas, who proved to be a greedy bully and unsuitable either as a husband or a stepfather. On the grounds that James IV's will had nominated her for the regency only if she remained a widow, the Scottish Estates sent for the Duke of Albany, descendant of that Stewart who had plagued James III. He had married well in France, and tendencies now swung again towards the Auld Alliance, much fed by the lingering grief of Flodden. Conflicting interests drove Albany out in due course. The queen mother, impatient for a more vigorous husband, divorced Angus, who was now conspiring with Henry VIII, and married another Stewart. Angus disappeared for a while, but returned to reclaim all his old honours and become one of a new group of guardians. The young James found himself a virtual prisoner of the Red Douglases in Edinburgh castle. In May 1528, while Angus was away, James disguised himself as a groom and made a dash for Stirling. With supporters opposed to the Douglas braggarts he set off towards Tantallon castle, where Angus had precipitately fled on learning that the king was loose and in vengeful mood.

Built to last by William Douglas, at a time when the family was in high favour because of its support of Robert the Bruce, the massive red sandstone ruins of Tantallon on its seagirt rock above the mouth of the Forth look virtually unassailable even today. In its prime the solid curtain-walled castle could not have been taken by storm up the sheer cliffs rising from the sea on three sides; and a deep ditch hewn from the rock on the landward side made any surprise attack on the gatehouse or drum towers improbable. Even though James V had brought artillery with him to pound the walls, it made little impression, and in the end the besiegers ran out of gunpowder. Starving the defenders out seemed to be the only course, and that would take a long time. Negotiations led to Angus being allowed to surrender unharmed on condition that he went into exile in England, while the Red Douglas possessions were declared forfeit.

Systematically demolishing his enemies, imprisoning some and descending on Border troublemakers for summary hangings, James combined military decisiveness with a great love of the arts and, as both his admirers and detractors admitted, of regal pomp. Henry VIII of England, busy destroying monasteries and confiscating their wealth, suggested in friendly fashion that his nephew should do the same in Scotland. But James remained true to the Roman faith, and to provide funds for his extravagant tastes sought a rich wife from Catholic Europe. His first choice was Madeleine, daughter of King Francis I of France. Their wedding took place in Paris on New Year's Day 1537 with all the pomp James could have wished for, accompanied by the substantial dowry which he also fancied; but six weeks after reaching Scotland his fragile wife died, unable to survive the rigours of the Scottish winter. He wasted little time in finding a replacement, choosing the widowed Mary of Guise. While waiting for her to produce a legitimate heir, he managed to father a number of illegitimate children on his six mistresses.

Franco-Scottish ties were stronger than they had ever been. When Mary arrived in Scotland complete with the second dowry, James set about transforming a number of his favourite residences. French masons were brought in to work on the glorified hunting lodge of Falkland in Fife until it came to resemble a French Renaissance palace in miniature, with the courtyard's south range richly decorated with Scots thistles, French fleurs-de-lis and pictorial medallions. A part of the grounds is still called the Fleurs, and the Royal Tennis court is one of the type, originating in France, known as *jeu quarré*. The ambience was the same at Stirling, where a Renaissance palace was inserted within the curtain walls, graced by delicate stone columns rising above the starker battlements. Mary herself praised the work done at Linlithgow; and for her comfort and his own, James began augmenting Holyroodhouse in Edinburgh.

What was once the abbey's guest-house had been increasing in size and grandeur as successive monarchs used it for their Edinburgh residence. While Edinburgh itself was growing in importance as a centre of government, the temporary residence was refashioned into a palace. James IV had added new ranges of rooms. His son planned a whole new courtyard and other buildings, but before his death had got little further than a north-west tower, later to be incorporated in further developments by Charles II's architect, Sir William Bruce.

Between palace and castle runs the processional route of the Royal Mile, for long the arena for the city's most important activities, climbing as it does up a narrow ridge cramped between steep slopes carved out by ancient glaciers to either side. In 1724 Daniel Defoe described it as 'perhaps the largest, longest and finest street for buildings and number of inhabitants, not in Britain only, but in the world'. The character of the whole place is best assessed by walking down from the castle rather than climbing east to west. Urban development does not, unfortunately, keep itself within strict chronological order, so that a geographically direct descent of the Royal Mile skips disconcertingly in and out of a far from direct historical sequence.

One of the first things to catch the visitor's eye when starting down from the castle esplanade is a cannonball lodged in the wall of a house, believed to have been fired from the castle at Holyroodhouse in 1745 when anti-Jacobite forces on the Castle Rock were at odds with Prince Charles Edward at the lower end of the town. A glance to the left gives glimpses of the spacious Georgian squares and terraces of the eighteenth century, when the North Loch and surrounding swamps were drained to allow construction of the New Town. Names in its neat gridiron of streets reflect the Hanoverian ascendancy of the time: George Street, Queen Street, Princes Street, Hanover

Street and Charlotte Square. Contrasted with that prospect of classical elegance is the tangle which the visitor sees ahead down the older thoroughfare: the spire of St Giles's cathedral, entrances to courtyards in which lived men as diverse as the philosopher David Hume and the Jekyll-and-Hyde rogue Deacon Brodie, and high tenement blocks wedged against one another as if to prevent them toppling backwards into a chasm.

Lack of space in which to build laterally resulted in this characteristic Edinburgh townscape of early tower blocks, often with additional lower floors invisible from the street, clinging to the cliffs and reached through narrow wynds, vennels and closes overshadowed by the dark flanks of buildings stained by the smoke of those 'Auld Reekie' years. The smoke of fires was not the only reeking element in the atmosphere. When Boswell lodged Dr Johnson in James's Court off the Lawnmarket his guest promptly remarked on the 'evening effluvia' which Boswell admitted 'could not be masked'. The markets themselves must have contributed greatly to this. From medieval times the street itself had accommodated market traders, their chief area being the Lawnmarket – once called the Landmarket – to which people from neighbouring farmlands brought in food and goods. A heart-shaped stone inlay in the road marks the site of the old Tolbooth where market tolls were collected, causing even more constriction in the narrow, lurching street. It also served as a prison, and features as such in Walter Scott's novel *The Heart of Midlothian*. St Giles's cathedral nearby is more properly known as the High Kirk, having been formally designated a cathedral for only a brief period during the reign of Charles I. It was here that Charles attempted to impose a High Anglican liturgy, virtually a Mass, upon a Presbyterian society which responded with brawls in the church and outside, still remembered as the Jenny Geddes Riots after a vegetable seller from the market who was reported to have thrown her stool at the Dean's head.

John Knox's House in High Street recalls the opposition of the fiercest of all Scottish Reformers to the Catholic beliefs (sometimes thinly veiled, sometimes undisguised) of the house of Stewart. It may or may not have been his home for any length of time, but it is certainly the only survivor of that contemporary period of timbered houses with thatched roofs which frequently caught fire and were eventually forbidden. The stone houses and tenements which replaced them, however, often continued to sport timber galleries above the street. Below Knox's supposed home once stood the Netherbow Port, a gateway in the town wall, outside which began the abbey's separate burgh of Canongate.

Canongate had its own Tolbooth, which has survived because it was set into the building line instead of blocking the thoroughfare. It now thrusts a clock out high above that thoroughfare. Among some fine town houses are Moray House, built after James VI had abandoned his capital for the greater adulation of London but when a Scottish parliament still endeavoured to preserve its autonomy in Edinburgh; and relics of ancient inns more accessible to coaching traffic than those in the congested upper reaches.

And finally, at the foot of the Royal Mile, one confronts Holyroodhouse, resplendent behind its gates and opulent courtyard.

While James was still in the middle of grandiose schemes for embellishing his more cherished properties, murmurs of trouble with England began to rumble once more. Henry VIII agreed to an amicable meeting at York to discuss differences between the two countries, many of them fomented by Douglas troublemakers exiled in England. James's advisers, especially churchmen who feared that one of Henry's main motives was to coax their king towards Protestantism and an anti-French alliance, warned against any venture on to English soil. When James failed to arrive at York, Henry was furious and vengefully launched attacks on the Borders. In return James decided on a full-scale invasion of England, and marched from Edinburgh with 10,000 men, adding some reluctant levies on his way.

At the battle of Solway Moss the superior numbers of the Scots were too disorganized to withstand the English troops.

Many deserted before the battle even started, and a number of nobles surrendered as soon as they could decently do so. James himself, ill with some ailment which has never been reliably diagnosed, and perhaps debilitated by a variety of medicines in which he dabbled, fled despondently to his palace at Linlithgow to see his pregnant wife. From there he moved on to Edinburgh, and finally shut himself away in his much embellished palace of Falkland to die.

His ill-starred daughter, of whose birth on 8 December 1542 James heard on his deathbed, was kept at Linlithgow for seven months, by which time it had been agreed that she should in the fullness of time marry Edward, heir to Henry VIII of England. Henry relied on the Douglas family and hostages taken at Solway Moss to support this arrangement on their return to their homeland.

The infant queen was crowned at Stirling, and her mother was appointed Regent. Mary of Guise, as leader of Papal and pro-French elements among the nobility, was dubious about English proposals for a proxy marriage before the queen was 10, and a subsequent upbringing in England. In due course the whole idea was rejected. Henry at once launched destructive raids into Scotland in what became wryly known as the 'Rough Wooing'. His troops under the Earl of Hertford devastated the great Border abbeys, ravaged defenceless villages, set fire to the Canongate in Edinburgh, and inflicted heavy damage on Holyroodhouse. In Argyll and the Inner Hebrides some pro-English Scots were equally ruthless against their own countrymen. The invasion was briefly halted at Ancrum Moor near Jedburgh, where a heavy defeat was inflicted on the English by an army under the command of the sixth Earl of Angus, hitherto one of Henry's supporters but now a bitter opponent because of the desecration of his family's graves at Melrose abbey. At the same time help was sought from France, which sent troops to the east coast.

At Henry's death his son Edward was 9 years of age. Hertford, now Duke of Somerset, proclaimed himself Lord Protector of England, and resumed the carnage in Scotland.

He led an army of some 18,000 to meet the Scots at Pinkie, six miles east of Edinburgh. The invaders were backed up by warships which from the mouth of the river Esk poured a crippling cannonade into the Scottish ranks. More than 10,000 were killed. Somerset wreaked further damage on Holyroodhouse and established English garrisons in Leith and other key positions.

One of the strongest of these was Haddington, the county town of East Lothian. The town's appearance today is that of a compact, prosperous market centre still clinging to its medieval street plan and to memories of the Franciscan priory once known as the 'Lamp of Lothian', a designation transferred in our own century to the church of St Mary. This church suffered cruelly when French and Scottish besiegers bombarding the English garrison destroyed the roof and vaults. The French reinforcements had arrived in answer to a plea from Mary of Guise, who had accompanied her daughter to safety in an island priory on the Lake of Menteith, about fifteen miles west of Stirling. In return for this co-operation the French asked that the child queen should be affianced not to Edward VI but to the Dauphin of France, and that she should be brought up there. A treaty was signed outside Haddington, and within a few weeks Mary, Queen of Scots, was on her way from Dumbarton to Paris.

Another son of Haddington was, it has been claimed, the fervent Protestant evangelist John Knox. After the dislodgement by French forces of agitators who had hanged the Catholic Archbishop of St Andrews from the walls of St Andrews castle and then sustained a protracted siege, Knox served a term in the French galleys until released by the intervention of Edward VI of England, to whom he became a royal chaplain. He preached fierily in England until the advent of 'Bloody Mary' Tudor caused him to flee to Switzerland and study with Calvin. Frequently reviled by the Catholic party under the queen mother, neither Knox nor his followers could view with any optimism the continuing presence in their country of French troops. The English, with no hope now of consummating the Rough Wooing, finally withdrew; but the French were proving almost equally unwelcome, provoking fears among committed Protestant reformers that Scotland was to be swallowed up by yet another powerful nation, and this one Papist.

During young Mary's absence in France, her mother acted as Regent of Scotland. The queen mother's religious views and those of the French advisers she gathered around her did little to allay the reformers' fears; nor would they have been happy to know that on Mary's marriage in 1558 to the Dauphin, who the following year became King Francis II, she secretly signed an agreement that if she should die childless her kingdom of Scotland and her claim to the throne of England should become her husband's. In a drift away from the Auld Alliance, leading magnates appealed to the newly crowned Queen Elizabeth of England to help rid them of the French. Already disturbed by Catholic accusations that she herself was illegitimate and that Mary was rightful successor to the English throne, Elizabeth hastened to oblige.

Combined English and Scottish forces drove the French out of Leith. Mary of Guise took refuge in Edinburgh castle, and conveniently died in June 1560. By the Treaty of Edinburgh both French and English agreed to withdraw and to recognize the independence of Scotland, while in return Mary would recognize Elizabeth as rightful Queen of England. Once the foreign troops had gone, the Scottish Parliament denounced Popery, forbade the celebration of Mass, and introduced a Protestant confession of faith. John Knox returned to a tumultuous welcome, having been flatteringly described as a reformer who not merely 'lopped the branches of the papistry' but struck 'at the root, to destroy the whole'.

In August 1561 Mary, widowed after a short marriage and a short reign, and seeing little future in a country under the influence of her powerful mother-in-law, returned to her own kingdom, landing in the mist at Leith and making her way to Holyroodhouse.

Thus there came into being a national jurisdiction which

had forsworn Catholicism, ruled over by a queen who refused to abandon her Catholic faith. For a while she behaved wisely – or cunningly – by allowing her ministers to give formal recognition to the ways of the reformed church on condition that she herself was allowed to worship in the old way in the privacy of her own chapel at Holyrood. Her other inconsistencies presaged more awkward problems. She had refused to sign the treaty recognizing Elizabeth as legitimate Queen of England, still considering her far from legitimate; yet, once returned to Scotland, she compromised far enough to say that she would accept Elizabeth's tenure during her lifetime on the understanding that her own eventual right to the succession was acknowledged. The English monarch repudiated any such understanding. The fact that Mary and her late husband had after their coronation in Rheims formally assumed the titles of King and Queen of England and Ireland had not provoked any great trust in Elizabeth's always suspicious mind. The stage was set for years of mutual mistrust and recrimination.

Whatever their differences, the two queens had one quality in common: Mary, like Elizabeth, sensed that the best way to win her subjects' affection and loyalty was for her to be seen moving among them. It helped that she was in herself such an impressive figure. Like Elizabeth too she had red hair, but unlike her cousin she was some six feet tall, towering majestically over most men, with a narrow face, high brow and broodingly sensual eyes – 'a miracle of nature', according to an Italian visitor to her court. She loved to dress in vivid colours, garnished with necklaces, bracelets, rings and other glittering jewellery which was the envy of every other monarch in Europe. She travelled regularly, taking in scattered places such as Inverness, Inverary, Dunoon, Aberdeen and the Border towns which needed encouragement after English depredations. Every spring she was to be found visiting Fife. In Argyll and Ayrshire she enjoyed herself hunting and playing golf. But Edinburgh was her capital city; and in Edinburgh most of the significant dramas of her life happened, or at least came to a head.

John Knox, at the time of the queen's return established as minister of St Giles, denounced her religious compromises from the pulpit and in a series of interviews endeavoured to persuade her to give up her idolatrous views, regretfully concluding that she was 'indurate against God and his truth'. Certainly she was indurate against Knox's sermonizing, and their clash of ideologies was one of the factors leading to passionate outbursts against Mary whenever one of her enemies wished to force her into an awkward situation.

Knox had trained at St Andrews as a priest, but under the influence of the Reformation advocate George Wishart became devoted to Lutheran ideals. When Wishart was burned at the stake on the orders of Scotland's primate, Cardinal Beaton, Knox had joined protesters and rejoiced at Beaton's eventual hanging at St Andrews. Sheltering abroad, in 1558 he wrote *The First Blast of the Trumpet against the Monstrous Regiment of Woman* – the 'regiment' actually meaning a regimen or government by women, which he condemned as 'a thing most contrarious' to God's 'revealed will and approved ordinance'. His tirades were reinforced, according to a contemporary, by a commanding physical presence and manner.

Rather below the normal height, his cheeks ruddy and somewhat full, the eyes keen and animated, large lips, his thick black beard flecked with grey falling down a hand and a half long, he bore an air of authority, and in anger his frown became imperious.

The question of remarriage and the provision of an heir to the unstable throne was inevitably rearing its head. Any possibility of a suggested match between Mary and the heir to Philip II of Spain was ringingly denounced by Knox. The wild offer by Elizabeth of England of her discarded favourite, the Earl of Leicester, met with justifiable incredulity. The whole matter was not so much solved as channelled in another direction by the sudden love match between Mary and her first cousin Henry, Lord Darnley, whom she described as the 'properest and best proportioned long man' she had ever seen. He was a suitable husband in one way: through the second marriage of his grandmother, Margaret Tudor, he stood next in line to Mary in the succession to the English throne. In other ways he proved far from ideal. Effeminate, spoilt and faithless, he was a bitter disappointment to her, and was so thoroughly despised by the rest of the Court that when she became pregnant there were rumours about the child having possibly been fathered by one of her favourites. Giving birth in Edinburgh on 19 June 1566, Mary was at pains to declare loudly to Darnley before a number of witnesses: 'God has given you and me a son, begotten by none but you.'

Apart from that she was now showing little but contempt for him. Only a few months earlier he had, as she was soon to discover, been involved in a plot to murder her secretary and musician David Rizzio, believing or half-believing that the two of them were lovers. Led by the brutish Patrick, Lord Ruthven, a gang burst in upon Mary, her ladies and Rizzio at supper in one of her private inner rooms in Holyrood. Rizzio was dragged into a neighbouring closet – now a feature of every visitor's tour through the palace – and stabbed about fifty times. Darnley's own dagger was found still in the body. Fearing for her own safety, the queen slipped out of the palace at night and, in spite of being unsure of Darnley's own part in the murder, rode with him to Dunbar castle on the coast of East Lothian. She returned to Edinburgh a week later, having acquired a dependable escort under the leadership of the Earl of Bothwell. John Knox made capital out of the murder by praying to God to 'destroy that whore in her whoredom'.

Darnley himself was the next to die. Mary's nobles detested her insolent consort almost as much as she did and, either from genuine loyalty to her or in devious application of their own power politics, conspired to remove him. The leader of this band was that dashing Earl of Bothwell who had shown signs of becoming Mary's latest favourite, and who was soon to show even higher ambitions. On the face of it the queen herself was innocent of any involvement. Yet the favours and appointments she showered on him must surely have given Bothwell reason to assume that he could interpret her secret wishes. Mary's own conduct towards her dissolute husband was also open to a number of interpretations.

Darnley had not attended his son's christening at Stirling. Soon after the ceremony he went to Glasgow, where he fell ill with what would seem to have been smallpox, and from vanity kept a taffeta mask over his face. During a visit to him there, Mary is supposed to have written a letter to Bothwell which, discovered later in a silver casket with some poems in French and a written agreement to marry Bothwell, pointed clearly to her complicity in a plot to murder her husband. Arguments over the authenticity or otherwise of these 'Casket Letters' have continued over the centuries. Nevertheless it was as an outwardly devoted wife that she took charge of Darnley's transfer from Glasgow to Edinburgh, where she lodged him not in Holyrood, in case he infected the infant prince, but in a house belonging to the Canon of Holyrood. This building, Kirk o' Field, stood well apart from other properties by the south wall of the city.

Mary spent a number of days and nights close to the sick man's bedside. On the evening of a masked ball in the palace she came visiting with Bothwell and other lords, and while she chatted to her husband they – with or without her knowledge – went down to the cellar to prepare the gunpowder stored there. In the small hours of the morning, after they had all gone, there was an explosion which shook the whole town. Darnley and his attendant were dead. But they had not been destroyed by the explosion: bewilderingly, their bodies were found in the garden some distance from the house, and they had obviously been strangled. As with the Casket Letters, conflicting theories concerning the event have proliferated ever since.

Public outrage at the enormity linked the names of Mary and Bothwell. A hasty burlesque of a trial exculpated Bothwell, but instead of keeping tactfully out of sight for a while he abducted the queen on the pretence of seeking to protect her.

She found herself again in Dunbar castle where, according to stories later defensively circulated by Mary herself, Bothwell raped her and she had to agree to marry him. A rushed divorce from his wife was arranged, and he and Mary returned under a strong guard to Edinburgh, where on 15 May 1567 they were married in Holyrood palace by Protestant rites. As a wedding present the queen created Bothwell Duke of Orkney and Lord of Shetland. Even nobles who had at one time covertly recommended such a union were alarmed by the unseemly haste, and realized that in any case the tide of national opinion was against the match. Diplomatically changing sides, they joined with forces planning rebellion.

Bothwell carried Mary off again, this time to Borthwick castle, a dark tower house in Midlothian south of Edinburgh which is still inhabited today. Pursued there and besieged, they fled by night to raise a loyal army, but found it pitiful in numbers. Superior forces led by the Earl of Morton met them at Carberry Hill near the earlier battlefield of Pinkie. The two armies waited while messengers conveyed to Mary the offer of her rebel nobles to support her once more if she would discard her husband's murderer. Since she knew by now that some of them had abetted Bothwell in that very matter, she angrily repulsed them. In the end Bothwell himself saw that there was no hope. He rode off towards Dunbar and set sail for his dukedom of Orkney and then for Norway, where he was arrested and confined in due course in the castle of Dragsholm in Denmark. Until well into our own century his embalmed body was displayed in a glass-topped coffin in Faarevejle church on the Danish island of Fyn.

Mary's submission to her lords brought none of the forgiveness which they had implied. She was kept prisoner in Edinburgh and then in a castle on an islet in Loch Leven near Kinross. Forced to abdicate and agree to the appointment of the Earl of Moray, one of her father's illegitimate sons, as Regent on behalf of her son, she languished in the bleak tower which now looks so romantic with its nineteenth-century addition of trees. Beside the laird's hall on the third floor a window embrasure was converted into a small private oratory for her use. After a year she used all her wiles to coax a young man into helping her escape, and crossed the Forth at Queensferry.

Along a route taking in the castles of Niddry, Cadzow and Craignethan she rallied sympathizers who still regarded her as rightful queen. The always quarrelsome and largely Catholic Border lords made moves to join her. High hopes of a triumphal return lasted just over ten days. She was defeated at Langside, south of Glasgow, and fled to Dumfries and at last to the banks of the Solway. Her last night on Scottish soil was spent at Dundrennan abbey. On 16 May 1568 she crossed the firth to land in England at the 'lytle prety fyscher town' of Workington and appeal, fatefully, for help from her cousin Elizabeth.

For five years after her departure, Edinburgh castle was loyally held in the queen's name under the command of her secretary, William Maitland of Lethington, and the distinguished soldier Sir William Kirkcaldy of Grange, in spite of Kirkcaldy's having led the forces opposed to her at Langside. A plaque on a courtyard wall pays tribute to his defence of the castle, which collapsed only when cannon on loan from Elizabeth devastated the main east front, which later had to be entirely rebuilt.

Custody of the refugee monarch in England became a matter of immediate local pride. She was lodged in Carlisle castle by the Deputy Warden of the West Marches of England, whose authority was immediately challenged by the Earl of Northumberland, premier Catholic nobleman of the region. Nor thumberland failed to take her into his personal custody, but their exchanges of letters during her incarceration in Carlisle were to contribute largely to the disastrous Rising of the North in 1569. This Northern Rebellion soured any possibility of Mary ever being trusted by her cousin Elizabeth, and spelt little but trouble for the always uneasy Border.

SELECTED SITES OF INTEREST

Antiquities

CAIRNPAPPLE HILL   Near Torpichen off the Linlithgow to Bathgate road. An extensive ritual and burial site with henge and cairns from 3000–1400 BC. A chamber open to visitors displays an Early Bronze Age beaker burial, and magnificent views take in the mountains of Arran, the Trossachs, the Bass Rock in the Firth of Forth, and the Border hills.

CHESTERS HILL-FORT   North of Haddington, signposted a mile south of Drem. A substantial, well-preserved Iron Age settlement with two encircling ramparts and supplementary earthworks. Traces of stone circles interrupting the main defences suggest later, less defensive occupation from the second century AD onwards.

RATHO   Cup-and-ring rock markings on Tormain Hill, off the B7030 near Ratho, beyond south-west suburbs of Edinburgh. On a ridge with fine prospects over Edinburgh, the Pentlands and the Firth of Forth are outcrops and boulders with the stylized incisions of circles, cup shapes and concentric grooves which appear at ritual sites in many countries from Ireland to India, and in especially large numbers in Scotland.

TRAPRAIN LAW   2 miles south-east of East Linton. A 500-foot high volcanic plug which was a tribal centre for over 1,000 years, with series of defensive outworks being added by successive occupants. It probably grew to the status of a town with special civic privileges during the Roman occupation, and seems to have survived well into the Saxon period.

(*For a general study of the foregoing see also Chapter 1.*)

Historic Buildings

DIRLETON CASTLE   Rises from a rocky crag above the village of Dirleton, west of North Berwick on the A198. Appearance today largely due to sixteenth-century work of the Ruthvens.

In the grounds, a beehive doocot and seventeenth-century bowling green.

EDINBURGH *Castle* Includes Scottish United Services Museum of weapons, uniforms and other regimental relics.

Georgian House, Charlotte Square Characteristic Adam building in the New Town, furnished in appropriate style.

Gladstone's Land, Lawnmarket Seventeenth-century block with period furnishings. Takes its name from Thomas Gledstane, a wealthy merchant.

Canongate Tolbooth Sixteenth-century tolbooth with gun-loops in its tower. Regular exhibitions, including permanent display of tartans and clan insignia.

HAILES CASTLE Off narrow unclassified road near East Linton. Overshadowed by Traprain Law, the castle in a tranquil river-side setting was a Bothwell property to which the earl brought Mary, Queen of Scots, during their flight from Borthwick in 1567. It had been seized by the English during the 'Rough Wooing', and was largely demolished by Cromwell in 1650.

LENNOXLOVE A country mansion in parkland just outside Haddington. It was originally a tower house called Lethington, property of the Maitland family who produced many influential royal advisers including Mary's 'Secretary Lethington' and her son's Chancellor; and the Earl of Lauderdale who became dictatorial Secretary of State for Scotland under Charles II. In Charles's time the house was bought by 'La Belle Stewart', Duchess of Lennox – the model for Britannia on British coinage – who, after her husband's death, insisted the house should be renamed Lennoxlove as a sign of her devotion.

LINLITHGOW The palace overlooking a beautiful loch was the birthplace of Mary, Queen of Scots. Much of interior destroyed by fire during garrisoning by troops after 1745 rising. In 1914 King George V held a court here in the Lyon Chamber. Parish church close by has a modern open spire in the style of the medieval crown steeple which was removed in the early nineteenth century.

Museums

DUNBAR   Near ruined castle, lifeboat house displays collection of models of early lifeboats and rescue apparatus.

EAST FORTUNE   Museum of Flight on airfield from which airships once set off. Display of early aircraft and space rockets.

EDINBURGH   *Holyrood Park Visitor Centre*   Exhibition of prehistory, history and conservation of the park's plant and animal life.

Huntly House, Canongate   Museum of local history in sixteenth-century town mansion.

Lady Stair's House, Lawnmarket   Seventeenth-century town house in a secluded close with collections of material relating to Robert Burns, Sir Walter Scott and Robert Louis Stevenson.

Museum of Childhood, High Street   History of children's dress, toys and environment through the ages.

NEWTONGRANGE   Scottish Mining Museum provides a 'coal trail' linking the Lady Victoria Colliery to the beam engine, brickworks and colliery remains at Prestongrange, past traces of a medieval coal heugh and later developments of the Lothian coalfield. Displays of working steam engines.

SOUTH QUEENSFERRY   Museum in Council Chambers has a local history display, including particularly interesting material on the building of the Forth railway bridge.

4

---◆---

The Borders

THE MODERN region called simply Borders encompasses the older shires of Berwick, Peebles, Selkirk and Roxburgh; but in this case the 'new' name reverts to an older over-all description of a swathe of land between England and Scotland whose boundaries were repeatedly overrun and violently contested throughout the centuries. Even after the Union of the Crowns there remained a long period during which old traditions and suspicions simmered uneasily, and old local enmities flared up at the slightest provocation.

Although the landscapes on both sides of the Border are very similar, from the lowlands north and east of Carlisle through fells rising to the Cheviot range and falling again to the coastal plain, it is still noticeable that permanent settlements of any size are fewer along the Scottish side. Scottish kings were rarely powerful enough, or could muster an army large and united enough to keep permanent guard along the frontier against major English invasions. They had their work cut out in simply trying to provide defences against the incursions of cattle raiders from the North Tyne valley, over Bewcastle Waste, or through that tract of the western fringe so unsure of its ownership that it was known as the Debatable Land; and their own people were themselves frequently as unruly as their enemies. Even the heavily fortified town of Berwick-upon-Tweed, on the Scottish bank of the river, was wrested from them by the English over and over again, and finally lost. Under both governances it somehow managed, in friendly or hostile fashion, to draw supplies of meat, poultry and other foodstuffs from the fertile riverside plain known as the Merse (or Marsh), which with its moderate rainfall was from early times one of the most productive agricultural regions in the country.

Northumbrian villages, though protected to some extent by castles and garrisons such as those at Carlisle, Naworth, Harbottle and Norham, tended to be built in a sort of miniature bailey around a large square green which could be gated when cattle were brought in for the night. Scottish villages were so frequently attacked and burned, and were so lacking in adequate fortified protection, that farmers and small gentry could survive only by building stone tower houses with barmkins, or walled enclosures. After the defeat at Flodden every Scottish Borderer with land above the value of £100 was ordered to build such towers and enclosures to safeguard tenants, workers and livestock. Any flimsy homesteads of clay and brushwood outside the defensive walls (or even inside if those walls were breached) were liable to be set on fire regularly, but their hardened inhabitants could usually manage a replacement within a few days 'provided we have five or six poles and boughs to cover them'. Little was permanent, and comforts were minimal. A traveller in the early seventeenth century wrote of a thatched house in Langholm that the wall had 'one course of stones, another of sods of earth, a door of wicker rods, and the spider webs hung over our heads as thick as might be in our bed'. Celia Fiennes, riding through the same region towards the end of that century, found the Border dwellings 'worse than booths at a fair', and so smelly that she preferred to lunch with her horses in the stable.

Records of clothing and the other necessities and niceties of life are scanty. The historian D.L.W. Tough comments that the main pointers are in what is omitted rather than what is mentioned: barely a reference to shirts or nightshirts, and the possibility that even adult Borderers had their underclothes sewn on and removed as seldom as those of slum children in later industrial cities. 'There is certainly little to suggest', he adds, 'that personal cleanliness was thought a necessity, or was even a rare virtue.'

Between the warring factions on both sides of the Border lay many stretches of infertile wilderness known as wastes. Rocky outcrops ('edges' or 'rigs') on the fells were the only landmarks to guide the knowledgeable around the boggy patches of moss or flow. For inveterate cattle-lifters it all added up to a convenient no-man's-land across which to launch thieving raids. Only gradually were these treacherous areas brought into profitable use from peat digging to farming or, especially in our own time, for afforestation.

In the north of the Border shires, along the flanks of low hills such as the Eildons, medieval monastic establishments built up their extensive sheep runs, denuding the cover of the hills and destabilizing the soil. In the fertile valleys they acquired large agricultural granges, some to be farmed by their own lay brothers, others let out to tenants who formed clusters of farm 'townships'. Here as in other regions the system of ploughed riggs, or ridges, and strip cultivation in fields shared by different families was common for many centuries. Marks of these furrows can be detected on many a gentle slope, especially when slanting sunlight casts regular shadows. The main crops were oats and barley. The mill was usually under monastic supervision, and the miller was allowed to take a proportion from each sack as his fee. Those who wished to brew beer for their own household could use the abbey brewery – again upon a proportional payment. In the less fertile, wilder southern fringes it was on the whole more rewarding to raise stock whose meat could be salted down and whose hides could be tanned and made into clothing, shoes and cooking or storage pots.

In the case of secular centres, most burghs had strips of land leading back from the market-place for burghers' houses, vegetable plots and space for livestock. Outside the town wall there would be common land for grazing, and strips of arable land. The burgesses of the 'husband town' allocated such divisions on behalf of the Crown, the arable land being measured to assess its user's liability for military service: a 'hus-bandland' was the area of ploughland sufficient to provide a man with a living that could afford him a horse and harness when called on in a Border emergency.

At appointed intervals the burgesses formally rode the boundaries to make sure that no encroachments or neglect had occurred. These surveys became a major symbolic cer-emonial, and are recalled in the colourful annual Common Ridings of Jedburgh, Langholm, Hawick and other towns. One of the most moving is the Common Riding at Selkirk, whose Flodden memorial with its inscription *O, Flodden Field* recalls the single local survivor who staggered back from the battle with an English standard, now lodged in the town museum. Each June a young lad chosen by popular vote to carry the town standard concludes the pageant by 'casting the colours' in the market-place. Not one of the Hawick contingent returned from Flodden, but each year a flag is carried through the town by the 'Cornet', this time a young married man. It is the replica of one seized from a gang of English raiders from Hexham the year after the battle. In 1988, offered the honour of taking part in the Lord Mayor of London's Show and carrying the Burgh Standard, the town of Langholm proudly declined on the grounds that the cherished flag was never displayed other than on Common Riding Day and never left the town, and that 'It would be demeaning for the Principals to take part in a "fancy dress" parade'.

Emergencies demanding the swift rallying of armed men arose not just in times of national conflict, but when large or small bands of rustlers swooped on livestock and rode off with them, as those Hexham raiders had intended. The movement of cattle, legal and illegal, had a much greater influence on Border life, particularly in its less amenable wilds and wastes, than did agricultural developments.

Prehistoric and Roman tracks were duly appropriated by drovers from the Highlands, bringing their cattle down for sale in the Lowlands and, when the two nations were at peace, in England. Some routes were planned, climbing from valleys to moorland pastures and shielings for summer grazing. Many more came into being simply by use rather than by calculation. Paths were worn between one friendly community and another, between markets and recognized assembly points. They could also, of course, be used by less friendly rustlers descending unawares on those communities: one hill track between St Mary's Loch and a ford across the Tweed was ruefully dubbed 'Thief's Road'; but most such raiders preferred to shun known tracks and ride straight across wild countryside on their sturdy little Border horses, known as hobblers or hobbys.

When a drover's or farmer's beasts went missing, they were liable to find their way into rogues' hiding-places such as the deep cleft of the Devil's Beef Tub near the source of the River Tweed above Moffat, where encircling hills seemed, according to Sir Walter Scott, to be 'laying their heads together to shut out the daylight from the dark hollow space between them'. Between the unruly vales of Teviotdale, Eskdale and Liddesdale, animals could be hidden in the wilds of the Tarras Moss into which only the bravest of pursuers would dare follow. The story of the Borders is largely one of cattle-rustling on a scale which would have amazed even the American Wild West, of internecine feuds as violent as those of Sicily, and of cliques of racketeers who brought into the language the term 'blackmail', meaning 'black meal' or 'black rent' – in other words, protection money.

As early as 1249, when England and Scotland were nominally at peace and recognized each other as separate kingdoms, a commission of English and Scottish knights framed a code of Laws and Customs of the Marches for use in local and national disputes and transgressions, though it was to be honoured more in the breach than in the observance. Edward I, considering himself sovereign lord of both countries, appointed his own Warden not so much to keep the peace along a border whose very existence he denied, but for the whole Keeping of Scotland. Only when Scottish independence was once more recognized did there come about the establishment of separate Wardens for each of the three main regions either side of the Border: West March, Middle March and East March. Appointments to these posts were in the gift of the monarch on either side, but the power of local lords made the choice a foregone conclusion in most instances if the said lords wished to serve, which was not always the case. For long periods there were Homes in the East March, the Kerrs of either Ferniehirst or Cessford (related but mutually hostile) in the Middle March, and the Maxwells in the West, save for periods when their feuding rivals the Johnstones took possession. On the English side, reluctance to accept office was a frequent occurrence. The Border was a long way from the intrigues of the Court in London, a good thing at times but a disadvantage if one were planning a profitable intrigue of one's own.

In due course the usages of the frontier included regular meetings of Wardens from either side, seeking to control unrulier elements in their own jurisdiction and obtain redress for robberies or killings inflicted from the facing March. They convened Days of Truce at which to reach mutual agreement on 'clearing' bills against the accused (that is, finding them not guilty), or 'fyling' them ('fouling' or finding them guilty). Although these were supposed to be held monthly, devious excuses were manifold when one side or the other wished to dodge an awkward issue. And although safe conduct was officially guaranteed to either faction during the time it would take to reach the site, parley and then ride home, many truces failed to hold.

One regular meeting place was at the Redeswire or Reidswire, close to the present Border crossing of Carter Bar. On 7 July 1575 Sir John Forster, the Warden of the English Middle March, took offence at an insult offered him by his opposite number, supporters of the two men began to jeer at each other, and a skirmish ensued in which several men were killed and Sir John and his son-in-law Lord Francis Russell were carried off as prisoners. Since the rulers of neither country were inclined to full-scale war at this time, diplomatic moves were made to sort the matter out, and the captives were hastily returned.

Ten years later Lord Francis Russell was less fortunate. Another meeting place in the Cheviots was at Windy Gyle, a bleak height difficult to reach even today unless one is a committed long-distance walker along the Pennine Way. Two prehistoric cairns stand above what was described in the sixteenth century as

> a great waste ground of four miles broad and more ... and the side thereof that lieth towards England is the common pasture of the uttermost inhabited towns of England, and the side thereof towards Scotland is so wet a moss or marshy ground that it will neither bear corn nor serve for the pasture of any cattle, also their way scarcely any man pass over it.

One of the stone mounds is now known as Lord Russell's Cairn. Close to it at a March meeting in 1585 accusations of a theft of some Scottish spurs and counter-accusations of 'a pretended matter beforehand' began to fly to and fro, until without warning someone on the Scottish side shot and killed Russell. Sir Thomas Kerr of Ferniehirst and Sir John Forster told conflicting stories in the subsequent enquiry. Ferniehirst was removed from office on English insistence, and gradually calm was restored.

A flagrant breach of truce in 1596 made history, and led to the creation of one of the most famous of the Border Ballads collected by Sir Walter Scott and others: the tale of Kinmont Willie. William Armstrong of Kinmont, a celebrated reiver or raider, was among the Scottish representatives at a meeting at Kershopefoot in Liddesdale, where the English frontier runs down the middle of the Kershope burn to its junction with the Liddel Water, and then south down the Liddel. Today it is a delightful corner, a tranquil meeting of the waters below a modern bridge with a road sign for England and Cumbria at one end. That spring day almost four centuries ago began quietly and formally enough, but ended in uproar. As Armstrong was riding homewards along the river bank at the end of the session, a group of English horsemen set off in pursuit, captured him, and bore him off to imprisonment in Carlisle castle. This defiance of the Border code so enraged the Keeper of Liddesdale, Sir Walter Scott of Buccleuch, that after diplomatic protests had failed he gathered men about him, rode to Carlisle, daringly broke into the castle, and rescued Kinmont Willie. Later it was suggested that he had received help from dissident Englishmen who preferred Border ruffians of like mind to their own unpopular Warden; but nobody could deny the rescuer the sobriquet bestowed on him in the ballad – 'The Bold Buccleuch'. The feat was all the more admirable in that the notorious Armstrongs had been among the major headaches in the region under his own jurisdiction, and Willie was among the worst.

One of the rare similarities between Highland and Lowland customs was the resemblance between the northern clans' loyalty to a chieftain who in return owed his family and retainers an equal commitment, and the mutually supportive 'surnames' of Border groups – usually known on the Northumbrian side of the Border, especially in Tynedale, as 'graynes'. Leading Scottish families included the Armstrongs, Elliots, Grahams and Scotts, though there were holders of those names also in the English borderlands. Since many associates who were not blood relations often assumed the surname but between them could muster only a limited number of Christian names, confusion was avoided by the bestowal of what we might call a nickname, or what has been more justly described as a 'to-name'. Thus one John Armstrong could be distinguished from another as John of the Park or Jock of the Side, the Laird's Jock (son of the chieftain), Jock Stowlugs, and so on. The worst fate that could befall any relative or follower was to be declared a 'broken man': that is, either by punitive official proceedings or by some family banishment, to be removed from the protection of the surname and so become an outlaw, fair prey for any enemy, English or Scottish.

A tombstone in the tiny graveyard of Caerlanrig in Teviotdale, down a tree-lined country lane which seems quite incongruously cosy in the shadow of windswept fells, commemorates the fate of an Armstrong who relied too much on the power of his name and his supporters.

Johnnie Armstrong of Gilnockie had defied an agreement between the Wardens of the Marches that no building should be erected by either side within the confines of the Debatable Land when he set up a tower above the Esk. This is usually identified with Hollows Tower, still to be seen in a fine state of repair beside the A7 near Canonbie, though it was in a poor state after Lord Dacre had ridden in from England to burn it. In reprisal the Armstrongs set off in force and burned Netherby in Cumberland. Their incursions into England were not mere hit-and-run raids: the Armstrong reiving, riding clan could put hundreds (they boastfully claimed thousands) of horsemen into the field for private raids as devasting as any military campaign. These reivers would round up cattle and horses and drive them back to their own lands. If sufficient forces could be raised at short notice, the robbed would pursue the robbers on 'hot trod', with the right to reclaim their goods by force and deal with the wrongdoers out of hand. If there was a delay, a 'cold trod' gave them the same privileges provided the retaliation was completed within six days. Local inhabitants on either side of the Border were legally obliged to offer assistance to the pursuers; but it was a brave man who opposed the Armstrongs, knowing that brutal vengeance would be exacted sooner or later, however much the law might theoretically be on his side.

Johnnie Armstrong's power over the region became so great, and the ill doings of his 'riding family' and associates so flagrant, that protests from England and the growing wrath of young James V in Edinburgh brought about a fatal confrontation. The king himself led an army into Liddesdale, rounded up the better-known thieves and 'tuik of thame to the number of xxxii personis of the greitest of them', including Armstrongs and Elliots. There was then apparently an offer of pardon to others who submitted willingly to the royal authority without delay. Johnnie Armstrong, distinguished from others of that surname by the to-name of Black Jock, dressed himself up in all his finery and rode with fifty of his best men to meet the king in Teviotdale, obviously hoping to impress him as a near-equal.

The normal attire of reivers in action included a shirt covered by a sleeveless quilted leather coat or 'jack', usually stiffened with strips of metal or horn, leather breeches and sturdy leather boots. On their heads they wore a steel bonnet, either a 'salade' like a rimless upturned bowl, a peaked version known as a burgonet, or a morion with curved brim and raised centrepiece like a cockscomb. Some of their leaders, however, indulged in richer displays: in moments of leisure or on a Day of Truce a chieftain might sport a satin doublet or gold-buttoned jerkin, satin hose, and velvet breeches and cloak. Certainly when Johnnie Armstrong arrived for his meeting with the king he was arrayed in the most ostentatious items from his wardrobe.

Instead of being impressed, James was mightily displeased. 'What wants yon knave that a king should have?' he demanded. When Black Jock protested loyalty to the Crown and his native land, and offered to carry out any raid James might choose in England, he and his followers were summarily hanged from the nearest trees. The reiver's last proud defiance has passed into Border history: 'It is folly to seek grace at a graceless face'.

Although intermarriage between Scots and English Borderers was officially forbidden during many periods, and could be punishable by death, it frequently took place. Some alliances between, say, a Fenwick of Tynedale and a Croser of Teviotdale might ensure a lull in raiding and cattle thieving for a while, though there was usually an excuse for it to be resumed at fairly short notice. Some families, across the Border or on their own side of it, pursued deadly feuds which could be settled only by the extermination of an entire family or, grudgingly and with much pressure from the Wardens, a compensatory payment in money or goods. The Tynedale Fenwicks and the Liddesdale Elliots were involved for a long time in a savage, unyielding feud; and the Armstrongs, among their many clashes, quarrelled simultaneously with the Scottish Turnbulls and Johnstones and with the English Bells, while the Bells were also feuding with the English Grahams. The intensity of these hatreds was such as to ensure that at the christening of a male child his right hand was kept clear of the water so that it would be free for unhallowed retribution upon family enemies.

Of all the turbulent valleys and fells, the most violent and troublesome territory continued to be Liddesdale. The raids and executions of James V provided only temporary respite from reiving and feuding. This 'cockpit of the Border', too volatile and time-consuming to be included in any of the three main Scottish Marches, had been allocated a Keeper of its own. Although there were profits and national prestige to be made out of all the Wardens' privileges and untold opportunities for corruption, it was often difficult to find anyone to shoulder this particular responsibility. Some Wardens could supervise matters from the reasonable comfort of homes such as Ferniehirst outside Jedburgh; but Hermitage castle, the 'Strength of Liddesdale' in the middle of inhospitable fells and mosses, was one of the most chill and sinister strongholds in all Scotland.

Hermitage has existed since the thirteenth century, standing within older earthworks. Fact and legend mingle inextricably within its grim walls. An early occupant is said to have been the villainous Lord Soulis, who in the ballad of the Cout of Keilder forces the head of his noble visitor under a pool in the Hermitage Water to drown him. He met his own fate when the wizard Thomas of Ercildoune instructed Soulis's enemies how to capture him and boil him to death in a cauldron on the Nine Stane Rig, a Bronze Age stone circle which can be reached by a scramble up the hillside above the modern B6399 between Newcastleton and Hawick. Whether or not there was ever such an owner, there is no doubt about the family which held the castle longest. Sir William Douglas captured it from one of Edward Balliol's English supporters, though he himself was later to join the English cause. Furious at the decision of young King David II to appoint Sir Alexander Ramsay rather than himself as sheriff of Teviotdale, Douglas captured Ramsay and threw him into the Hermitage dungeon. He then went off, leaving his rival to starve to death. After his defection,

David presented the castle to another William, later the first Earl of Douglas. Taking no chances, this Douglas killed his predecessor in Ettrick Forest.

After a couple of decades in English hands, Hermitage came back once more to the Douglases. They set about reinforcing and extending their property to give it much the appearance it has today, apart from some modern restoration. Their grip was relinquished only when, playing their usual game of under-hand negotiations with the English, they aroused the suspicions of James IV, who installed Patrick Hepburn, Earl of Bothwell, in their place. The Hepburns proved hardly more reliable, but did keep a hold on the castle and – so far as anyone could keep a hold on such a region – the lordship of Liddesdale. James V had failed to subdue the Armstrongs and their kind. His daughter was fated to face the same problem.

After the scandalous murder of her secretary and the rumours surrounding her dismal husband, Queen Mary was anxious to re-establish her qualifications for wise, firm rule. Combining the public relations exercise of showing herself to her people with the need to exhibit her legal powers, she set off on court circuits or justice ayres which inevitably had to include the crime-ridden Borders. One such court was sched-uled for Jedburgh in October 1566. Here the queen was, according to local records, accommodated in a turreted tower house known since as Mary Queen of Scots House, though a few researchers have concluded that it could not have been built until many years after her stay in the burgh. How-ever that may be, it is a sturdy example of a defensive town house of the period, and serves today as a repository for souvenirs of the queen (some of dubious authenticity), in-cluding a replica of her death mask, the Communion plate she used on the morning of her execution, and her royal seal.

At this time there were few suggestions of any relationship between Mary and James Hepburn, the then Earl of Bothwell, other than that of queen and devoted lieutenant. Yet when news reached Jedburgh that Bothwell was lying seriously wounded in his Liddesdale stronghold of Hermitage, Mary set off to ride the 50 miles there and back in a day.

The earl had gone on ahead in order to round up malefactors and provide the court with some impressive numbers for trial. He and his men succeeded in wheeling a satisfactory batch of Elliots into custody in Hermitage. Then, in a further foray, Bothwell encountered Little Jock Elliot of the Park, one of the most savage of that reiving family, and shot him off his horse. He approached the fallen man, either to arrest him or make sure he was dead, whereupon Elliot came to life and stabbed Bothwell three times. Some chroniclers say that Elliot then died; others that he escaped and continued to be a thorn in the flesh of the authorities. Bothwell's men had to carry their leader back to Hermitage, where he was greeted by the mortifying news that the prisoners had overpowered their guards and taken charge of the castle. In order to gain admittance and nurse his wounds, Bothwell had to strike a deal which involved letting all the Elliots go free.

There are two versions of subsequent events. Writers who disapproved of Mary claimed that her impatience to be at her lover's side

> could not temper itself, but needs she must bewray her outrageous lust, and in an inconvenient time of the year, despising all discommodities of the way and weather, and all danger of thieves, she betook herself headlong to her journey with such a company as no man of any honest degree would have adventured his life and his goods among them.

Others record that she patiently concluded the business then before the court, and went off with a reliable escort to hold a council with Bothwell about the taming of Liddesdale and empower him to hold courts in Hermitage itself.

Whichever may be the true explanation, it is certainly known that on her way across the wilderness north of Hermitage the queen was thrown by her horse into a peat bog, marked on modern maps as the Queen's Mire. Here she lost her watch.

When she returned to Jedburgh that evening she was in great pain from what is likely to have been a haemorrhage, of which she had suffered several since her son's birth. At one juncture it was thought she had died, but gradually she recovered. Local gossips noted that her husband, Darnley, did not appear in Jedburgh until the crisis was over; and then, incensed by the attendant nobles' cool reception, he stayed only one night and possibly did not even visit Mary. Bothwell had already been fetched here on a horse litter from Hermitage.

In 1817 the lost watch was unearthed by a mole, and a stirrup and horseshoe were found in the Queen's Mire, though there is no firm evidence of their having come from Mary's horse. In 1987, the four-hundredth anniversary of her execution, events throughout the country included a ride by Jedburgh men and women in costume retracing the royal route to and from Hermitage. In that same year the watch was stolen from the museum.

Although Mary herself was never to return to the town above the Jed Water or to venture again into the valley of the Liddel Water, her tragic history was soon to involve others in the turmoil of Liddesdale.

When she arrived in England in 1568 she claimed to be seeking the protection of her cousin Elizabeth, but at the same time began scheming for support in her claims to both thrones, having earlier told a priest that she 'trusted to find many friends when time did serve, especially among those of the old religion'. Of those readiest to succumb to her personal charm and regal pretensions, the most influential was Thomas Percy, Earl of Northumberland. He and fellow Catholic lords began to murmur of an uprising against Elizabeth; and there were even plans for Mary to marry the Duke of Norfolk, in the hope of producing an acceptable successor to the throne of England. Elizabeth soon discovered what was afoot and frightened the mooted consort into a hasty retreat to his Norfolk estates, though she misinterpreted his sudden flight as a prelude to the rising of the north. When he reappeared apologetically in London to plead for clemency he was sent to the Tower, while in the north itself the Earls of Northumberland and Westmorland blundered into ill-planned revolt.

The Northern Rebellion began with a march upon Durham cathedral, where Protestant furnishings were torn down and mass was celebrated. It did not take long for forces from the south to march upon the rebels and throw them into abject retreat. As their pursuers closed in near Hexham and Naworth, when 'the beacons burned all night, and every hill was full of horse and foot crying and shouting as though they were mad', the two leaders fled across the Border into Liddesdale. Westmorland and a few followers were lucky: after joining with the reivers in attacks on the English Marches, they ultimately fled to the Netherlands and lived there as pensioners of Catholic Spain.

Northumberland was less fortunate. Having been offered shelter by one of the Armstrongs, Hector of Hardlaw, whom he had helped some years previously, he was treacherously handed over to the Earl of Moray, Regent of Scotland since Mary's enforced abdication. Himself an illegitimate son of Mary's father, James V, and a collaborator in the murder of Darnley, Moray held on to his captive for a time in that Loch Leven castle where the queen had also been imprisoned. His successor, the Regent Morton, was anxious to keep the peace with England at least until he had consolidated his own position, and ingratiatingly delivered Northumberland up to the East March Warden at Berwick in June 1572 in return for a large cash payment. The rebel lord was beheaded two months later at York.

Meanwhile his Countess had been rescued from a Liddesdale cottage 'not to be compared to any dog kennel in England' by the chivalrous Kerr of Ferniehirst, in spite of past feuds with her husband's family. He and Buccleuch then went to Hector of Hardlaw's house and burned it to the ground. 'Taking Hector's cloak' became a Border catch-phrase for the betrayal of a friend.

The Border was aflame once more. Matters had not been helped by the murder of the Earl of Moray at Linlithgow by a member of the rival Hamilton family, who aimed his musket from an upper window behind a line of washing. After some shifts and confusions, a new Regent was appointed, the Earl of Morton, one of the ubiquitous Douglas family. Taking advantage of the ebb and flow of state politics and power, Border reivers swept in force over the Border in the company of English refugees who were now their grateful allies. In retaliation, English troops inflicted a scorched-earth policy on the Border valleys and towns, burning Hawick, battering Ferniehirst castle and Jedburgh, and boasting that they would leave 'never a house nor tower unburnt'.

In the aftermath the Border needed time to breathe and recuperate, and while religious civil war threatened Scotland as a whole, the far from religious reivers bided their time. Whenever the preoccupations of monarchs on either side of the frontier distracted attention from local outrages, the riding families rode again, incapable of forswearing the pleasures of rustling, pillage, murder and blackmail. When James VI came to manhood and attempted to assert himself over both the Borderers and the disruptive Highland clans, he tended for a while to concentrate on the Highlands rather than the Lowlands. Troublesome as the Armstrongs, Elliots and the rest might be within his own kingdom, they were quite useful as a thorny, lacerating palisade against their English neighbours.

In any case he had dangerous worries on his own doorstep. Shuffled from one power group to another during the regencies of his childhood, he was not safe even when he became a fully fledged king. Falling under the spell of an older, flamboyantly dressed and well-educated kinsman, Esmé Stuart, who had come over from France, he was suspected of dangerously Papist leanings and of some unnatural sexual habits. Such suspicions were reinforced when he made this pampered favourite Duke of Lennox and granted him the revenues of Arbroath abbey. In August 1582 Protestant lords under the Earl of Gowrie kidnapped James while he was hunting near Perth, and took him to Gowrie's castle of Ruthven outside the town. Their excuse was that they feared the influence of those Catholic

THE BORDERS·

lords who, pretending to be the king's loyal advisers, were in fact anxious to restore his mother to the throne. Mary herself, in captivity in England but forever smuggling out letters and appeals, dealt slyly in shrouded half-promises and suggestions, but made one thing quite clear: she still regarded herself as rightful Queen of Scots and, even towards the end, offered no more than a grudging suggestion of James being 'associated' with her in ruling the country. The Gowrie faction guarded James for almost a year, issuing decrees in his name while claiming that he was their willing guest. In July 1583 he escaped to St Andrews, and set about destroying his tormentors or pardoning some in return for abject submission.

Yet Gowrie's son was, in 1600, apparently prepared to risk abducting the king yet again, luring him to the House of Gowrie in Perth with a fanciful story about a mysterious pot of gold. The 'Gowrie Conspiracy' was to leave a lot of puzzling questions which have never been satisfactorily answered. The king had his attendants with him, and in a very short time they overpowered and killed Gowrie and his brother, whose bodies were hanged, drawn and quartered, the quarters being displayed at Edinburgh, Perth, Dundee and Stirling. There have been suggestions that James owed Gowrie a great deal of money, and contrived the incident to rid himself of the debt; or that he had had homosexual designs on the young man, and had murderously silenced him when rejected.

Ruthven lands were forfeited. An Act of Parliament abolished the very surname and ordained that the property outside Perth should henceforth be called Huntingtower. Although its great hall and courtyard buildings have crumbled, its linked tower houses make an impressive sight from the A85 towards Crieff, and the interior still contains fine tempera painted ceilings, plasterwork and moulded fireplaces.

When the clumsy plotting of the Queen of Scots against Elizabeth finally exasperated the English beyond endurance, Mary was beheaded at Fotheringhay. Her son, who had scarcely known her but felt that his own throne was conceivably under threat so long as she lived, made no great show of grief when the news was brought to him. James had for some time been accepting an annual pension from Elizabeth in return for promises of assistance against foreign invaders – meaning, at this period, Spain – and on the tacit understanding that he would in no way connive at his mother's return to Scotland. Now he renewed pressure to have his own right of succession to the English throne acknowledged. Elizabeth played one of her characteristically tantalizing games, and kept him waiting until the very moment of her death.

Although contemporary witnesses leave no doubt that James was a practising homosexual, he knew his dynastic duties, and at the age of 23 set off to bring home a bride. Calculating that neither Elizabeth nor the Scottish parliament would favour a Catholic marriage, he settled on a Protestant princess of Denmark. Whatever his proclivities, he carried out the wooing in gallant style. When gales prevented Anne from sailing to Scotland, James went himself to fetch her, and they were married in Oslo. She was 15 at the time of the wedding, and was to present him with seven children, among them the future Charles I. She also presented him with an embarrassing situation by deciding after a while to become a Roman Catholic.

During the king's absence on his romantic mission, a bitterly familiar name was involved in strange moves against his person. The Earl of Bothwell, nephew of the earl who had done James's mother so much harm, was what today would be called a tearaway: he revelled in leading Border raids, once broke into the Edinburgh Tolbooth to free one of his men from custody, and was widely believed to hold the office of chief warlock to various covens of witches. At North Berwick he was reported to have assembled a band of 200 witches to raise a magic storm which would drown the king and his new queen on their voyage to Scotland. The site of this unsuccessful venture in the black arts is marked today by the few stony fragments of St Andrew's twelfth-century church above the harbour. James was terrified of witchcraft and became a ruthless persecutor of anyone suspected of it. When he heard of the incident he imprisoned Bothwell in Edinburgh castle, but continued to fear the earl's powers. He had reasons other than supernatural ones: Bothwell soon escaped into the Borders to cause further disturbances, twice forced his way into Holyroodhouse to plead with and simultaneously threaten the king, and once cornered him in Falkland palace. He was both courageous and physically attractive, but deranged, and it was a great relief even to his associates when he left Scotland to die a pauper in Naples.

When Elizabeth of England died early on the morning of 24 March 1603 it had already become obvious to her entourage that James VI of Scotland was her only possible successor. Many who had earlier worked against Scottish interests had for some time been making covert approaches and promises through envoys between the two Courts. It is said that on her deathbed Elizabeth, unable to speak, signified assent to the succession by a movement of her head or hand. In any event, the decision was made. Sir Robert Carey, Warden of the English Middle March, had been in London visiting the queen, but had prudently arranged for relays of horses to be ready for him between the capital and Edinburgh, so that he could ingratiate himself with the King of Scots by being the first to arrive with the news that he was now King of England also. The moment Carey was confident that Elizabeth had breathed her last he was in the saddle, racing for the Border. It took him two and a half days to reach Edinburgh. James had gone to bed by the time he arrived, but the travel-stained messenger was admitted and graciously allowed to convey the news.

The favours for which Carey had hoped were somewhat disappointing. Courtiers in London, angry at his arrogant seizure of responsibility for notifying the new king, blocked various royal appointments. Fortunately he was allowed to become Master of the Household to the young Prince Charles, treated his royal charge with intelligence and genuine affection, and on Charles's accession was created Earl of Monmouth.

The Union of the Crowns did not mean that England and Scotland had ceased to be separate countries. Full national union would be another century in coming. But now that King

James VI of Scotland was also King James I of England he was determined to rule both kingdoms so as to allow no further violence between them. As far as he was concerned, there was no longer a borderline. Reiving and feuding must stop. He saw little hope of achieving this by gradual measures or appeals to newly established unity. Wasting neither time nor mercy he set about dispersing the riding families.

They had undoubtedly been asking for trouble. Within a few days of Elizabeth's death the reivers had taken what they imagined would be the opportunity for easy plunder, and swarmed over the Border in what their victims and the Wardens referred to as 'Ill Week'. James appointed new guardians with wider powers on each side of the Border, and troops were moved north. A couple of thousand men were allowed to leave the country and serve as mercenaries in the struggle of the Netherlands against Spain. Those remaining were placed under strict rules and penalties. No one must own any horse other than a work horse; arms were forbidden; informers were planted in every community to report on breaches of regulations or even suspicions about a man's trade or lack of it; and in all cases of doubt, summary hanging was in order. The riding families were broken up: many, like the Grahams, were transported to the Low Countries and Ireland, leaving their lands and stock to be appropriated by grateful Marcher lords. Those who fought back were declared outlaws and hunted down.

Peace was at last enforced on the Border. Yet in the blood of the quelled freebooters and their descendants there would always be a pulse of rebelliousness, a longing to ride again as their ancestors had done. After a couple of decades of comparative calm, the names of Armstrong and Elliot began to reappear in familiar practices. There was no possibility of large-scale raiding into England now; but in spite of sharing a crown, the two countries were still separate and old cross-Border temptations still beckoned. Small groups went in for spasmodic cattle thieving with familiar equipment and familiar methods, including blackmail. In an Act of 1662 in the reign of Charles

II there is reference to 'a great number of lewd disorderly and lawless persons, being thieves and robbers, who are commonly called Moss-troopers'. Rewards were offered, including some to moss-troopers themselves provided they betrayed their companions. It took a long time for the plague to be controlled and for strongholds of the riding families to be overthrown. In our own time the Armstrongs' Hollows Tower has been romantically restored; but Mangerton, home of the most powerful of the Liddesdale branch of the family, is no more than an overgrown knot of stones on a knoll beside an equally melancholy, abandoned railway line.

One substantial surviving tower house, about five miles north-east of Sir Walter Scott's grave in Dryburgh abbey, is that of Smailholm:

> That mountain'd tower,
> Which charm'd my fancy's wakening hour.

In 1773 Scott was sent as a sickly child to stay with his grandparents at Sandyknowe farm, below the rocky plinth from which rises a fortalice with sturdy walls and gun-loops. It captured his imagination, as he later showed in *Marmion*; and that imagination was further fed by books in the farmhouse window seat and by the Border tales his aunt and grandmother told him. The Pringle lairds who built and occupied the tower had frequently been beset by reivers from Tynedale and Redesdale, who on one occasion took away with them 600 cattle, 100 horses and 100 prisoners. In despair John Pringle accepted a blackmail deal which, however irksome, seems to have been honoured and left him unmolested afterwards. Later the family ran into financial difficulties and sold the property to Sir William Scott of Harden, whose direct descendant was the young Walter Scott. Throughout his life the author loved and drew inspiration from the whole region, from Smailholm to 'Scott's View' above the river Tweed and the house he built for himself at Abbotsford.

Smailholm tower today provides a worthy setting for a

collection of tapestries and spell-binding costume figures evoking characters and scenes from Scott's *Minstrelsy of the Scottish Border;* and there is a compelling tableau of Queen Mary and her ladies, the 'Four Maries'.

Researches into Border ballads were to lead to the composition of Scott's immensely popular *Lay of the Last Minstrel.* He had started his career in the law, but while attending court at Jedburgh in 1792 he met and became friends with Robert Shortreed, Sheriff-Substitute of Roxburghshire, and was invited on expeditions into Liddesdale to listen to old tales and verses. Within the gate of what is now the Bank of Scotland's premises in Jedburgh is preserved a 'Loupin'-on Stane' from which they used to mount their horses before setting off.

Liddesdale was still a sullen, untamed region populated by people as prickly and hostile as they had always been. It was only Shortreed's family connections with the Elliots which guaranteed a friendly reception. One of these relatives, a Dr Elliot, had already collected many ballads. When he saw Scott's interest in the history of the valley he arranged for men to clear out the rubbish which had accumulated in Hermitage castle so that the visitors could inspect the dungeon. The 'Border Warhorn' which was to hang in Abbotsford was found in use as a grease vessel for a local labourer's scythe. Scott and his friend returned year after year in search of poetic treasure, and Scott is recorded as having been the first man ever to tackle the rough tracks into Liddesdale in a carriage. Roads were few and uncomfortable in the Borders. In 1832 a fellow poet, James Hogg, the 'Ettrick Shepherd', wrote of Selkirkshire:

Not a vestige of a road formed before the last century. The county was overrun with underwood that made it impervious to the traveller.

The first settlement of any size in Liddesdale was the purpose-built village of Newcastleton, established in 1793 by the third Duke of Buccleuch as the basis of a weaving community. In the following century it was linked with Edinburgh and Carlisle, and with the larger textile centres of Hawick and

Galashiels, by the 'Waverley Route' railway. This disappeared during the Beeching era, and most of the employment in the neighbourhood is now in the expanding forests, including the vast spread of Kielder spanning the Border into Northumberland.

Wool has been an important product of the region since the earliest days of home spinning and weaving produced a coarse grey cloth known as 'hodden'. When monks from France and Flanders were settled in the Border abbeys in the twelfth and thirteenth centuries they introduced new skills, and also devoted themselves to the expansion of sheep rearing to provide the necessary basic material. Profitable exports were handled through the port of Berwick-upon-Tweed until, in the middle of the fifteenth century, the kings themselves saw the advantages of taking over pastures for their own flocks, storing the wool at Selkirk and then shipping it out via Leith. Experiments over the centuries resulted in the predominance of the Cheviot breed with a fleece eminently suitable for finer grades of cloth. Water for fulling – cleansing and thickening the cloth – and in due course for driving the industrial mills which were to replace the looms of individual home-based workers was also an important factor.

The bridge over the river Tweed at Peebles was once an important part of the Kailzie Drove Road, a main route for cattle driven from the Highlands for sale in English markets and with side paths for transporting local woollen goods to similar markets. Stretches of this can still be found descending on Peebles from the north and, south of the town, across a ford on the Haystoun burn and over Kailzie hill, heading onwards over the Ettrick Water towards the Border.

The name of 'tweed' now associated with a rough-surfaced, hard-wearing cloth arose from a misunderstanding between Scot and Sassenach. Correctly called twill, it was heard by London dealers in Scottish pronunciation as 'tweel'. On one occasion, it is said, this was written down mistakenly as 'tweed'. When enthusiastic repeat orders for such an admirable product began to roll in, shrewd manufacturers along the river Tweed saw the advantage of association with the river name and set about exploiting it.

There was a great expansion in the nineteenth century with the coming of power-driven mills, and a corresponding growth in their parent townships. Selkirk, Peebles, Kelso and Jedburgh all flourished. It was Jedburgh weavers who first combined two colours of yarn to produce the now familiar look of 'tweed'. At Walkerburn, a few miles along the river from Peebles, a mill shop and wool museum display all the processes of shearing, cleaning, spinning, carding, dyeing and weaving. Ironically the adjoining mills, which for more than a century provided employment for almost the entire village and supplemented the picture now provided by the museum, were abruptly shut down in 1988: bought up by a large firm, the premises were paid an afternoon visit by a director who announced imminent closure and drove off.

It is true that demand for coarser gauges of knitwear has fallen off and that the export market has been infiltrated by products from countries with lower wage rates. Yet, although commercial competition is tougher, there are still weaving and spinning mills in Selkirk, one of which won the Queen's Award for Export Achievement. The large enterprise of Jedburgh Kiltmakers stands beside the A68 north of Jedburgh, and large-scale mills and knitwear houses still provide most of the employment in Hawick on the Teviot. Hawick's sheep auction mart is the oldest in the country, while Kelso is still the centre for the huge annual Kelso Ram Sales.

Another important stream was that of the Gala Water. The name may have derived from the old British *gala* or *gwala*, describing a full or swiftly flowing stream, though some etymologists think it may be the Cymric *gal*, meaning 'scattered'. *Shiels* or *shields* are cottages, direct from the Anglo-Saxon, so the town of Galashiels may be regarded as cottages by a stream, or as scattered cottages. A modern statue of a shepherd carrying a ram on his shoulders symbolizes the place's dependence on the wool trade. In the thirteenth century wool was exported from here to Flanders. In return, Flemish weavers eventually came to settle in the neighbourhood and teach local workers their 'mysteries'. By the middle of the eighteenth century the main product was a coarse cloth known as Galloway Grey. Although there had been fulling mills along the river for several centuries, the first industrial age mill was not built until 1790. As others followed, the Gala Water was dammed and its course altered to create three mill lades. Production expanded so rapidly that home supplies of wool were insufficient, and imports from Australia and South America increased.

All raw materials had to be washed before processing, and especially in the case of imports there was a need to get rid of dirt, seeds and insects. Great quantities of effluent pouring into the river added to the stench of local skin and tannery works to produce appalling smells and what one official report referred to as 'gross pollution'. The seeds, however, had one interesting effect: well over 300 separate plant species arrived in the wool, and when flushed away into the Gala Water began to grow profusely along its banks.

Before chemical dyes were discovered in the mid-nineteenth century, the colouring of cloth had been achieved by boiling plants in dye kettles. Such hues included:

Red	Rock lichen
	Blaeberry (bilberry)
	Nettles
Bright red	Yellow bedstraw
	Tormentil (also used for tanning)
Yellow	Applewood
	Ash
	Buckthorn
Bright yellow	Teasel
	Sundew
	Rhubarb
Orange	Ragwort
	Peat soot
Magenta	Dandelion

The discovery of chemical substitutes led to the founding of a dyestuffs industry and helped the mills develop into extended factory production, gradually mechanizing processes which had hitherto been done by outworkers in their own homes. Cloth manufacture and the knitting of garments became separate industries, though close working partnerships remained essential. The *Guinness Book of Records* confirms the fastest example of co-operative production on 30 January 1974 when wool was sheared, dyed in Selkirk, carded and spun in Galashiels, and knitted and finished in Hawick, with a sheep-to-wearer time of 4 hours 35 minutes.

Tartan, the style most commonly associated with Scotland, had never been produced in the Borders before 1826. Then Sir Walter Scott ordered a pair of trousers in black and white shepherd check, adopted the pattern as the family tartan, and started a fashion. Prince Albert, Queen Victoria's consort, helped this trend by designing his own Balmoral tartan and having it made up at Walkerburn. At the Great Exhibition of 1851 in the Crystal Palace, eleven Galashiels firms exhibited woollen worsteds over a hanging space of 2,000 feet.

A local family, Hoppringle, later changed its name to Pringle, still a familiar one on sportswear. They came into possession of the 'forest stead' of Gala at one of the most troubled times in the Borders. Other all too familiar names come into the story. In 1563 one Hoppringle had been set upon and murdered in his house by a joint force of Armstrongs and Elliots, which gave rise to a long Border feud. Those days are remembered in a fine statue in Galashiels of a mounted reiver with typical steel bonnet and lance. The town's brief motto, 'Soor Plums', is a memento of an English invasion when a few stragglers misguidedly stopped to help themselves to some wild plums. Set upon by the locals, they were killed and tossed into a trench still known as Englishmen's Syke. The incident must also have inspired the melancholy bagpipe tune, 'Soor Plums of Galashiels'.

Only the most starry-eyed optimist could have supposed that the Union of the Crowns and then, at last, the Act of

Union in 1707 making the two countries one would somehow bring immediate peace in a region with such memories. The amalgamation of kingdoms was itself carried out with the greatest animosity on both sides. England had thrown out the Stuart monarch, James II, and brought in his daughter Mary and her husband William of Orange, followed by the heirless Queen Anne. A Protestant Hanoverian succession looked inevitable. The Scottish Parliament was split on this as on so many other matters. Catholic elements still regarded the exiled James II as rightful James VII of Scotland, and would continue to extend this loyalty to his son and grandson. The Protestant element favoured complete union with England, in spite of warnings that this would mean subjugation – by peaceful means rather than the warlike ones of the past, but subjugation nonetheless. To force the Scottish Estates to acknowledge the Hanoverian right of succession, the English authorities banned the sale of Scottish cattle and other products in England as part of a programme of arm-twisting economic sanctions, and threatened to treat all Scots as aliens unless they toed the line.

Commissioners were appointed on either side to work out an agreed formula which would cover differences in legal systems, taxation discrepancies, the coinages – which were still quite distinct – and above all the religious rights of Epis-copalians, Presbyterians, Cameronians and others who had reason to be wary of the Church of England. The Scots aimed at a federal system which would allow them some autonomy. There were outbreaks of violence in the Borders and down the Royal Mile in Edinburgh. But England held the whip hand: it was a matter of amalgamate or be crippled by economic meas-ures. On 16 January 1707 the Treaty of Union received its royal assent. Within a few months many assurances were broken; there were wistful, unfulfilled hopes of James Edward Stuart landing and asserting himself as King James VII; and in the House of Lords an attempt by Scottish members to repeal the Act was defeated by only a small majority. But it was all too late.

'Now there's ane end of ane old song,' James Ogilvy, Earl

of Seafield, had said as he signed the engrossed exemplification
of the Act of Union. The music was by no means ended: there
were many discords still to come.

SELECTED SITES OF INTEREST

Antiquities

EDINSHALL BROCH   On a side of Cockburn Law near Abbey
St Bathans, Duns, reached along farm path from the B6355.
An early oval fort of pre-Roman times with a later broch in
one corner, perhaps added by the Votadini even though they
were supposed to be collaborators with the Roman occupiers.
Later came a walled but obviously peaceable settlement.

EILDON HILLS   On the northernmost of the three peaks,
reached from Melrose by the B6359 or from Eildon village on
the A6091, are remains of a fortified British town which was
probably the *oppidum* of the Selgovae, to which the Romans
added a circular enclosure. Visible for miles around, this was
obviously an important signal station, serving the supply depots
and fort of the Newstead settlement at the foot of the hill.

GLENRATH SETTLEMENT   Manor Water road off the A72
between Peebles and Lyne leads to a Celtic settlement and
field system of lynchets and dykes, with cairns made of stones
dug from the earth during cultivation, and fragments of circular
houses.

WODEN LAW   About 8 miles south-east of Jedburgh, reached
from the A68 via eastbound by-road below Carter Bar. From
the summit there is a view of the Roman supply route, Dere
Street. The fort started with a single stone wall, to which
were added ramparts and another wall. There are also Roman
siegeworks which may have been used for exercises by troops
from nearby temporary camps still visible around Pennymuir.

(*For a general study of the foregoing see also Chapter 1.*)

Historic Buildings

ABBOTSFORD   Off the A7 just over 2 miles south-east of Gala-shiels. Romantic 'Scottish baronial' mansion built by Sir Walter Scott between 1817 and 1822. The author's study is preserved as he left it, along with his collections of books, armour and historical records.

FERNIEHIRST   Off the A68 a mile south of Jedburgh. Six-teenth-century Border castle with fairy-tale turrets (now for holiday let as luxury apartments!), home of the Kerr family restored in recent years by their descendant and current chief-tain, the Marquis of Lothian. The stables have been converted into an information centre with displays of Border reiving history and battles in which the family has been involved over the centuries.

GREENKNOWE   (The word means 'green hill'.) Beside the A6089 about 9 miles north-west of Kelso, a sixteenth-century turreted tower house complete with its original iron yett, or gate, behind a sturdy timber door.

JEDBURGH   Most extensive remains of all the ravaged Border abbeys, with glass-less but beautiful rose window known as St Catherine's Wheel. A Visitor Centre provides graphic back-ground details to the history of the abbey and town.

NEIDPATH   On the western outskirts of Peebles, a medieval castle set high on a wooded bank above the Tweed. In essence a massive L-shaped tower with walls 12 feet thick, a well and a pit dungeon, it was adapted in the seventeenth century for more comfortable and less defensive living. The gateway carries the goat's head and coronet crest of the Hay family, Earls of Tweeddale.

THIRLESTANE   Castle off the A68 just outside Lauder. It has been in the hands of the Maitland family for more than 400 years since its creation by John Maitland, Chancellor of Scotland, and later enlargement by the Duke of Lauderdale.

The state rooms were redecorated by plasterers from Holyrood. Splendid display of toys in the family nurseries.

TRAQUAIR Tower house converted into a lavish mansion, off the B709 2 miles from Innerleithen. Claiming to be the oldest inhabited house in Scotland, it was a favourite hunting centre for royal visitors. Among its treasures are the cradle used by Mary, Queen of Scots, for her son James; a quilt woven by her and her 'Four Maries'; a secret staircase used by recusant priests and Jacobite refugees; and a collection of Jacobite glass including one with a portrait of Prince Charles Edward. When Bonnie Prince Charlie left after a brief visit during his march on England in 1745, the Earl of Traquair vowed that the resplendent Bear Gates (the 'Steekit Yetts') should not be opened again until the Stuarts were restored to the throne. They remain shut to this day. Ale is still produced in the eighteenth-century brewhouse, and sold on the premises.

Museums

COLDSTREAM Military and local museum in the original head-quarters of the Coldstream Guards, founded here in 1659 from what had originally been Monck's Regiment, formed under Oliver Cromwell's auspices.

EYEMOUTH Museum opened in 1981 to commemorate the great east coast fishing disaster in which 129 local fishermen were lost. Displays include Eyemouth tapestry, history of Berwickshire farming and fishing, and the wheelhouse of a modern fishing boat.

GALASHIELS Anderson's textile museum with daily guided tours and the largest range of worsted textiles in the world.

HAWICK Museum in Wilton Lodge Park, on western outskirts of the town, has extensive displays of Border history and in particular of the textile industry.

HEXHAM (Northumberland) Although in England, this must be recommended for its imaginative displays in the Middle

March Centre of Border reiving history, with chillingly convincing soundtrack backgrounds to colourful life-size tableaux.

JEDBURGH   On hilltop above the town, Castle Gaol, a nineteenth-century model prison in the shape of a turreted castle, has been converted into a museum of prison life and local social history.

PEEBLES   The Tweeddale Museum is housed in the Chambers Institution, a gift to the town from the brothers William and Robert Chambers, founders of the famous dictionary and encyclopaedia publishing company. Noted for its fine geological collection. Frequently changing exhibitions of local history.

SELKIRK   Halliwell's House off the main square, actually an entire terrace of eighteenth-century dwellings, has become a museum of local and national history, with a special display of the town's long-standing ironmongery trade, and sad souvenirs of the battle of Flodden. In the nearby Municipal Buildings is a courtroom with the bench and chair used by Sir Walter Scott during his 30 years as Sheriff of Selkirk.

5

Dumfries and Galloway

THE EASTERN fringe of Dumfriesshire has always been virtually part of the Borders, from Annandale across Eskdale and down to the borderline itself, encompassing a large tract of the Debatable Land and the fateful battlefield of Solway Moss. To the west one moves gradually into a quieter, more withdrawn and mysterious country. To either side of the busy main road, the A75 between Stranraer and Gretna, lies a remoter world bathed in a hazy light which softens all harsh edges, seeming to pulse with the breath of old ghosts and whispers of old folklore and stubborn religious memories. Tales are still told of little dark men living underground and coming out only to wreak mischief or charitable deeds according to their own whim; and there are still the carved stones of early Christianity, and the sad, humbler stones commemorating persecuted Covenanters. Small fields climb in and out of rocky outcrops which have supplied many a drystone wall, overlooked by low whitewashed cottages and byres, only a few of which still shelter the plump Galloway Beltie cattle with their broad white cummerbunds. Once the sturdy little Galloway pony was famous, but now it is almost extinct.

The ancient lands of Galloway comprised what were later the counties of Wigtownshire and Kircudbrightshire. The names of their subdivisions are still used locally, on maps and on road signs: Galloway has its Rhins (peninsula) and Mull (headland); the Machars (or Machairs) of Wigtownshire are low-lying fields and pastures by the sea; and Kirkcudbright ('Church of St

Cuthbert') still calls itself the Stewartry, in memory of times when lands of the troublesome Douglases had been forfeited and were administered by stewards or sheriffs answerable directly to the king.

Galloway's long boot of a peninsula has throughout the centuries been a natural stopping-off place for sea traders and raiders, a point of entry for settlers and missionaries, and one terminus of a regular two-way traffic with Ireland: some contemporary mockers have called the local accent 'Stranraer Irish'. Ancient settlements, fortifications, burial grounds and cairns abound, though the generally undulating rather than spectacular landscape accommodates few hill-forts until one reaches the heights further inland above Nithsdale and Annandale. Western shores and sheltered bays such as that of Glenluce continue to yield up the bone hooks, harpoons and tools of fishermen and primitive farmers.

The Stewartry and the blunt Wigtownshire peninsula, itself rather like a flint axehead, provided a pleasantly mild climate and fertile land for early settlers. At Drumtroddan they set standing stones on a ridge. The cairns of their rural communities can still be seen at Cairn Avel near Carsphairn, at Cairnderry just over ten miles north-west of Newton Stewart, and most awesomely at the two Cairnholy groups above the A75 south-east of Creetown. Although stones from the southern mound have been quarried over the centuries to build field walls, the remains still have a commanding dignity. A passage leads from an exposed burial chamber towards an arc of stone pillars, facing a small courtyard in which ritual ceremonies took place. There must have been a similar arc at the entrance to the northern block, of which only a single pillar remains upright, while others have been shattered across its forecourt. One wonders if the farmers who tilled these slopes found time to stand and stare, deriving as much pleasure from the splendid view across the bay as the modern visitor surely must. Thomas Carlyle is said to have told Queen Victoria that the coast road from Creetown to Gatehouse-of-Fleet was the most beautiful in her realm, and when asked if there was no other as good, to have replied: 'Yes – the coast road from Gatehouse-of-Fleet to Creetown.'

In a number of lochs such as those at Lochmaben and near Crocketford, and in Carlingwark Loch on the outskirts of Castle Douglas, is another form of primitive settlement, apparently less solid than the stone buildings of the moors but in fact in an admirably defensive position. Crannogs were wooden forts and living quarters built on islands of boulders or of logs driven into the bed of a lake and covered with brushwood. Only the inhabitants knew the zig-zagging configurations of the approach track just below the surface. When Carlingwark Loch was partially drained two hundred years ago four crannogs were revealed, together with a causeway and finds including Iron Age tools and weapons, dug-out canoes and a Bronze Age sword.

As the Pictish power bases moved to the east, many tribal leaders stayed in this remote south-western corner, keeping themselves to themselves and keeping the lordship of Galloway independent from other power politics. In effect it was a separate kingdom: a twelfth-century ruler, Fergus, was referred to in records of the time as 'King' until he was conquered by Malcolm IV, King of Scots, and a century later there was a King Alan. A major stronghold of such rulers was at Cruggleton castle on a headland overlooking Wigtown Bay near Garlieston. Excavations of its ragged ruins have unearthed traces of Iron Age timber houses, over which a timbered hall was built in the eighth century: post-holes in the rock are still visible. Later lords of Galloway strengthened the fortress with stone walls and towers, sheltering a complex of workshops and kitchens. Most of that stone is now to be found in the field walls of neighbouring farmland.

Other stone castles appeared at a slower rate than in those places which had come more directly under Norman influence, and forts often remained little more than earth mottes crowned by wooden buildings and palisades. Galloway has more of these mounds than any other region of Scotland; and the Motte or Mote of Urr, in a fine defensive position above low-lying marshland and with a ditch encircling its bailey, is the largest motte-and-bailey construction in the country. Standing five miles north-east of Castle Douglas, just south of the Haugh of Urr, it was set up to guard the feudal possessions of William de Berkeley, a late twelfth-century royal chamberlain. South of Castle Douglas, less impressive and perhaps erected by a lesser lordling, is a motte at Ingleston – a 'settlement of the English' – without any sign of a ditch or bailey.

Although Robert the Bruce was crowned at Scone in the east, and is best remembered for his achievement at Bannockburn in the central region below Stirling, his family was more closely associated with the south-west. There are two major claimants in the matter of his birthplace: Turnberry castle, whose sketchy remains lie near the lighthouse north of Turnberry village in the Bruce lands of Carrick; and Lochmaben castle in Annandale, a much more substantial though overgrown ruin hidden in trees on the shore of Castle Loch, south of the town. During the many Anglo-Scottish conflicts this castle was captured and recaptured twelve times, and was also attacked and besieged another six times.

The Bruce became sixth Lord of Annandale on the death of his father, and at the time of his shifting alliances with Edward I was Earl of Carrick. Two rugged memorials to his change of heart and his fight for independence stand in one of the most beautiful parts of the Galloway Forest Park. At the head of Glen Trool, reached by a winding road through shadowy woodlands, under the shoulders of hills climbing towards the Merrick, southern Scotland's highest peak, is the Bruce Stone. In its setting of hill and loch, heather and rock, it marks the site of one of Bruce's first successful assaults in 1307. Dispiritedly scrambling over such harsh alien terrain, English forces were thrown into disarray when huge boulders came rolling down on them from the hillsides above the glen. Beside the gleaming expanse of Clatteringshaws Loch, rich in wildfowl, another stone is surrounded by a respectful body-guard of trees. Here in that same year Robert inflicted a further defeat on the invaders. He is said to have leaned on the stone while directing the course of the battle. Its inscription reads:

The Bruce's Stone:
Upon this Moss Raploch
Robert the Bruce,
Earl of Carrick, Lord of the Garrioch,
defeated the English in 1307.

Cairn Edward forest south of the diminutive royal burgh of New Galloway is named after Robert's brother Edward, who fought a number of supplementary battles in the cause of independence.

One of the Bruce family's greatest rivals had strong local connections. Devorguilla, daughter of Alan, the last King of Galloway and Constable of Scotland, married John de Balliol of Barnard Castle near Durham. Her husband rashly quarrelled with the Prince-Bishop of Durham, and as part of his penance was forced to establish a hostel in Oxford for poor students. When he died in 1248 his disconsolate widow had his heart embalmed and took it around in a casket wherever she went. She gave further endowments to the hostel which now became Balliol College; paid for the building of a bridge across the Nith in the heart of Dumfries, whose fifteenth-century replacement still bears her name; and south of Dumfries founded an abbey whose pink sandstone tower, walls and windows form what is surely the most graceful and warmly appealing of all architectural skeletons. Originally called New Abbey to distinguish it from Dundrennan abbey to the west, it acquired another name after Devorguilla's death: taking her husband's heart with her to the grave, she was buried beneath the high altar, since when it has been known as Sweetheart Abbey.

A further resonant name in the Stewartry and Galloway was that of Douglas. The name probably derives from the Gaelic *dubh glas* ('black water'), and one strand of the family became known as the Black Douglases, possibly because of the swarthy countenance of Sir James, Lord of Douglas. One of Robert the Bruce's most trusted supporters and the one ultimately chosen to carry the dead king's heart on Crusade, 'The Good Sir James' had distinguished himself during the wars of independence in the recapture of Roxburgh castle. Cunningly he ordered his men to crawl towards the walls at twilight under their cloaks, so that the sentries mistook them for cattle and realized their mistake too late. His 'goodness' was regrettably far from apparent in his ruthless Border raids, creating such fear that mothers used to scold their children into obedience with the threat 'The Black Douglas will get you.'

His nephew William became first Earl of Douglas, and had a son also called James, the second earl, who took part in one of the most celebrated battles in Border history:

> It fell about the Lammas tide
> When the muir-men win their hay,
> The doughty Earl of Douglas rode
> Into England to catch a prey.

There had been a long-standing feud between the Scottish family of Douglas and the great Northumbrian family of Percy. Their clash in 1388 seems to have started when the English went hunting in the Cheviots – Chevy Chase – on lands which the Douglases regarded as their own. After burning Percy lands in revenge, Douglas seized Harry Hotspur's standard and tried to carry it home across the Border. The English pursued and gave battle at Otterburn. Harry Percy was captured; but the earl was killed.

He left no heir. The earldom was bestowed on the Lord of Galloway, an illegitimate son of the Good Sir James, known to his contemporaries as Archibald the Grim because of his ferocious expression when in battle. He built for himself on an island in the river Dee the equally grim pile of Threave castle. Its ponderous four-storeyed tower was originally more than 70 feet high, and within the 8-foot thick walls a garrison of up to a thousand men could be quartered to maintain Douglas control over the surrounding countryside.

The Douglases, like so many noble Scottish families, were frequently in revolt against their king, and just as frequently at odds with their fellow nobles. At the age of 16 the sixth earl presented, in the eyes of James II's regents, such a threat to their own manipulation of the boy king that he and his younger brother were lured to Edinburgh castle and murdered at the 'Black Dinner' *(see also Chapter 3)*. Still the family estates and power continued to grow, and oppression of the people on their lands raged on unchecked. William, the eighth earl, boasted that the stone knob used for hanging malefactors above Threave castle gateway 'has not been without a tassle for fifty years'. When there was no criminal to be hanged, the earl kept up the tradition by seizing any passing peasant and hoisting him up. Local hatred of the Douglases was such that a much quoted tale recounts how, when James II led troops towards the castle in 1453 to put an end to their pretensions and disloyalties, the local blacksmith and friends were delighted to help in the forging of a huge cannon known as Mons Meg (today displayed at Edinburgh castle) for an assault on the otherwise impregnable walls, taking its name from the blacksmith's wife Meg. Unfortunately this colourful legend has been contradicted by records which show that the gun was cast at Mons and presented to James by the Duke of Burgundy in 1457.

The Douglas himself was not at home, but his wife, the Fair Maid of Galloway, was at table when the cannon was first fired. As she was raising a cup of wine, unperturbed by any possible attack on the family stronghold, a massive granite ball smashed right through the wall and took off her hand. The castle nevertheless withstood the siege for more than three months.

James personally killed the eighth earl at Stirling castle, and when his brother the ninth earl rose in vengeful revolt, marched on another Douglas castle at Inveravon, near Linlithgow. Although the earl fled to England and continued conniving against the king, the power of the Douglases had been effectively broken, and their estates were forfeited. In due course these lands were granted to the fourth Earl of Angus, of the family known as the Red Douglases because of the colour of their hair. One of them was to marry James IV's widow,

Margaret Tudor, whose red sandstone tomb is set into a wall of Lincluden abbey church outside Dumfries. Their daughter became the mother of Lord Darnley, and descendants include the Dukes of Hamilton, Buccleuch and Queensberry. The Castle Douglas near which Threave castle stands does not, confusingly, take its name from the family of Archibald the Grim. Originally no more than a small hamlet on the eighteenth-century military road built for the passage of troops to Stranraer and Portpatrick *en route* for Ireland, it was bought in 1789 by William Douglas, a rich Glasgow merchant. He laid out a planned estate village, which developed into a major market and textile manufacturing centre.

Two other arrogant, feuding families caused decades of terror and bloodshed in the south-west. Today there are few more moving and beautiful sights than the bronze otter high above the bay near Port William, commemorating the life and work of Gavin Maxwell, whose favourite spot this was in childhood. The Maxwells have been associated in recent centuries with the building of model villages such as Monreith and Port William, and their family chapel and graveyard cling to the cliff below the otter statue. But they were not always philanthropic. They and the Johnstones were so involved in conflict over such a long period that one warden of the English West March reported that between them they had turned the Debatable Land into a wilderness. For a large part of the time they were themselves struggling for possession of the perks and pickings of that wardenship. No two families could have better exemplified the violent antagonisms that James VI denounced in his *Basilikon Doron:*

> For anie displeasure, that they apprehend to be done unto them by their neighbours, take up a plaine feid against him, and (without respect to God, King or commonwealth) bang it out bravely, hee and all his kinne, against him and all his.

Of Annandale origin, the Maxwells played a tricky game during the swings of fortune between Edward I and those who defied him. When it seemed politic to do so, they supported English claims. In the early fourteenth century it was a Maxwell who held Caerlaverock castle for England. This glowing pink triangular castle within its moat and massive earthworks has undergone many alterations over the centuries, but from the earliest times was a key to control of traffic across the Solway and along the coastal plain. The original was almost certainly built by the English to maintain a bridgehead for their frequent incursions into Scotland. After the death of Edward I, Sir Eustace Maxwell slyly did a financial deal with the feeble Edward II, then promptly switched his allegiance to Robert the Bruce and held out against a siege by the enraged English. Shortly afterwards the castle was dismantled on Bruce's orders to safeguard against an all too likely return of enemy forces anxious to re-establish that bridgehead. The fortification must nevertheless have been in repairable condition, since by 1347 it was in the possession of Herbert of Maxwell – again a careful hedger of bets, who submitted to Edward III and was granted letters of protection for himself and the castle with all its contents.

There are several references to renewed demolition, but the building has repeatedly managed to regain its strength. Henry VIII took possession of it, then the Scots won it back. When the Earl of Sussex was devastating the countryside it was recorded that the castle had been besieged and 'thrown down'; but by 1593 Lord Maxwell was setting up 'great fortifications' and had 'many men working at his house five miles from Dumfries'. The remains today present a remarkable sight, with a gatehouse mightier than the actual castle behind it, wide gun-ports inserted into earlier masonry, in complete contrast to graceful seventeenth-century ranges within the courtyard sug-gesting a Renaissance mansion rather than a fortress. These civilized living quarters were the work of Robert Maxwell, first Earl of Nithsdale, who during the Civil War held the castle for Charles I until it was accepted that the siege by the

Parliamentarians could not be relieved, when the garrison was allowed to capitulate on honourable terms.

In 1557 Sir John Maxwell had been appointed Warden of the West March of Scotland, becoming fourth Baron Herries in 1566. A couple of years later he was in rebellion, and was dismissed. A Douglas held the post briefly, but in 1570 Herries reappointed himself Warden in Queen Mary's name. He had built himself the stronghold of Hoddom castle from which to dominate the West March – the setting for much of Scott's *Redgauntlet*. Today surrounded by caravans, its massive tower still carries the beacon platform on which a 'balefire' could be lit to warn the valley of imminent invasion. Another Maxwell building on a hilltop to the south, the Repentance Tower, bears the word REPENTENCE in Gothic lettering over its door, probably as a sop to the Bishop of Glasgow, whose local chapel Maxwell had pulled down to use its stones in his castle.

Thereafter for a quarter of a century, with only a few inconsequential interruptions, the pendulum swung between a Maxwell and a Johnstone, until the final great open battle between the two families in 1593.

The Johnstones went raiding and pillaging not just in England but across Maxwell lands. Whenever a Johnstone was made Warden, the Maxwells would immediately instruct their families not to obey him. Sometimes the Wardens of the English West March would, on instructions from London, try to keep the feud at boiling point in the hope of both parties exhausting each other; at other times they viewed with alarm the possible devastation of the entire region.

During a spell when John Maxwell, Earl of Morton, was in disgrace and the king had instructed John Johnstone to arrest him, hatred between the two blazed up to new heights. Instead of lying low, Maxwell gathered some hundreds of the Armstrong reiving clan together and attacked Johnstone's castle at Lochwood in Annandale, which had grown from a timber tower into a substantial stone fortification. He killed six Johnstones, burned surrounding houses, and set fire to the castle itself. The king ordered troops into the region; but Maxwell warned local people that if they helped the royal forces in any way he would repay them in kind. Throughout the spring of 1585 Johnstone villages and houses were sacked; the Johnstones retaliated by burning the Maxwell village of Duncow north of Dumfries; the Maxwells rounded up Johnstone cattle in the Dryfe valley and hanged four Johnstones outside their own doors in Lockerbie. Royal commands and denunciations made little difference. There was even a time when, in despair, the Border wardens and the king himself contemplated calling on England for help.

In 1593 the final confrontation came. Restored to favour in spite of his known collaboration in the assembly of the Spanish Armada, John Maxwell, Earl of Morton, was reappointed Warden of the West March. There had been a spell of calm between the two notorious families, helped by the marriage of young James, the Johnstone chief, to a Maxwell girl. Then, following a very minor reiving episode which led to some skirmishes and further thieving in Nithsdale, including attacks on the property of Lord Sanquhar and the Laird of Drumlanrig, Maxwell had to take action in his official capacity against the Johnstones. He assembled 2,000 men at Lockerbie, ready to return to Lochwood castle and finish the job that had been started a few years before. Johnstone had been able to summon only 400 supporters, among them a number of Elliots and English Grahams, so at first had to resort to cunning rather than brute force. He lured Maxwell's advance party into an ambush of men 'lyand darnit in a wood', and frightened it into turning back and crashing into its own main body on Dryfe Sands, outside Lockerbie. A ferocious battle was joined, raging into the streets of the town itself. In spite of being outnumbered, the Johnstones fought so savagely that they killed 700 of Maxwell's men, mutilating them and others by cutting their ears off with cleavers – a wound known along the Borders as a 'Lockerbie nick'.

Maxwell himself was brought down from his horse and stretched out his hand in surrender. It was immediately chopped off, and he was then hacked to death. The Johnstones were at last victors, though for a time they were outlawed; but later James Johnstone was appointed the last Warden of the West March. In 1608 he agreed to meet the then Lord Maxwell to put an honourable end to the family feud. At the meeting Maxwell shot him twice in the back, and was arrested and executed. Among relics of their internecine warfare are the last fang of Lochwood tower above cellars and a dungeon, in ancient woodland south of Beattock; Lochmaben castle, which was for some time the Warden's official residence; Caerlaverock castle; and the Johnstone Tower in Lockerbie.

Beside a footpath from the admirably landscaped Caldons camp and caravan site in Glen Trool, a modern stone commemorates less noble deeds than those performed in the neighbourhood by Robert the Bruce. On its two sides it records the slaughter in 1685 of six Covenanters by a party of dragoons under the command of a Colonel Douglas. The original stone was vandalized in our own time and had to be removed for repair and safe-keeping to Newton Stewart Museum.

Galloway had been accustomed to the inroads of various preachers and sects since the arrival of St Ninian in the fourth century. Probably born in North Wales, Nynia or Ninian was consecrated a bishop in Rome by the Pope and sent to preach Christianity to the southern Picts. So persuasively did he do so that, according to Bede, they readily 'abandoned the ideas of idolatry'. In due course his diocese spread from the environs of Glasgow to the northern fringe of Westmorland, though in effect the Celtic church depended less on a diocesan pattern than on monastic and lingering tribal customs – one of the factors which was to bring it into conflict with the authorities in Rome. It must be from this period that the stones of Kirkmadrine originate, shielded now behind glass in the porch of a disused chapel near Sandhead in the Rhinns of Galloway. Among the earliest Christian memorials in Britain, the Latin dedication of one of these slabs to three bishops suggests an important see, and it has even been suggested that Ninian himself was one of the bishops.

In the low cliffs in the south-west tip of the Wigtownshire

peninsula is St Ninian's Cave, in which he is supposed for a time to have led a hermetical existence. Early Christian crosses have been carved into the rock, and a number of stones have been moved for safety to Whithorn Museum. A few miles to the east, a roofless thirteenth-century building known as St Ninian's Chapel stands on a breezy promontory beside the bright little harbour village of Isle of Whithorn. The most substantial relics of Ninian's presence, however, are to be found in Whithorn itself, 10 miles south of Wigtown.

Tradition has long held that it was here that St Ninian founded his *Candida Casa* (White House); and certainly the town of Whithorn takes its name from the Northumbrian translation – *hwit aern*. This was the first Christian church in Scotland, although the surviving priory ruins date only from the twelfth century. When Ninian died, the site became a shrine which remained so popular even after the Reformation that a special Act of Parliament had to be introduced forbidding pilgrimages there. The twelfth-century buildings were largely demolished, and a newer kirk stands on the slope above the remains. In 1986 a major five-year excavation of the site was begun, with some surprising results. The 'Whithorn Dig' revealed an unsuspected palimpsest of successive cultures. Below a nineteenth-century schoolhouse lay both Anglo-Saxon and medieval burial grounds; and painstakingly there was exposed a substantial Viking settlement, which appears to have survived for a considerable time at peace and on prosperous trading terms with its neighbours. Then, deeper still, there were indeed the Christian buildings and graves of the fifth century. Alongside the priory and excavations a small museum displays a collection of Christian stones, including the Monreith Cross.

One of the most awe-inspiring stones is that in the church of Ruthwell village, about 8 miles south-east of Dumfries. Dating from the so-called 'Dark Ages', the Ruthwell Cross is a triumph of light and beauty, all the more so since its installation within the church apse, illuminated to bring out its features. Biblical scenes by an unknown seventh-century sculptor include the Annunciation, the Flight into Egypt, Mary Magdalene washing Christ's feet, the Crucifixion, and Christ in Glory. In runic text on the narrower sides is Caedmon's *Dream of the Holy Rood.* The 18-foot high pillar had lain broken for a long time in the churchyard before being rediscovered by the minister, Dr Henry Duncan, who carefully reassembled it. Dr Duncan has other more mundane claims to fame: in 1810 he founded the first Savings Bank in a nearby cottage, now a museum of the Savings Bank movement.

In AD 563 another evangelist, later to be canonized as Ninian had been, arrived in the land of the Picts. Calumcille, whose Irish name was to be Latinized as Columba, was of royal blood and might well have become a High King of Ireland if it had not been for his ungovernable temper. Although he was an eager divinity student who duly entered the church and founded several monasteries in his homeland, he was also possessed of a regal arrogance in which religious humility seems to have played no part. After declaring war on the High King Diarmid and waging a particularly bloody battle, he was threatened with excommunication unless he could produce as many converts as the men he had caused to be slain. Setting off across the sea to proselytize in the infant kingdom of Dalriada, he is believed to have lived for a while in what is now called St Columba's Cave on the shore of Loch Killisport in Argyll. It seems to have been in regular occupancy since the Middle Stone Age, with additions in Columba's time of a rock altar and carved crosses. At some stage the preacher moved to the island of Iona and established it as the holiest centre of the Celtic church. From here he travelled out as 'Apostle of the Highlands', building up what became for a century and a half the effective national church of Scotland, offering little more than token respect to the church of Rome.

On the eastern side of Luce Bay, near Mochrum, the rectangular foundations of Chapel Finian stand close to the coastal road. This was probably named after another sixth-century Irish saint who is known to have been educated at Whithorn, and may have been set near a landing-place for pilgrims on their way to St Ninian's shrine.

The following century produced St Cuthbert, thought to have been born in Northumbria of Lowland Scottish parents. He entered the monastery at Old Melrose before settling in Lindisfarne and then secluding himself in a hermit's cell on the Farne islands. In due course he was interred within Durham cathedral, to have his rest disturbed by Viking raiders, while in later centuries the Scots were to inflict iconoclastic damage on the cathedral itself.

As we have seen at St Andrews, the Culdees and other Celtic sects were in due course coaxed or bullied into surrendering to Roman rites. Such takeovers or attempted takeovers and reclamations were to be a bitterly recurrent feature of Scottish Christianity over the centuries to come. The frequent attempts at permanent alliance with France against the English led, after Henry VIII's assumption of ecclesiastical as well as secular power, to even more troublesome splits between different factions than those which occurred in England. Pro-French elements remained staunchly Catholic, and accused the Reformation zealots of being in the pay of England. This was indeed true of several of them. The militant John Knox worked in England and was to a large extent subsidized by the English until the accession of the Catholic 'Bloody Mary'. When he returned to his native land after a spell in Frankfurt and Geneva imbibing Calvinist doctrines, he found many nobles willing to listen to him because they saw possible rich gains if the church could be despoiled of its possessions.

The Protestant ethic made steady advances from the 1540s onwards, partly from a genuine revulsion against the Catholic church and partly from motives of greed. In 1557, mistrustful of the Regent, Mary of Guise, herself a French Catholic, the Protestant Lords of the Congregation signed a bond or Covenant, the first of a number similarly entitled, each seeking with increasing fervour to establish a religious observance free from papal hegemony and to maintain a Presbyterian system in which presbyters or elders replaced Roman or Anglican

bishops. By 1560 a Calvinistic Confession of Faith had superseded Roman usages.

The reign and opinions of Mary, Queen of Scots, threatened
the new freedoms; but her own behaviour, in particular her
dismal marriages, led to her downfall and to a strengthening
of the puritanical element. As in all such abrupt changes, there
was an outbreak of vindictive destruction, the wanton smashing
of 'idolatrous' church furnishings and of the buildings themselves, and persecution of those who refused to subscribe to
the rigorous new ethic. While the mob was occupied in this
way, lords and landowners appropriated church land and incorporated it into their own estates, though in 1561 it was
grudgingly agreed that some revenues should be set aside for
ministers of the Reformed church.

In 1599 James VI began cautious attempts to restore the
episcopacy, believing that its very existence provided spiritual
and practical support for the monarchy: 'No bishop, no king.'
After becoming King of England as well as of Scotland he
adopted what suited him from the Church of England, put in
hand the compilation of the Authorized Version of the Bible
based on the 1568 'Bishops' Bible', and in 1618 managed to
get ratification from the General Assembly of the Five Articles
of Perth. These included contentious points such as a return
to kneeling rather than sitting during Communion; the observance of Christmas, Easter and Pentecost; and the necessity of
Confirmation. It took three years for Parliament to give its
ultimate sanction, on a day which opponents were to call Black
Saturday. James died shortly after, and his son inherited not
only the troubles obviously lying in wait but a self-righteous
determination even more wilful than that of James.

Although born at Dunfermline and as much King of Scotland as of England, Charles I showed little concern for the
distinctive interests of his ancestors' homeland. Approaches to
the Scots came only when he was desperately in need of help
against the Parliamentarians during the Civil War; and then he
was shameless in making promises which he had little intention
of keeping.

James had expounded a belief in the divine right of kings in his treatises, *The Trew Law of Free Monarchies* and the *Basilikon Doron*. 'Hold no Parliaments', he advised, 'but for necessities of new Laws, which would be but seldom.' Such laws, obviously, were to be only those required by the king to raise taxes and repress any challenge to his own holy power and in no way to bestow rights on lesser mortals. The devotion with which Charles followed such a philosophy led to his inevitable clash with the English Parliament, while his secret Catholicism linked with overt Anglicanism led to attempts in Scotland to turn back the Presbyterian tide.

There is a tragic irony in this adherence to his father's precepts, when one considers how little that father had cared for him. James's first-born son Henry had been expected to succeed to the throne, and every care was lavished on him. Charles, a weakling child warped by rickets, and only 5 feet tall when fully grown, was despised and received no training whatsoever for kingship. When Henry died of typhoid in 1612, it was too late for James to switch his affections or set about educating this poor second-best heir. Charles had to learn his own way; and soon showed signs of doing so without accepting the advice of anyone else.

During his years in England, James had left the day-to-day administration of Scotland to his Privy Council in Edinburgh, never bothering to attend any of their meetings but expecting them to handle routine matters without distracting him from more important things. Charles, naturally secretive and stubborn, ignored them even more offensively and simply issued royal commands which he expected to be obeyed and put into effect without question or comment.

In 1637 he decreed that Archbishop Laud's revised Anglican liturgy should be adopted throughout Scotland. This provoked the 'Jenny Geddes riot' in St Giles, Edinburgh. The committees known as the Tables, established to resist the king's attacks on their Reformist beliefs, proclaimed a National Covenant 'to recover the purity and liberty of the Gospel'. The General Assembly denounced episcopacy and re-established

Presbyterianism. Attempting to raise an army and march into Scotland to enforce his will, the king provoked the disjointed Bishops' Wars of 1639 and 1640. In the first, Charles found that without the backing of the English Parliament – which he refused to call – he had no way of assembling adequate levies. In the second, he managed to get supplies from Ireland but was swiftly defeated at Newburn on the river Tyne, whereupon the Scots overran most of Northumberland and Durham. In an ignominious armistice the king had to agree to pay these occupying forces £850 a day until he could recall the English Long Parliament to conclude a peace.

A year after the outbreak of the Civil War in 1642, the English Parliamentarians and the Scots signed a Solemn League and Covenant by which, in return for the supply of a Scottish army at a fee of £30,000 a month, it was mutually agreed that Presbyterianism should be established throughout England and Ireland. Towards the end of his stubborn contest with Cromwell's forces, Charles changed tack and tried to make a deal with the Scots after surrendering to them at Newark; but they handed him over to his enemies. In a very short time the Scots themselves were at odds with the Parliamentarians, and after the execution of Charles I they acknowledged his son as King Charles II on condition that he signed the Covenant. This the young man did, and was crowned at Scone. His first spell of kingship lasted only a short time: Cromwell marched into Scotland, won the battle of Dunbar, and seized Edinburgh. After a year of intrigue Charles led a Scottish army into England but was defeated at the battle of Worcester and had to flee to France.

Scottish disillusionment with the Commonwealth administration, which dismissed the General Assembly and, so far from honouring the pledge to advance Presbyterianism, proved hostile towards it, was followed by worse disillusionment on the Restoration of Charles II. He, too, renounced his agreement to the Covenant, reintroduced bishops into the Scottish church, threw out a third of the existing clergy and forbade them to return within 20 miles of their parishes. Only the most subservient Presbyterians were licensed to preach a muted form of their gospel. Rejecting any such compromise, the stricter Covenanters had to meet at secret conventicles in the hills and remoter vales. Persecuted beyond endurance by posses of bullying dragoons sent in to break up conventicles by the sword, Covenanters in Galloway rose unexpectedly in November 1666 and captured the leader of their tormentors in Dumfries. Several thousand then marched on Edinburgh, but their numbers dwindled, and troops under Sir Thomas Dalyell of the Binns easily defeated them. Captives were tortured, deported to the West Indies, or taken back to be hanged in front of their own homes.

A grim memorial in a Lanarkshire churchyard recalls the dismembering of four Covenanters who died for their convictions:

> Stay passenger take notice
> what thou reads:
> At Edinburgh lie our bodies,
> here our heads:
> Our right hands stood at Lanark
> these we want,
> Because with them we sware
> the Covenant.

In spite of such measures, rebellion continued, and the more earnest and restrained preachers found themselves distanced from armed and openly defiant groups. In the end the Duke of Monmouth led an army into Scotland and defeated Covenanting forces at Bothwell Brig on the Clyde. More than 200 prisoners were penned, half-starving, in the Greyfriars churchyard in Edinburgh to await transportation to the American colonies as slaves. The *Crown*, the vessel in which they finally embarked, was caught in a gale off the Orkneys on 10 December 1679. The captain spurned their pleas to be allowed to struggle ashore, and battened down the hatches. When the ship was finally pounded on to the rocks the entire crew escaped by using one of the masts as a bridge to safety; but only 50 prisoners survived, to be put aboard another ship and sent off to Jamaica and New Jersey. In 1888 a tall memorial pillar was set up at Deerness, a few hundred yards from the scene of the wreck, and a smaller obelisk was installed in front of St Magnus's cathedral in Kirkwall.

Charles II's brother James, Duke of York, was appointed royal commissioner and, himself avowedly Catholic, set about the systematic obliteration of the Covenanting faith with a brutality which continued after he had become King James VII of Scotland, James II of England. The years of terror inflicted by Scottish vassals seeking his favour, proud of being known as the Persecutors, were to be remembered as the 'Killing Times'.

In condemning the atrocities of these Persecutors, one must reluctantly take into account the previous record of the persecuted. When they had been on the winning side, the Covenanters themselves had behaved as arrogantly and bloodily as any other fanatical sect. They had destroyed opponents' buildings and their very lives. Tolerance of any creed other than their own was regarded as heresy. During Charles I's attempts to assert himself, a Covenanting army which had defeated Irish troops at Philiphaugh near Selkirk felt no compunction in their handling of such Papists. Men who surrendered were slaughtered, all the women and children among the camp followers were hacked to pieces, and those who attempted to escape into the hills were hunted down and hanged, drowned, or had their throats slit. Much the same now happened to the anti Papists at the mercy of others; and much the worst of it in darkly obdurate Galloway.

Two of the most dedicated and sadistic leaders of the suppressors were Sir Robert Grierson of Lag ('Bloddy Lag') and John Graham of Claverhouse ('Bloody Claverhouse'), who was such a fervent royal acolyte that he was created Viscount Dundee when James II needed support against a greater threat, that of William of Orange. Modern listeners may find the song about the 'bonnets of Bonnie Dundee' rousing and inspiring; many of the viscount's contemporaries did not. Little mercy was shown on either side. Covenanters announced in the Apologetical Declaration their intention of assassinating those enemies who attacked their faith. The said enemies responded with an inquisition whereby anyone suspected, on any pretext whatsoever, of complicity with such views must solemnly abjure what were called the criminal elements in the declaration, or be executed. And all the time the pursuit and killing of both peaceful and militant worshippers in remote corners went inexorably on.

In the trim little royal burgh of Sanquhar in upper Nithsdale, a granite monument marks the spot where Richard Cameron, the 'Lion of the Covenant', uttered in 1680 the Sanquhar Declaration calling for the abdication of the tyrannical Charles II, usurper and enemy of the true Kirk. James Renwick renewed those principles in 1685, in the face of worse threats from the new King James.

Cameron had died at Aird's Moss at the hands of Claverhouse. His fervour inspired his followers to keep faith and to head for Sanquhar five years later to support the equally respected Renwick in his Second Declaration, in spite of the risk of being informed on. A group travelling from Kirkcudbright heard whispers of such an informer and switched their route to a little-known track across Dumfriesshire, leaving one of their number behind to see if the spy could be flushed out into the open. This volunteer was John McClurg, a blacksmith from Minnigaff, on the river Cree by Newton Stewart. He did not have long to wait before the traitor appeared – a traitor indeed, since Grier had himself been a vociferous Covenanter until lured into royal service by the promise of good payment for betraying the secret meeting-places and regular movements of his old co-religionists. McClurg shot Grier and divested him of his armour and weapons, the most potent of which proved to be a flail.

This agricultural tool had probably been used as a primitive weapon before the times of muskets and well-made swords – and employed by peasants who could in any case never afford more sophisticated weapons with which to protect themselves.

As a blacksmith by trade, McClurg found it easy to adapt its iron links so that they enwrapped and stunned an opponent. His first effective use of it was on the last stretch of the path to the Sanquhar rendezvous, where he and his colleagues were intercepted by some of Bloddy Lag's men. McClurg threw himself at them so devastatingly that they broke up in confusion. Thereafter the 'Galloway flail' became a fearsome weapon in the hands of desperate Covenanters. One of the greatest testimonies to its efficacy is that it was adopted in later years by the arch-persecutor Claverhouse: having seen it in action, he resorted to it when he was himself a refugee from the forces of the Protestant William III.

It is significant that the 'Highland Host' of mercenaries brought down from the north to subjugate the Covenanters, living off the land and treating the entire local population with indiscriminate savagery, left behind such a foul odour of cruelty that not one man from the south-west responded to the call to join Bonnie Prince Charlie and his Highlanders during the Stuart rising of 1745.

In the year of the Second Sanquhar Declaration the persecutions were at their most intense throughout Galloway. This was the time when the hapless worshippers in Glen Trool were surprised and

MOST IMPIOUS

LY AND CRUELLY

MURTERED FOR THEIR

ADHERENCE TO SCOT

LANDS REFORMATION

COVENANTS NATIONAL

AND SOLEMN LEAGUE

North of Glen Trool and the Galloway Forest Park, whose hills once sheltered many conventicles, another Covenanters' memorial stands in the old graveyard of Dalmellington. Later a weaving centre and then prospering briefly from an ironworks and small colliery, Dalmellington was for a time forced to house Claverhouse's soldiers at the town's expense. Its Interpretation

Centre in a row of old weavers' cottages records incidents from Covenanting days and the lives and deaths of local heroes, as well as displaying a re-creation of the interior of a weaver's home and the tools of his craft. In Biggar, a farmhouse found in ruinous condition 10 miles away has been moved and reassembled as a Covenanters' House, with relics of the movement's history and tribulations. A memorial to John Hunter stands on the edge of the Devil's Beef Tub above Moffat. On the flanks of the Lowther Hills, the churchyard of Durisdeer – its slim steeple visible for miles up the southern river valley, often bathed in sunlight while the Lowthers are cloud-shadowed – shelters the bleak table tomb of a Covenanter, in complete contrast to the grandiose tomb and burial aisle of the second Duke of Queensberry within. In St Michael's churchyard, Dumfries, a nineteenth-century obelisk marks Covenanters' graves close to the Robert Burns mausoleum.

One memorial of the Killing Times has become a gruesome tourist attraction. Below Wigtown church a boardwalk leads out across the marshy shore of the bay to a stone replica of the stake to which two women were tied and deliberately drowned. As the tide came in they were abjured to forsake their beliefs, but neither gave way, and the water closed over their heads. Their graves are enclosed by railings in the churchyard above the scene. Even higher, overlooking the town, is an obelisk commemorating them and other martyrs.

The preservation of Covenanters' memorials in lonely rural settings owes much to the activities of Robert Paterson, an itinerant stonemason from the village of Balmaclellan near New Galloway. Distressed by neglect of the scattered graves and fearful that the names of the dead would be forgotten, he tramped the Lowlands tidying up plots, cleaning inscriptions, and in some cases carving crude stones of his own. His nickname, 'Old Mortality', became the title of one of Sir Walter Scott's novels. Paterson was buried in Caerlaverock, and there is a statue of him, recumbent on a slab with his horse beside him, at Dumfries museum. Another lifesize statue of him clad in his plaid, cloth leggings, stout shoes and large cloth bonnet, once stood near his birthplace in Balmaclellan, but because of threats of vandalism has been moved, like the Caldons stone he carved, to Newton Stewart museum.

The flight of James VII and II and the arrival of William III in the Glorious Revolution of 1688 came too late to save the much admired James Renwick, executed in February of that year. There is a monument to him in Moniaive village, around which many conventicles were held. On Skeoch Hill a memorial and four rows of 'Communion Stones' recall one attended by 3,000 of the faithful in 1679.

Welcome as the new régime was, however, it did not produce an undivided and uncontentious Church of Scotland. Presbyterianism was officially restored in 1690, while those who preferred the formalities imposed by Charles II formed their own Episcopalian Church of Scotland. Within the main body of the church, argument broke out about the question of patronage. Most benefices were in the control of patrons who often forced unwelcome clergymen upon the congregation. The more severe Calvinists resented this, but attempts to eject such nominees were thwarted in the law courts. Two secessions by protest groups took place in 1733 and 1752; but the real 'Great Schism' came in 1843. The General Assembly of the Church of Scotland, having failed to get a Veto Act accepted by the state, giving any congregation the right to reject a patron's nominee, was split between moderates and evangelicals. Defiantly, a number of the clergy seceded to form the Free Church of Scotland, taking half the membership with them. Oddly enough, in the usually staunch Nonconformist regions of Teviotdale, Dumfries and Galloway only a quarter of the clergy seceded, as against three-quarters in the Highlands, and every single one in Aberdeen.

Shorn of patronage and state support, the Free Church had to raise money by collections from its congregations, even the poorest. When it could afford its own churches it deliberately built them as close as possible to the older ones: hence the foreign visitor may be perplexed by the close juxtaposition of a Church of Scotland and a Free Church of Scotland. Some landowners treated it with outright hostility. In the Strontian district (later to give its name to the metallic element *strontium*), the Free Church sought a piece of land to build a place of worship, but was refused. So in 1846 a boat was specially built and launched on Loch Sunart as a floating church, in use until 1873. Local observers reported that one could tell the size of the congregation on any given day by the depth of the vessel in the water.

With the complete abolition of patronage, the Free Church united with the Presbyterians to form the United Free Church in 1900, which was reconciled with the Church of Scotland in 1929.

Such amalgamations were not to the taste of the more ascetic Calvinists. Claiming to be the true inheritors of the Free Church, they retained its title but because of their limited numbers have been more generally known as the 'Wee Frees'. An even tinier and more austere breakaway sect is that of the Free Presbyterian Church of Scotland, where historic intolerance of other creeds has continued to flourish. In 1988 the Lord Chancellor, Lord Mackay, was suspended as an elder of this body and banished from communion for six months because he had attended a requiem mass for a Roman Catholic colleague.

With the Act of Union in 1707, when 'Scotland was sold for England's gold', fresh secular troubles sprang up. Now that the Border was abolished, Scottish meat was free to enter the English – or British – market, but could profit from this only if the old system of small-scale farming on peasant smallholdings could be replaced by enclosures and less labour-intensive stock rearing and despatching. This had to be accompanied by better transport and better communications with the outside world.

Until late into the seventeenth century the roads of Galloway were no more than mud tracks, and any long journey involved innumerable detours to find the few bridges across river and stream. The commonest vehicle was a creel or 'carr', a wicker basket slung between two shafts and dragged along the ground behind a horse. Wheeled carts did not appear until the middle of the eighteenth century. Cottages were lit by oil obtained from whales cast up on the coast, and heated by burning peat and bracken. The sea also provided salt in salt-pans, building mortar made by burning seashells in primitive peat-fired kilns, and fertilizer from seaweed. Farming was crude and wasteful, divided between run-rig strips of arable land and common areas for pasture and grazing. Faced by new commercial prospects and challenges, the more alert lairds saw that Gallovidians had to be shaken out of their old stubborn ways.

The cattle trade with England offered healthy profits, with excellent pastureland on the Scottish side of the now abolished Border, and the reasonable proximity of English markets. But to build up good stock and move it when necessary, land had to be enclosed and drove roads well protected from weather, strays and rustlers. Tenant farmers were served with eviction notices. The landlords began vigorously building walls and dykes. With equal vigour gangs of 'Levellers' roamed the countryside tearing them down and filling them in. One of the protesters' most effective leaders in Galloway, Billy Marshall, had been a soldier, but was now known as the King of the Gypsies. Yet again the dragoons rode out, as they had ridden in pursuit of the Covenanters. The revolt was inevitably suppressed, but Billy himself lived on to the age of 120, and was reputed to have fathered several children after he had passed his hundredth year.

Some of the landed gentry tried to soften the impact of this agricultural revolution by setting up other employment for the dispossessed and at the same time profiting themselves from burgeoning industries such as textiles, tanning and brewing. Ideally it ought to be possible to balance an adequate but not excessive labour force on the land with employment in rural and small-town industry. One of the most ambitious schemes of this kind was put in hand by James Murray of Cally at Gatehouse-of-Fleet. From 1763 onwards he supervised the creation of an entire community with tanneries, breweries, a soap works, and supplementary crafts and shops. Above all he planned an expanding textile industry, especially in cotton spinning. In due course four mills were built, powered by water fed down from Loch Whinyeon in the hills above. Business had fallen away by the beginning of the twentieth century, but the layout of the village today remains as trim and practical as its sponsor could have wished.

Many peasants driven from the land did find employment in weaving, but there was not enough for all of them in spite of the opening up of American as well as British markets. Some emigrated, driven by forces presaging those of the later Highland Clearances.

Another export to America was a man born in 1747 at Kirkbean, in a little white cottage which still overlooks the Solway, whose shores he was to harry for some years as a daring pirate. John Paul Jones had been a garden boy on the Arbigland estate surrounding his birthplace, but felt the call of the sea and shipped as mate on a slaver. When serving as captain of a merchant ship he was arrested and imprisoned on a charge of murdering a member of his crew. His brief period of imprisonment was in the Kircudbright Tolbooth, whose outer wall retains the iron jougs to which malefactors were manacled. Leaving his own country, he won a commission in the American navy during the War of Independence, and made several attacks on the English and Scottish mainland. His influence was so great that he became known as the Father of the American Navy; and went on to become an equally formative power in the Russian Navy.

One of Jones's best remembered exploits was a surprise raid on St Mary's Isle in Kirkcudbright Bay. He had been hoping to capture the Earl of Selkirk, whose home was there, and carry him off as a hostage for American prisoners in British hands. As the earl was away at the time, Jones's men helped themselves to his silver plate; but their leader, perhaps feeling this was not gentlemanly behaviour in the land of his childhood, returned the plate some years later.

It was while staying at the Selkirk Arms in Kircudbright that the poet Robert Burns wrote his *Selkirk Grace*. Although born at Alloway in Ayrshire and brought up nearby on farms of which his incompetent father could never make a success, Burns spent his later creative years in and around Dumfries After their father's death, he and his brother took a farm at Mossgiel, but were equally inefficient, and relied for income on the lyric poems and rumbustious satires which Robert was now writing. It was at this time that he fell in love with Jean Armour, about whom he wrote several moving poems and whom he made pregnant. He had already had a daughter by another girl, Lizzie Paton, word of which had caused them to be summoned before the Kirk, where they were forced to sit on the 'cutty stool' or sinners' seat through three successive Sunday services. Burns tried to write jokingly about it later, but wrote more affectionately about his daughter in *A Poet's Welcome to his Bastart Wean*. The attitude of the Armour family to his later outrage drove him into the arms of yet another girl, Mary Campbell, for whom he also composed many songs, including *Highland Mary*.

Just when he was planning to take Mary with him to a post he had been offered in Jamaica, he was hauled to the 'cutty stool' yet again, this time accompanied by Jean Armour. Jean was shortly delivered of a twin boy and girl; Mary, now also pregnant, died of 'a malignant fever' before her child could be born; and all Burns' plans were revised when his first printed book, *Poems Chiefly in the Scottish Dialect*, proved an outstanding success. He was soon drawn to Edinburgh and lionized there. On a visit to Dumfries in June 1787 he was at once created an honorary burgess. While toying with the affections of well to-do ladies and calculating his chances of a profitable marriage, he managed to fit in visits to Jean Armour once more and again to father twins upon her.

Since writing poetry was not, in spite of his growing reputation, enough to provide him with a reasonable standard of living, Burns set about doing two other jobs at once, as well as adding to his personal responsibilities. He bought a farm at Ellisland, north of Dumfries; accepted an appointment as gauger or Excise officer at Dumfries; and married Jean Armour after the early death of her second batch of twins.

Work was arduous. While battling to make a success of the farm, he had to ride a couple of hundred miles each week in all weathers on his Excise duties. Yet in spite of weariness and illness he produced during this period some of his most inspired work, including *Auld Lang Syne*, and contributed about 160 songs of his own to the *Scots Musical Museum* in Edinburgh, as well as 'mending and patching' many others. Eventually he and Jean decided to give up the hopeless farming venture and move into Dumfries itself. In 1796 he was advised by his doctor to take a course of sea bathing in the Solway Firth, and at the same time drank a great deal of water – not one of his usual beverages – at the little spa of Brow Well near Ruthwell. His last home is maintained as a museum in the cobbled Dumfries street now called Burns Street. On his deathbed at the age of 37 he referred to himself as 'a pigeon not worth the plucking'. For some years his body lay in an overgrown grave in St Michael's churchyard until, in 1815, a large white pseudo-classical mausoleum was erected to house his remains along with those of Jean and five of their children.

Other places associated with the poet include his cottage birthplace in Alloway; Ellisland farm off the A76, with museum rooms; a monument at Brig o' Doon, setting for part of *Tam o' Shanter;* his favoured taverns, the *Globe* in Dumfries High Street and the *Hole in the Wa'* in Queensferry Square; the *Black Bull* in Moffat, still displaying one of his derisive verses scratched on a window; and the modern Robert Burns Centre installed in an old sandstone mill beside the river Nith in Dumfries.

SELECTED SITES OF INTEREST

Antiquities

BARSALLOCH   On the bluff of Barsalloch Point near Monreith, about $1\frac{1}{2}$ miles south-east of Port William. Iron Age fort shielded on landward side by ramparts and a wide, deep ditch.

BORELAND   About $1\frac{1}{2}$ miles north of Minnigaff (Newton Stewart), reached by footpath from by-road. A chambered cairn of the Clyde-Carlingford type, over 6 feet high and 70 feet long, in a good state of preservation.

GLENQUICKEN   Off a by-road just over 2 miles east of Creetown. A circle of 28 squat boulders, 50 feet across, with a 6-foot high rectangular pillar in the centre.

LOCHMABEN (or CLOCHMABEN) STONE   Misleadingly, nowhere near the town and castle of Lochmaben, but just under a mile south-west of Gretna. A standing stone on a knoll close to the Solway Firth, thought to have been a focus for market trysts and the administration of justice since Roman times. It was one of the regular meeting-places for West March Wardens from both sides on Days of Truce.

TORHOUSE (or TORHOUSEKIE) STONE CIRCLE   Beside the B733 4 miles west of Wigtown. A Bronze Age circle of 19 boulders with, at the centre, three others which are probably the remains of a ring cairn.

(*For a general study of the foregoing see also Chapter 1.*)

Historic Buildings

CARDONESS   Beside the A75, a mile south-west of Gatehouse-of-Fleet. Remains of a fifteenth-century four-storeyed tower house with thick walls and inverted keyhole gun-ports, on a fine vantage point overlooking Fleet Bay. Interior still has original stairs and ornate fireplaces.

CASTLE KENNEDY   Beside the A75, 3 miles east of Stranraer. Early seventeenth-century castle was ravaged by fire in late October 1716 and never rebuilt. Instead, beautiful gardens were laid out around the ruins and the two lochs, some of them by soldiers under the command of the second Earl of Stair: hence the names of features such as Mount Marlborough and Dettingen Avenue. In 1867 Lochinch castle was built to one side of the estate, and further formal gardens were developed.

DRUMLANRIG Off the A76, 3 miles north of Thornhill. Though called Drumlanrig castle, the building in its present form is a seventeenth-century Renaissance mansion in pink sandstone, set in parkland on the site of earlier Douglas strongholds. In 1810 the Douglas line of the Dukes of Queensberry died out, and the dukedom and much of the estate passed to the Dukes of Buccleuch. Both names are prominent on statues and public houses in the region.

DUNDRENNAN Beside the A711, 7 miles south-east of Kirkcudbright. A twelfth-century Cistercian house built by the monks of Rievaulx, with later medieval additions. Alan, last of the Lords of Galloway, was buried here, and it is probably he who is commemorated by the effigy of a knight in one of the tomb recesses. Mary, Queen of Scots, spent her last night here before crossing the Solway to England *(see also Chapter 3)*.

ECCLEFECHAN The 'Arched House', birthplace of Thomas Carlyle, consists of two linked houses with a central pend (passageway), built by his father and uncle, both master masons. Contains memorabilia of the writer, who used Ecclefechan as 'Entephful' in his *Sartor Resartus*. He is buried in the village churchyard.

KIRKCUDBRIGHT MacLellan's castle on greensward overlooking the harbour is a sixteenth-century castellated mansion built by Sir Thomas MacLellan, then provost of the town, who married the daughter of Lord Herries, one of the powerful local Maxwell family. Their son became first Lord Kirkcudbright, but a mixture of misplaced Royalist fervour and bad estate management led to the family's ultimate downfall.

LANGHOLM The 'Muckle Toon' (big town) on the Esk was the birthplace of the poet Christopher Grieve, who under the name of Hugh MacDiarmid revived the use of the vigorous 'Lallans' form of Scots-English language and campaigned ceaselessly for Scottish independence. A striking metal memorial to him stands beside the winding, narrow road over Tarras Moss, favourite haunt of the Border reivers when in trouble.

ORCHARDTON   Off the A711 just outside Palnackie. A unique round tower house, not unlike a Martello tower, dating from the late fifteenth century. It must once have been a small-scale castle, as there are traces of storage and living accommodation beside it; but the wide, unprotected valley seems an odd setting for such a construction, which has always baffled historians.

Museums

CLATTERINGSHAWS   Off stretch of the A712 designated The Queen's Way in honour of Queen Elizabeth II's Silver Jubilee, Galloway Deer Museum stands above Clatteringshaws Loch. Exhibits of deer and other wildlife in Galloway Forest Park, and history of the region. Nearby are a replica of a prehistoric settlement discovered in the bed of the loch during work on the reservoir, and one of the Bruce stones.

KIRKCUDBRIGHT   Stewartry Museum in St Mary Street has displays relating to local prehistory, history (including material from the seventeenth-century tolbooth), and crafts. There is a special section devoted to the story of John Paul Jones.

MAXWELTON HOUSE   Beside the B729 near Moniaive. Dating from the late fourteenth century, originally the home of the Earls of Glencairn and later the birthplace of 'bonnie' Annie Laurie, whose 'promise true' in the famous song was in fact speedily broken, since she married a man other than the author of the verses. Now houses a museum of domestic life through the centuries.

SHAMBELLIE HOUSE   Beside the A710 above New Abbey. Museum of costume, administered by the National Museums of Scotland, with annual changes of exhibits.

WANLOCKHEAD   Museum of Scottish Lead Mining, with a walkway through eighteenth-century mine, and outdoor exhibits including beam engine and smelt mill (*see also Chapter 6*).

6

Glasgow and Strathclyde

A FTER THE Romans had finally gone, the British kingdom of Strathclyde remained powerful until well into the tenth century in spite of Northumbrian, Pictish and Viking attacks. At the peak of its power it embraced Cumberland, Westmorland and the Scottish shires of Ayr, Dunbarton, Lanark, Renfrew and Stirling. Its first capital was at Carlisle, but was moved to *Alcluith* or *Alcyde* (Clyde Rock), 'a castell stronge and harde for to obteine' on a double-peaked volcanic plug in the mouth of the river Clyde. The Irish called it *Dun Breatann* – Fort of the Britons – from which it came ultimately to be known as Dumbarton. Today the fortress woven around the rock is a mixture of medieval and post-medieval elements, including additions made after the Jacobite rising of 1715, and a few made during the Napoleonic Wars.

In AD 945 the English handed Strathclyde over to the King of the Scots; it struggled free for a brief period; and then in 1034 was swallowed up in Scotland again, and in due course divided into the shires with whose names we were familiar until 1974. The present reconstitution of Strathclyde lacks Stirling and the English segments, but has won for itself Argyll and some pieces of the Inner Hebrides.

Although there has long been an amiable rivalry between Edinburgh and Strathclyde's major city, Glasgow has in fact come into prominence only in the last couple of centuries, as its architecture shows. Its name derives from the Celtic *Gleachu* and later *Glasghu*, meaning a 'dear green spot', and there was certainly already a settlement here when St Mungo (or Kentigern) came from Culross in Fife as 'Apostle of the Strathclyde Britons'. He became Bishop of Glasgow around AD 543, and in due course the city's patron saint. The cathedral which he founded took on its present shape in the thirteenth century, with a lower church below the choir housing a shrine for the saint's relics. A spire and nave were added 200 years later. Nearby is the extensive Necropolis, populated by great headstones recording the achievements and worthiness of city merchants – not to mention the less ponderous William Miller, author of *Wee Willie Winkie*.

It was the merchants who fashioned the Glasgow we see today. As the commercial centre of Scotland, the city could afford the most grandiose Victorian offices, banks, civic buildings and residential terraces. In its haste to expand, it condemned its poorer inhabitants to live in tenement blocks which soon became slums, such as those in the notorious Gorbals; but at the same time its City Chambers dominating George Square were provided with lavish interiors, buildings such as Hutchesons' Hall (now most fittingly headquarters of the National Trust for Scotland) raised elegant spires above the wide streets, and architects of successive decades found themselves being granted exhilarating scope to impose their styles on many a corner.

The university, the second to be established in Scotland, had its home in High Street for just over four centuries from 1451, and then was moved out to Gilmorehill into Gothic buildings designed by Sir George Gilbert Scott. A more controversial and influential architect was Charles Rennie Mackintosh, whose Glasgow School of Art became a stimulus for designers who considered themselves modern in 1896. Even better loved by several generations were his Willow Tea Rooms in Sauchiehall Street, now restored and preserved as a shop. Perhaps of equal symbolic significance, related to one strand of the city's prosperity, are the cast-iron structures of Ca D'Oro and Gardner's Warehouse, the latter designed by John Gardner and generally referred to as the Iron Building.

It was the discovery of lead, coal and iron in a belt across the Lowlands, together with the proximity of the navigable river Clyde and its seagoing trade, which helped to make the region one of the most productive as the age of industrialization dawned. The sources of these riches cannot be neatly apportioned to one county or administrative region: the coal was there before men drew their boundaries; the veins of lead crossed borders without any care for customs posts or local government jealousies.

The Lowther Hills, straddling the divide between Strathclyde and Dumfries and Galloway, disgorged traces of silver-bearing lead as early as Roman times. The monks of Newbattle were mining lead in the thirteenth century; but the area really began to expand after the discovery of alluvial gold in the sixteenth century. Foreign prospectors were encouraged to lease mineral rights and produce gold for coinage and for the Scottish regalia. The remains of opencast workings can still be seen in the valley of the Elvan Water.

In the 1640s the village of Leadhills was built on the slopes east of the Lowther ridge by James Hope of Hopetoun House beside the Forth, while on the west side the Queensberry family set up the village of Wanlockhead. Since the lead workings of both estate owners continued operating until well into our own century, signs and relics of their activities are still plentiful, scarring the countryside and adding little clusters of mine buildings, spoil heaps and old tramways to the hillsides. Around some, such as the smelt mill at Sowen Burn, it is easy to see the ravages of lead poisoning on the vegetation, leaving only a bare, pitted landscape. There were once cart tracks along which consignments of smelted lead were transported to Biggar and from there to the port of Leith, but these were superseded in the middle of the nineteenth century by the Leadhills and Wanlockhead Light Railway. Although the line has been closed, stretches of track still survive and, now carrying only ghost trains, a fine brick viaduct curves across the valley.

The Museum of the Scottish Lead Mining Industry has a display of local relics in Wanlockhead, and has laid out a lead-mining trail. The showpiece is a beam engine used for pumping water out of Straitsteps mine, with the circular track of a horse gin beside it, round which a horse plodded to lift ore up the shaft. While raising water from the mine, the engine was itself supplied by water running down from a cistern on the nearby hillside. This poured into a bucket hanging from the beam, thus weighing it down and then at ground level emptying so that the beam naturally rose again. Part of the Lochnell or Loch Neil mine, connecting with the shaft to the Straitsteps drainage level, can be visited in the company of museum guides.

At Leadhills the son of a mine manager founded a Miners' Library in 1741. He was Allan Ramsay, who had left his birthplace to set up as a wigmaker in Edinburgh. Turning to bookselling, he published collections of his own lyric verse, and left the country forever in his debt as a collector of traditional Scots poems and songs. In Edinburgh he founded Britain's first subscription library before establishing the one in his home town. The Leadhills building has become a tourist information office, but in its original guise was so much valued that Wanlockhead hastened to establish a similar amenity. A bell on a wooden tower is a reminder of days when it was tolled to warn villagers of an accident underground; and there is grim testimony to the number of such accidents in the tombstone inscriptions of the churchyard.

Another distinguished son of Leadhills was William Symington, who studied at Edinburgh University and became critical of James Watt's steam engines. At the time this must have seemed the most appalling *lèse-majesté*, since Watt's acclaimed work on the power potential of steam was already transforming the whole industrial scene. But Watt was himself not, as is generally supposed, the 'inventor' of steam power: Newcomen had been ahead of him, and Watt's main contribution was his development of a separate condenser.

James Watt had been born at Greenock, on the Clyde, in 1736. He became mathematical instrument maker to the University of Glasgow, and later worked on surveys for the Forth and Clyde canal, the deepening of the rivers themselves, and the improvement of a number of harbours. While repairing a model of Newcomen's early steam pumping engine he realized how efficiency could be improved by condensing the steam in a separate vessel instead of in the actual cylinder. In 1774 he went into partnership with a Birmingham manufacturer, Matthew Boulton, originally as a consultant for customers wanting to build their own steam engines, especially pumping engines. Before long, however, the prestigious firm of Boulton and Watt began making its own machinery at its own foundry.

In 1790 William Symington devised and installed a steam pumping engine to drain the Wanlockhead mines; but the cost and complications of getting coal up to the site were such that the water-bucket system prevailed. His skill, however, had already been recognized. Ironing out some shortcomings of Watt's concepts, he was able to construct engines in smaller sizes, a great help when it came to production of a steam-driven carriage. Even more daring was his acceptance of a commission to devise an engine capable of propelling a small boat with paddle wheels. The result took to the water in October 1788 on Dalswinton Loch, close to Robert Burns' Ellisland Farm. Reports on the success of its trial are conflicting. All that can be said with certainty is that after the maiden voyage the engine was removed, sold half a century later to a scrap merchant, and subsequently recovered only in fragmentary condition. Conjecturally reassembled, it was housed in the Science Museum in London. In the same setting is to be found the model of a later, more famous steamship, the *Charlotte Dundas*, associated with the Forth and Clyde canal.

A linking of the rivers Clyde and Forth had obviously been desirable from the moment Lowlands industry began to boom. Indeed, various schemes for a canal had been mooted from the time of Charles II onwards. In 1798 substantial plans were at last put forward for

an easy communication between the Firths of Forth and Clyde, as also between the interior parts of the country, which will not only be of great advantage to the trade carried on between the two said Firths, but will also tend to the improvements of the adjacent lands, the relief of the poor, and the preservation of the public roads, and moreover be of general utility.

It was to be not merely for barge traffic, but wide and deep enough to carry sizeable ships between Grangemouth on the Forth and Bowling on the Clyde, with a spur into central Glasgow at Port Dundas. Estimates were prepared by John Smeaton, who supervised the project personally until it had to stop from lack of funds. Nine years went by before work was restarted with the help of a loan authorized by the government from assets seized from rebels after the 1745 rising, and the canals were at last completed by Robert Whitworth.

Passage of high-masted vessels was facilitated by the use of bascule bridges. Locks and bridges were so effectively organized that goods could be shifted between the east and west coast within a day. There also grew up a busy passenger traffic. Swift boats pulled by two or three horses were described by a contemporary as 'more airy, light and comfortable than any coach'. Road transport companies found themselves having to tie in special services and joint fares with their speedy and more comfortable rivals: in the 1840s 'Forth and Clyde Canal Coaches', for example, advertised omnibuses and coaches to and from Stirling to connect with the packet boats. Excursion steamers were to use the canal from the end of the nineteenth century until 1940.

It was closed in 1962, but the western terminus at Bowling Harbour is kept alive as a mooring for seagoing pleasure craft. Along the full course there are substantial relics of the locks, bridges and aqueducts which made it such an engineering marvel in its day. Of the 43 aqueducts, those over the Luggie Water at Kirkintilloch and over the Kelvin River near Maryhill, to the north-west of Glasgow, are especially worthy of a visit.

It was for this Forth–Clyde canal that William Symington was commissioned to devise a suitable specialized vessel. Unfortunately during its trials an attempt to drive it at full speed resulted in the paddle wheels disintegrating. Repairs were carried out, but the sponsor had lost faith, withdrew his support, and left Symington and his associates to get rid of the remains. It was at this juncture that the engineer went off to Wanlockhead to build his mine pumping engine. The Forth–Clyde waterway, however, was still challenging those who wished to exploit it to the full. Lord Thomas Dundas, one of its directors, put in hand a steam-powered vessel for towing barges through the canal, with two paddle wheels and an engine designed by Symington. Named the *Charlotte Dundas* after the sponsor's daughter, it proved too feeble to operate satisfactorily as a tug, and was ultimately abandoned in harbour at Grangemouth.

Dundas persevered; and so did Symington. Another *Charlotte Dundas* was built, and exhibited at Glasgow in January 1803. A couple of months later it proved its power by successfully towing two sloops more than 18 miles against a strong headwind. The other directors, however, were alarmed by the possibility of such a forceful machine damaging their canal banks. They left Symington's bills unpaid, so that after some years of struggle in Scotland and then in London, 'dying in want' he was buried in St Botolph's churchyard, Aldgate. The second *Charlotte Dundas*, shorn of its engine and ironwork, spent some years as a hand-operated dredger before rotting away like its impoverished designer.

In the year that work had begun on the canal, a new manager was appointed to an industrial centre beside the upper reaches of the Clyde. In 1784 a group of woollen mills had been built near Lanark to harness power from the river. One of the partners in the enterprise was Richard Arkwright, inventor of the water-powered spinning frame. In 1798 Robert Owen took over as manager and eventually became part-owner of New Lanark, which he set about turning into a model industrial village with good housing for the workers, including pauper apprentices, an infant school, a co-operative store and a co-partnership scheme. His social reforms, fuelled by the humanitarian conviction that mills and the life around them need not be dark and satanic, brought thousands of visitors in his own lifetime, and since restoration of the site from the late 1960s onwards the flow has continued.

In spite of tough competition from the river Tyne, the Clyde for long had no doubts of its claim to be the greatest shipbuilding river in the world. It flourished in the provision of sailing packets for the transatlantic passenger trade and cargo vessels for all the oceans of the world. Steam took time to replace sail on long voyages because of the problem of carrying huge weights of coal, and as late as 1869 a great sailing clipper was launched at Dumbarton to compete in one of the most important business ventures of the time. The speedy delivery of tea from China had become a matter of keen rivalry between companies supplying the main London purveyors. In 1868 the *Thermopylae* left the stocks at Aberdeen and was lauded as the fastest sailing clipper in the world. In the following year the *Cutty Sark* from Dumbarton offered a serious challenge. When the problem of bunkering steamships was rationalized and the demise of the clippers followed, the *Thermopylae* was switched to the Australian wool trade and finished her days as a Portuguese training ship. The *Cutty Sark* followed much the same course until reclaimed for permanent exhibition at a special dry dock at Greenwich, where her figurehead of Nannie from Burns' *Tam o' Shanter*, clad in her 'cutty sark' (a short shift), still stretches out an arm to grab the tail of Tam's grey mare.

One of the pioneering transatlantic steamship services for passengers and mails was founded by Samuel Cunard of Nova Scotia ('New Scotland'). He was wise enough to engage the services of the gifted engineer Robert Napier, 'Father of Clyde Shipbuilding', who is buried near his Dumbarton birthplace and a museum where the engines of one of his early paddle steamers are preserved. Napier had been responsible for the first iron battleship, HMS *Vanguard* and its successor, the ironclad *Black Prince*. He was awarded more than 60 Admiralty contracts over the years. In conjunction with the Fairfield yard of John Elder he produced the Cunarders *Umbria* and *Etruria*.

By the mid-1880s there had been a great increase in business and pleasure traffic across the Atlantic, paralleled by an increasing threat of competition from Germany and from the North Americans themselves. The American financier J.P. Morgan set about buying up and amalgamating as many of the North Atlantic lines as possible, and the major British company, Cunard, was saved only by an injection of government funds. As a direct result, building was commissioned of the *Lusitania* on the Clyde and the *Mauretania* on the Tyne. The much loved *Mauretania* was to hold the record for the fastest crossing for 22 years. The *Lusitania* was torpedoed during World War I. An even more luxurious liner, the *Aquitania*, had been completed on Clydebank just before the outbreak of that war, of such dimensions that the river had to be altered to allow for her launching and departure.

The luxury trade waned in the Depression years, and it was difficult to tempt the remaining wealthy travellers into ageing pre-war vessels. Trying, as it were, to keep afloat, Cunard put in hand the first of two new steamships, but when the hull was nearing completion a halt had to be called, as the money had run out. Unemployment figures rose, while work waiting to be done in John Brown's shipyard seemed unlikely ever to be resumed. Then the government offered a huge loan if the hitherto competing Cunard and White Star companies would amalgamate and concentrate their mutual resources on the North Atlantic trade. By April 1934 Clydesiders were back at work, and six months later the *Queen Mary* was launched by King George V.

For those not rich enough to cruise to the United States or desperate enough to emigrate, there were other steamship activities on the Clyde and down the coast. River and seaside resorts such as Helensburgh, Largs, Ardrossan and Troon had been served from the middle of the nineteenth century by paddle steamers. Helensburgh, being within easy reach, was a favourite with Glaswegians. A well-known marker on its western esplanade is an obelisk in memory of Henry Bell, hotelier and steamship promoter of the growing town.

1   The massive broch of Mousa in the Shetlands was built from the slate flagstone of the
tiny island on which it stands, and once had the
additional protection of an outer wall.

3 (*above*) In 1307 Robert the Bruce inflicted two surprise defeats on English forces, commemorated now by two 'Bruce stones'. This one stands above Loch Trool in Galloway Forest Park.

2 (*opposite*) Sueno's Stone on the outskirts of Forres carries a wealth of elaborate carving, believed to symbolize a victory by the Danish prince Sueno over the Scots in 1008.

4   (*above*) A print from John Slezer's 1693 *Theatrum Scotiae* of Linlithgow Palace. Begun by James I in 1424, this was to be the birthplace of both James V and his daughter Mary, Queen of Scots.

5   (*below*) A painting by John Opie of the murder of James I at Perth, in the presence of his wife, Queen Joan.

7 (*above*) Hermitage castle, 'the Strength of Liddesdale', changed hands between warring factions many times while developing from a small fortification into a massive tower-house.

6 (*opposite*) A Holyrood inventory of the wardrobe of Mary, Queen of Scots, included more than sixty dresses in gold, silver, and the brightly clashing colours and jewellery she loved.

8 (*above*) Urquhart castle stands on the site of a vitrified Dark Age fort on a promontory above Loch Ness. Most supposed viewings of the legendary Loch Ness monster have been made from here.

9 (*below*) By throwing her stool at the Dean of Edinburgh, the indignant Jenny Geddes unleashed riots against the imposition of Archbishop Laud's Anglican rituals upon Scotland.

10   (*above*) The dashing Prince Charles Edward Stuart, whose personality
when young won him affectionate sobriquets such as Bonnie Prince Charlie
and the Young Chevalier.

11   (*right*) A dramatic front page of *The Illustrated London News* in January
1888 depicting clashes between police, marines and Hebridean crofters
during attempts by landlords to replace their starving human tenants with
game reserves.

THE ILLUSTRATED LONDON NEWS

REGISTERED AT THE GENERAL POST-OFFICE FOR TRANSMISSION ABROAD.

No. 2544.—VOL. XCII.　　　SATURDAY, JANUARY 21, 1888.　　　WITH EXTRA SUPPLEMENT } SIXPENCE. BY POST, 6½D.

READING THE RIOT ACT AT AIGNISH FARM, NEAR STORNOWAY.

POLICE AND MARINES SEIZING THE RIOTOUS CROFTERS.

CROFTERS OF LEWIS, IN THE HEBRIDES.

12 (*above*) Cardhu whisky distillery on Speyside.
(*below*) The copper pot stills in which Cardhu single malt whisky is distilled.

The railways soon found it to their advantage to provide connections from further afield for excursions and holidays, in competition or liaison with the steamers, especially those serving the nearer Hebridean islands.

Extension of rival English railway routes into Scotland had caused headaches not just to directors and accountants but to the engineers who had to face difficult terrain even across the so-called Lowlands, and far more alarming problems in the Highlands. The two top priorities were to get profitable main lines across the Border to Edinburgh and Glasgow. Centuries earlier the Romans had laid out their own eastern thoroughfare of Dere Street from York across the Tyne at Corbridge and on over the Cheviots into Lauderdale and Lothian, much of it close to the modern A68. To the west they established a supply route from Carlisle up Annandale to Crawford and along the south-western edge of the Pentland Hills. The railway engineers flinched from tackling such a direct path over the Cheviots from the eastern side, and in any case needed to include the city of Newcastle in their crossing of the Tyne. Once Stephenson had flung his splendid viaduct across the Tweed at Berwick, mangling Berwick castle as he did so, the track stayed on the coastal plain all the way to Edinburgh.

On the Glasgow side there were no such easy solutions. What was to become, after many amalgamations, the London, Midland and Scottish had to achieve a fearsome climb up Shap Fell south of the Border, cross the treacherous Solway mosses, and then in Annandale make the long, steep climb of Beattock Bank. Today's electric trains hiss swiftly up that slope, startling many a car driver on the neighbouring road as they emerge unexpectedly from cuttings; but during the steam era a second locomotive had to be coupled on at Beattock station to help the train to the summit.

There is no longer a reserve engine, and there is also no longer another impediment to railway routine in Scotland. Strict Presbyterians outraged by 'the clink of buffers on the unlawful day' were for a considerable time able to prohibit shunting by the Glasgow and South-Western Railway on

Sundays, though they appear to have felt no qualms about the moral effect of such operations being shifted just over the Border into heathen England.

Linked with the main lines or served by minor companies of their own, a number of seaside resorts and would-be spas grew up mainly because they had been reached by the railways. Wemyss Bay, for instance, owed as much to the Wemyss Bay Railway Company and later the Caledonian Railway Company steam trains as to the Clyde steamboats. The graceful glass-roofed interior and clock tower of the pier station are still an ornament to the town, though immediately beside them is the symbol of competition which was to weaken the iron road and the steamer trade in the end – a large car park.

The motor car industry appeared at one stage to offer renewed possibilities for Lowlands work-forces when threatened by a decline in traditional shipbuilding and competition from the cheap labour and different methods of Eastern countries. In 1959 the British Motor Corporation built a new plant for heavy goods vehicles at Bathgate, between Edinburgh and Glasgow. The following year Rootes started up a new complex at Linwood, near Paisley, for production of family cars including the Hillman Imp. High hopes did not last long. After a series of takeovers, industrial disruption, and broken promises by owners and government, both centres were abandoned.

North Sea oil provided another beacon of hope, though most of it for the eastern and northern coastlines. Upper Clyde Shipbuilders had been allowed to go bankrupt with no hope of government intervention, but there were still facilities which ought to have made it possible to build rigs and drill-ships on the Clyde. Remnants of the old John Brown shipyard were hastily swept away to make room for the rig-builders, and Scott-Lithgow committed itself to manufacturing semi-submersibles – making disastrously optimistic estimates, and going broke. By the mid-1980s Clydeside was once more a depressed area. In March 1989 the wife of the Secretary of State for Scotland, Mrs Malcolm Rifkind, launched one of the last vessels ordered from the small Ferguson yard at Port Glasgow, the

Lord of the Isles, for the Caledonian MacBrayne line of inter-island ferries.

The decline of seaborne travel across the Atlantic which contributed to the decline of shipbuilding had itself been due in large measure to a huge increase in air travel. Representations were made from many authorities in the Midlands and Northern England as well as in Scotland for the redirection of air routes to provincial airports instead of concentrating all the traffic on London. Developed during World War II as a terminal for Transatlantic military flights, Prestwick on the Firth of Clyde was expanded to international airport status, and at least could offer its visitors easy access to a game which, whatever its origins and whatever its current international status, could claim to be in essence and by almost holy tradition Scottish — though there had been times when rigorous steps had had to be taken to prevent its unholy enjoyment on the Sabbath.

Golf is played at Prestwick on three superb courses, one of them the hallowed old Prestwick course. The Open Championship was instituted here in 1860, remaining for some thirty years the exclusive fief of professionals from Musselburgh and St Andrews. Its near neighbours, Royal Troon and Turnberry, are spectacular examples of 'links' courses: that is, sand and heathland immediately behind a shoreline. In this part of the world one overlooks the other: the fifth hole at Troon is called 'Turnberry' because from it the player can see Turnberry lighthouse; and the ninth hole at Turnberry itself is named after Bruce's Castle, the probable birthplace of Robert the Bruce visible from the tee.

The game is not perhaps as purely Scottish as patriots would like to make out. There are records of similar club-and-ball pastimes in Roman times, and the very word surely derives from the Dutch *kolven* or *kolf* which, like its German equivalent *kolbe*, means a club. Nor was the game in its pioneer stages played according to the now sacrosanct rules, or with the same equipment. Balls were originally made of wood. In the early seventeenth century a new style was introduced, consisting of a stitched leather cover into which boiled feathers were stuffed. The gutta percha ball was invented around 1848. Clubs were also wooden for many centuries. It was not until the late 1700s that iron plates called cleeks were added to the heads; and then in the twentieth century steel shafts became common. Whatever the impetus behind material developments, however, it was undoubtedly in Scotland that the now accepted rules of play were formulated.

The first registered association was that of the Honourable Company of Edinburgh Golfers, established in 1744 and playing at Leith, then Musselburgh, and ultimately on their specially created course at Muirfield. But the most significant year was 1754, in which the Society of St Andrews Golfers in Fife laid out its Old Course on a raised beach, formed at the end of the last Ice Age when the melting of glaciers relaxed their pressure on the earth. It was William IV who bestowed on the club its title of Royal and Ancient, signifying the interest shown by so many monarchs including the Stuart kings and Mary, Queen of Scots, and setting a seal of approval on its authority as effective governing body of British golf and the one most revered by foreign associates.

Golf links abound down the west coast; but so do historic associations of other kinds, especially literary ones. Ayr has a fine seventeenth-century church in which Robert Burns was baptized; Alloway has his birthplace and other mementoes, and his father is buried in the graveyard of the old kirk through whose window Tam o' Shanter saw the carousing witches and warlocks. Echoes of another character from that poem can be found at Kirkoswald in Souter Johnnie's cottage – 'souter' being Scots for a cobbler. In an upper room of a house now administered by the National Trust in Tarbolton were held dancing lessons and meetings of the Bachelors' Club, a debating society of which Burns and his close friends were drinking, discursive and argumentative members.

The mere name of the coastal village of Ballantrae evokes memories of Robert Louis Stevenson's novel, *The Master of Ballantrae*, though in fact the setting of the story is Borgue in Galloway. It is believed that Stevenson chose to tag the name on to such a grim tale as his revenge for having once been chased out of the place because the inhabitants disapproved of his unfamiliar clothes.

There are other grim tales about the neighbourhood. Ardstinchar castle, now in ruins, was the home of one of the rival Kennedy families who fought continually and bloodily for the lordship of Carrick. Another ruin, that of Carleton castle, is associated with a Kennedy of Culzean who outwitted the evil Sir John Cathcart. He had made a habit of marrying rich heiresses and then pushing them naked off the cliff at Games Leap so that he might profit from not merely their funds but also their finery. His eighth wife, May Cullean, modestly asked him to avert his eyes while she obediently undressed, since it was wrong for a man to see a woman naked; and then pushed him over the edge instead.

But the most notorious denizens of the cliffs were a family living under Bennane Head in the sixteenth century. Sawney (Sandy) Bean and his wife seem to have produced an inordinate number of children, who continued incestuously to multiply, keeping themselves fed by preying on travellers, eating them and pickling spare limbs for their store cupboard. So many disappearances led to terrifying rumours, and according to a contemporary record 'an abundance of innocent travellers and innkeepers were executed on suspicion of murder, yet all was in vain'. Although local inhabitants grew wary of going out and many moved away, there appears to have been a continuing supply of unsuspecting strangers, probably including pilgrims on their way to Whithorn. When at last someone was attacked but escaped to tell the tale, James VI himself led a posse into the region, seized the Beans, and had them executed in Edinburgh without trial. The menfolk had their limbs chopped off and were allowed to bleed to death in front of the public. The women were piled up and burnt. Numbering of the cannibals' victims in thousands may be a wild exaggeration, and many grisly trimmings have undoubtedly been added to the story over the years; but along that once violent coast, noted for its smugglers' caves and smugglers' misdeeds, the doings of the Bean family seem all too plausible.

Northwards into Argyll, we come across another enthralling blend of fact and fiction, in another Stevensonian adventure. When, in the novel *Kidnapped*, David Balfour and Alan Breck are cast on the rocks after the foundering of the brig *Covenant*, Alan foresees trouble with old enemies:

> Set me on dry ground in Appin, or Ardgour, or in Morven, or Arisaig, or Morar; or, in brief, where ye please, within thirty miles of my own country, except in a country of the Campbells.

Argyll is undoubtedly Campbell country, and today is inarguably lodged within Strathclyde. Alan Brett would not have recognized that reshuffle, and it is difficult for anyone with a sense of tradition and even of elementary geography to do so now; which is why I prefer to approach it in the next chapter where it belongs, part of the Highlands. It is, however, a journey which can incorporate one significant link with Glasgow and its environs.

After the Forth and Clyde canal had begun to pay its way and repay its borrowings, the government allocated some of this income as a loan to the newly formed Crinan Canal Company. There had long been felt a need for a short cut across the peninsula of Kintyre to shorten the passage for trade from the Caledonian Canal to the Clyde, and to save fishing vessels from the Hebrides the ordeal of rounding the stormy, unpredictable snout of the Mull. Authorized by Act of Parliament in 1793, the 9-mile waterway with its 15 locks between Loch Crinan in the west and Ardrishaig on Loch Gilp eliminated a sea passage of 85 miles. After various repairs, including some in 1816 under the supervision of Thomas Telford, the canal became a busy thoroughfare for the fishing boats of Tarbert and the Ayrshire coast ports, and most notably the sturdy steam 'puffers' which arouse such nostalgic daydreams among locals who remember them in their prime. The occasional puffer still travels along the canal, but nowadays the traffic is made up largely of pleasure craft. The canal is, in itself, a great pleasure when followed at a leisurely pace along the towpath. An adjoining road offers the most attractive vistas near the locks at Dunardry and, from Crinan basin a quite spectacular prospect of the Western Isles across the Sound of Jura and of the hills of Argyll to the north.

SELECTED SITES OF INTEREST

Antiquities

CLACKMANNAN STONE   In front of the town's tolbooth and beside its mercat cross is the standing stone of *Clach Mannan* (Stone of the Manau), associated with the Manau district of the Votadini tribe. Thought to have served originally as a meeting-point at the foot of a nearby brae, it was kept for some time in the hilltop Clackmannan Tower on the Bruce estate, then laid in a recumbent position outside the town gaol before being restored to upright dignity on its present site.

ELLERSHIE HILL   A characteristic Clydesdale feature is the Bronze Age unenclosed upland settlement, with field systems below the platforms on which timber houses would once have stood. The complex on Ellershie Hill, near the junction of the A74 and A702 roads and the main railway line, emerges in fragments from later agricultural developments. Some platforms are easily identifiable, as are three burial cairns on a ridge.

NORMANGILL HENGE   Close to the settlement in the preceding entry, this ritual stone circle was sliced across first by a railway and then by a minor road from Crawford, with a sheepfold dumped on one corner for good measure. In spite of this it remains an impressive example of an oval henge enclosed by a ditch, with wide entrances in the northern and southern arcs.

(*For a general study of the foregoing see also Chapter 1.*)

Historic Buildings

BOTHWELL   In its time one of the most magnificent fortresses in Scotland, this castle was built in a commanding position above the Clyde, 7 miles south-east of Glasgow, by Walter of Moray in the thirteenth century, and grandly extended by Archibald the Grim of the Douglas family in the late fourteenth and early fifteenth centuries. Even in its present ruined state the massive tower, walls and doorways are awe-inspiring, contrasting with the gentle sylvan setting.

CRAIGNETHAN   Off the A72 5 miles north-west of Lanark stands the last private castle of really defensive character built in Scotland, on a bluff above the Water of Nethan. It was the work of Sir James Hamilton of Finnart, known to his contemporaries as 'that bloody butcher', who rose to become master of works to James V and to influence the refashioning of Linlithgow, Falkland, Stirling and Edinburgh, only to fall out of favour and be executed on a dubious charge of intended regicide. His descendants espoused the cause of Mary, Queen of Scots, and suffered for it, as did the castle: much of it was hurled down into the river below. The original tower house which provided the centrepiece for later fortifications still stands, and excavations have disclosed what may have been the earliest example in the country of a *caponier*– a covered passage with gun-loops across a defensive ditch.

CROSSRAGUEL   Close to the A77 south-west of Maybole, a small thirteenth-century Cluniac monastery founded by Duncan, Earl of Carrick, as a daughter house of Paisley abbey. Although robbed of stones for local secular use, the extensive ruins include a substantial gatehouse and, unusually, a defensive tower house. In the fifteenth century a range of Corrodiars Houses were added for the accommodation of retired clerics and even a number of laymen who wished to spend their declining years in a religious atmosphere. They were presumably kept adequately fed from the beehive doocot on the western fringe of the site.

CULZEAN About 5 miles west of Maybole, a medieval tower house of the Kennedy family was supplanted in the late eighteenth century by a turreted, castellated mansion designed by Robert Adam, who was also responsible for the interior decoration, including some wonderful plaster ceilings. In addition he designed the Home Farm, with its courtyard and arched gateway, now converted into an information centre for visitors to the house and Country Park. An Eisenhower Room commemorates the general's association with Culzean and his part in the Allied victory of World War II; and his invaluable support for a public appeal in 1968 which raised an endowment fund enabling the National Trust for Scotland to restore and maintain the castle and its grounds.

GLASGOW *Provan Hall* Set in Auchinlea Park amid east end housing estates, this pre-Reformation manor house was probably once a medieval hunting lodge. After the Reformation the site was acquired by Sir William Baillie from Glasgow cathedral, and in the eighteenth century was joined to another house along one side of the courtyard, overlooking the Clyde valley. The courtyard gateway has a flight of steps leading up to a lookout platform. In the present century the property was falling into disrepair until bought by a group who later presented it to the National Trust for Scotland.

Provand's Lordship The sole survivor of more than 30 fifteenth-century prebendaries' houses once clustering round the cathedral. This, the manse of Barlanark's prebendary, is built of undressed stone in contrast to the commoner timber-framed merchants' houses of the period.

The Tenement House At No.145 Buccleuch Street is a typical tenement house of the late nineteenth century. One of its flats, little altered since Victorian times, was given to the National Trust for Scotland in 1982 by the actress Anna Davidson, who had enjoyed its 'antique' atmosphere while living there and preserved as much as possible of its original furnishings, including box beds, sink and kitchen range.

Museums

BIGGAR   Gladstone Court Museum in a nineteenth-century coachworks has displays of Victorian shops and shop windows. Nearby an open-air museum is being extended around a reconstructed seventeenth-century farmhouse and the buildings and gasholders of Biggar's early Victorian gasworks.

GLASGOW   *Hunterian Museum*   Archaeological and historical displays, including an exhibition on the history of Glasgow University. Collections of Roman material, much of it relating to the Antonine Wall.

Museum of Transport   History of transport, including a reproduction of a typical 1938 Glasgow street. Ship models, Glasgow trams, buses and a subway station.

GRANGEMOUTH   Actually in Central district, but of particular interest here because of its museum's evocative displays of the story of the Forth and Clyde canal, including material on the *Charlotte Dundas*, and local shipbuilding in general.

PAISLEY   Museum and Art Gallery house comprehensive collection of Paisley shawls, together with a history of weaving techniques and the development of the famous Paisley pattern.

7

Argyll and the Highlands

THE MERE mention of 'The Highlands' conjures up visions of great mountains and dark, secretive glens, peopled by noble stags such as that in Landseer's painting *The Monarch of the Glen*, game birds, and sturdy clansmen in tartans eating haggis while listening to sad laments about the king across the water. The word 'Lowlands', with its immediate suggestion of subservience, offers no such romantic stimulus. Yet most of the significant political history of the country was fashioned in the Lowlands, and kings of Scotland holding court in Perth, Stirling or Edinburgh regarded their northern peoples as little more than barbarians whom it was necessary – if difficult – to discipline every now and then. The borderline established by geological faults between the pastures of the plain and the skimpily clad heights was just as real and as dangerous as the national divide along the Marches with England. In return, the clansmen regarded the families and livestock of fertile Lowland farms as fair prey, and owed their allegiance only to clan chiefs, and virtual local kings such as the Lords of the Isles.

The region known baldly today as Highland imposes an arbitrary boundary around early lordships whose own original boundaries had frequently shifted from one grouping to another. Old elements swallowed up under this bureaucratic blanket are Inverness-shire, Nairn, Ross and Cromarty, Sutherland, and Caithness.

Evidence of early settlers is most plentiful in the extreme

north-east of Caithness, probably because of its proximity to the similar settlements of Orkney. The Grey Cairns of Camster are an impressive example of chambered tombs which have been adapted and extended over succeeding generations. One single round cairn of stones shouldering up from the rust-brown moor south-west of Wick has a well-preserved burial chamber divided into sections by large upright slabs. A couple of hundred yards away a mightier mausoleum consists of two circular cairns linked to form a 200-foot long mound with projecting horns at both ends. Irregularities in its outward shape are due to the depredations of later occupants of the region, robbing it of stones for walls: impertinently within sight of the great grey cairn is a solidly built sheep-stell showing an inarguable family resemblance. The awesome mounds are reached from the road by a wooden walkway across the boggy moorland, and can be crawled into by those prepared to risk pains in the knees and back.

Standing on the verge of another road, in the delectable glen of Loch Hope and Strathmore in Sutherland, is the beehive-shaped broch of Dun Dornaigil (or Dun Dornadilla), with a heavy triangular lintel over its entrance. In Glenelg on the west coast the two brochs of Dun Troddan and Dun Telve stand within a short distance of each other, commandingly tall but not as tall as they used to be, thanks again to the removal of stones from the top for other local usage.

One tract of Argyll is garnished by the most remarkable succession of stone creations. Across the valley below the village of Kilmartin runs a string of burial cairns and ritual monuments covering some two thousand years. The Nether Largie tombs have capacious burial chambers and a number of unusual axe-head decorations and cup-marks chipped into the stones. The slabs of a cremation cist in Ri Cruin cairn are grooved and rebated as if they were wood, so that they could be slotted together to form a stone box. At Temple Wood there are two stone circles (or, rather, ovals), one of whose stones is decorated with an incised double spiral. Most intricately decorated of all is the exposed rocky outcrop of Achnabreck near Lochgilphead. It has the largest spread in Scotland of the magic or ritual 'cup-and-ring' markings known from India to Ireland, with small cups gouged into the rock and surrounded by shallow-cut concentric circles. Here the carving is so detailed that one can almost begin to believe the theory that such configurations did bear some relation to the movement of planets round the sun.

A striking, rather eerie feature of the Kilmartin neighbourhood is the continuity of a tradition of sculptured stones well into medieval times and beyond. In the village churchyard are sequences of pictorial grave slabs, several now preserved in slightly tilted rows within an enclosure, like a recumbent art exhibition, the majority dating from the fourteenth and fifteenth centuries. Fragments of two crosses once stood close by, one from the sixteenth century with representations of Christ crucified on the front and Christ in Majesty on the back, but these are now sheltered within the church itself.

Whatever tribal rituals may have survived in disguised or assimilated form from early settlers, and whatever British, Anglo-Saxon and Norman influences various kings may have tried to disseminate north of the Highland Line, the social and military tradition remained obstinately that of the clan system. England and parts of the Scottish Lowlands succumbed to feudalism, in which a man held his land by a chain of obligations reaching up to the monarch himself. Highlanders held their land as a clan, the word deriving from the Gaelic *clann*, meaning children.

Individual clans held sway in different regions, though there were all too frequently some dangerous overlappings which led to internecine feuds. The larger clans were divided into septs, some of which had different names but were still glad to owe allegiance to one protective chieftain who controlled his family and retainers in a mutual acknowledgement of kinship which went emotionally far deeper than the purely materialistic concept of feudalism. Even when kings powerful enough to assert their authority (often a temporary one) over the Highland tribes sought to introduce a form of feudal charter, ties of kinship still prevailed. The individualism of the clans and the frequency of their devastating vendettas led eventually to a governmental decree that every clan should supply the Court with one high-ranking representative as hostage for his people's good behaviour. Any family defying the edict was termed a 'broken clan' and was denounced as being in outlawry. An obvious parallel is that with the feuding families of the Border and their 'broken men'.

The distribution of land under the aegis of the clan chief was usually handled by a 'tacksman'. This functionary, often the leader of a minor branch of the family, would rent a large area on 'tack', or lease, and sub-let sections of it at a profit to smallholders. In addition to the rent, and usually more import-ant than it, there would be military obligations to the head of the clan.

Clan or family names have unforgettable resonances in the Highlands. Any attempt to deal with each and every one of them in a short space would be to confuse rather than illuminate the matter. There are clan museums throughout the region, and in Comrie, 6 miles west of Crieff, the Scottish Tartans Museum with its exhibition of over 450 tartans and other features of Highland dress provides a background not just to the weaving of clothes but the interweaving of family fortunes and misfortunes.

There is also an interweaving of different inherited cultures. The familiar prefix 'Mac', meaning a son (Macdonald the son of Donald, MacNab the son of an abbot), has the authentic romantic ring about it; but there were just as many groups from other conjunctures. The Chisholms were Celtic tribesmen whose name arose from marriages into feudal Norman families. The Gunns are of Norse origin, via Orkney and Shetland. Anyone living in the Middle and West Marches would know – to his cost, maybe – that the Armstrongs were of Northumbrian and Cumbrian origin. The Hamiltons were also of Nor-thumbrian stock; the Grahams Anglo-Norman; and the Hays came almost direct from France. But undoubtedly the real blood tie is most clearly exemplified in the sons, the Macs, of ancient tribal leaders.

They defied kings or, as mercenaries, supported kings of their own country or any other with terrifyingly murderous vigour; but acquired a reputation for quitting the field the moment they realized that the battle was lost and there would be no profitable pickings. Aside from this opportunism and the love of fighting for its own sake, their main characteristic was a passion for quarrelling interminably and bloodily among themselves. John Major, fifteenth-century Scottish theologian and historian, contrasted the tolerably civilized life of Lowland lairds, merchants and tradesmen with that of the denizens of the glens and hillsides:

> They do not bring up their sons to any handicraft. Shoemakers, tailors, and all such craftsmen they reckon as contemptible and unfit for war; and they therefore bring up their children to take service with the great nobles, or with a view to living in the country in the manner of their fathers.

One of the earliest clans, or rather grouping of families into a loose federation, was Clan Chattan. A number of what the Borderers would call 'graynes' came together on the grounds that they were all of Pictish origin and had common interests. Among them were the Farquharsons, Macbeans, Mackintoshes and Macphersons. The latter two were soon in conflict as to who should be nominal head of the federation. It took a few centuries for the Mackintoshes to win the accolade on the grounds that by marriage they were entitled to consider themselves inheritors of the group's originator, a twelfth-century warrior Gilliechattan Mor ('Great Servant of St Cattan') who had established his own principality in Badenoch and Lochaber. The Macphersons nevertheless continued pressing their own claims, until all of them were caught up in the disaster of the Jacobite campaign of 1745.

Blood feuds were the cause of much of the Highland barbarism so deplored by monarchs in Edinburgh; or was it the innate barbarism that provoked the blood feuds? Whichever way one might interpret it, there came a time when a feud between two 'pestiferous caterans' (Highland freebooters) grew so lethal that they were commanded by royal edict to settle the matter once and for all by a conflict of 30 chosen warriors on the North Inch at Perth in 1396. It is generally believed that one of the clans was that of Chattan, the other the Camerons or Keays. The king himself, Robert III, was among the spectators. The two teams fought until only a few remained alive, though on the verge of death, and the sole survivor escaped only by plunging into the river Tay and swimming across to safety, later to commit suicide out of shame. It seems slightly hypocritical of the king to have demanded such a resolution, or somewhat naïve to have supposed there could ever have been one in such a violent climate: Robert's own younger brother Alexander, Earl of Buchan, was so contemptuous of his official duties as justiciary of the Northern Lowlands that he led gangs of robbers over the very areas he was supposed to protect, and earned himself the nickname of 'The Wolf of Badenoch'.

In 1427 James I, weary of continual turmoil, summoned Highland chieftains to attend a parliament in Inverness. Whatever they had expected to discuss, they were given no time. The king had a number imprisoned, and some of the less powerful ones hanged. He achieved a brief, shocked lull in the feuding and raiding, and established – in principle at any rate – that royal power was superior to that of local chieftains; but old habits and appetites soon reasserted themselves.

One of the most successful and most scheming of all the clans was that of the Campbells. Their name derives from the Gaelic *Na Caimbeulach,* meaning 'men of the twisted mouths', and many of their victims would have agreed with such a definition. It has been said of them that they had an instinct for picking the winning side, even at the eleventh hour. Of the several branches of the family, the most powerful was that of the Campbells of Argyll. Originating in Strathclyde, they had supported Robert the Bruce and were granted lands and privileges as a result. Among their still visible strongholds are Innischonnel castle at the southern end of Loch Awe, Castle Campbell or 'Castle Gloom' above Dollar, and historic Dunstaffnage, acquired after the MacDougall owners had fallen foul of Robert the Bruce and the Campbells had forced a deal upon their successors.

These successors were the Stewarts, Lords of Lorne. In 1463 the lordship was held by John Stewart, a widower whose three daughters were married to three Campbells, including the future first Earl of Argyll. The Campbells thus had every hope of acquiring the Lorne estates on Stewart's death. There was, however, a snag. John Stewart had an illegitimate son; and suddenly decided to wed the boy's mother and legitimize him as rightful heir. On the way from Dunstaffnage to the chapel the wedding party was ambushed, supposedly by a gang of outlaws, and Stewart was fatally wounded. He insisted on being carried into the chapel to go through the ceremony, dying an hour later in the knowledge that he had ensured his son's inheritance. The Campbells at once contested the validity of the marriage, but had to accept a compromise whereby the son was allowed to hold Appin on behalf of the Crown, and John Stewart's brother took over the lordship of Lorne until, in return for other lands, he handed it over to the Earl of Argyll. The heirs to the Earls and then Dukes of Argyll have since by custom held the title of Marquis of Lorne: one in the nineteenth century married Queen Victoria's daughter, Princess Louise, and gave his name to a number of English inns.

Of all Campbell rivals and enemies, the Macgregors were the most detested. Their possessions stretched from Glen Orchy in Argyll to Perthshire, and from their hilly fastnesses they persistently raided the farmlands along the Clyde valley. Claiming descent from Grogar, a son of Alpin, they had the swaggering motto 'Royal is my name'. Unfortunately for them, their Glen Orchy lands bordered those of the Campbells, who used every possible legal device and representation to the king to encroach on larger and larger tracts, as well as any number of illegal and unprincipled acts. On one occasion they managed to force a candidate of their own on the Macgregors in place of the legitimate chief, and continued eroding the estates until one sept of the Macgregors became no more than Campbell tenants. When their leader rebelled against this he was seized and summarily beheaded by Campbell of Glenorchy.

The nominal end of the Macgregor clan came in 1603. The previous year they had carried out one of their typical raids on lands belonging to the Colquhouns of Luss, who complained to the king. There may have been some diplomatic negotiations, but just at the time when James VI was about to become James I of England a pitched battle erupted near Glenfruin during which 200 Colquhouns were killed, as well as a number of innocent bystanders caught up in the sudden fury. In no mood to be distracted from his new responsibilities, James rushed an act through his Privy Council to outlaw the whole clan and even to deprive them of their identity: use of the name of Macgregor was proscribed, and anyone caught trying to retain it could be killed out of hand.

The move was by no means well calculated. Men deprived of their very name were unlikely to become all at once meek, submissive citizens. James could scarcely have devised a more reliable way of creating a whole race of full-time bandits from a clan already famed for its unruliness. In the next century one of the most notorious, Rob Roy MacGregor, horrified some relatives by adopting as cover the name of the clan's mortal enemies, the Campbells. In fact he was merely taking on his mother's maiden name. For a time he led a moderately respectable existence as a cattle dealer, until he made off with a large sum of money belonging to the Duke of Montrose. The duke appropriated his land and threw his wife out of their house; whereupon Rob Roy took to a life of banditry and protection rackets across the heaths and hills.

Playing shamelessly on the Campbell connection, he offered his services to the Duke of Argyll when it suited him, and stole Campbell cattle when it did not. It was rumoured that while professing devotion to the Jacobite cause he acted as a spy for Argyll, and it is equally probable that he was a double agent. Captured and sentenced to transportation in 1726, he was pardoned and managed to die a peaceful death at Balquhidder, wreathed in legend as a Highland Robin Hood. His supposed house is in Glen Shire, north-east of Inveraray; the Rob Roy's Cave and Rob Roy's Prison of folklore are on the east bank of Loch Lomond; and the grave slabs of his wife, two sons and himself are in Balquhidder churchyard.

James, with England and Ireland now at his disposal, had made further attempts to control the clans by expelling some to Ulster and by issuing in 1609 the Statutes of Iona, by which chiefs had to acquiesce in altering the structure of their clans, abandoning aggressive military organization in favour of agriculture and productive community life. They were to become landed gentry rather than tribal warlords. Their children were increasingly sent to Lowland schools to acquire some of the veneer of civilization.

Still old enmities and acquisitiveness persisted, and when William III turned his attention to the Highlands he found the clansmen just as disruptive and self-willed as his predecessors had done. Some of his advisers recommended tactful bribery of the chieftains to bring them round to acceptance of the new régime. The Campbells decided fairly promptly where the profit lay. John Campbell of Glenorchy invited influential leaders to a conference in Achallader castle by Loch Tay and persuaded them that for a tidy financial subvention they would be granted free title to their lands provided they swore allegiance to the new monarch. A number gladly took payment in return for loyalty. Others felt themselves still bound to James VII and II, who had fled to France after dislodgement from the throne. In August 1691 William offered a pardon to all rebels who would take an oath of allegiance before the next New Year's Day. After a great deal of soul-searching and pleas to the exiled James to release them from earlier vows, most clan chieftains were ready to toe the line; but James had been dilatory in giving his absolution, and it was impossible for some of the remoter leaders to travel through wintry conditions to register their new oath in time.

The ageing Alasdair MacIain, chief of the MacDonalds of Glencoe, took his oath at Inveraray on 6 January, not knowing that orders for the extinction of his family had already been issued by the Master of Stair, King William's most trusted representative in Scotland. Even after hearing of MacDonald's submission, Stair refused to withdraw his orders, rejoicing as a contemptuous Lowlander that he had an excuse 'to be exact in rooting out that damnable sept, the worst in all the Highlands'. Soldiers of the Earl of Argyll's regiment were sent under the command of Captain Robert Campbell of Glenlyon into the wild, rocky pass of Glencoe – in Gaelic the 'narrow glen'. Savage and sombre at the best of times, the ruptured valley between its contorted glacial volcanoes must have been at its least attractive in the bitter blizzards of mid-February. The even more bitter perversity of it all was that, inhospitable as Glencoe itself might be, its unsuspecting inhabitants gave a traditional Highland welcome to the Campbell troops.

For almost a fortnight these troops were billeted in the amicable company of 'that damnable sept'. In the meantime it had been planned that both ends of the pass would be blocked by other contingents on their way to the rendezvous, and then the order would be given for all those contained within the valley to be slaughtered. When the signal came, the weather and the incompetence of the planners meant that a number of MacDonalds were able to escape, perhaps helped by warnings from squeamish soldiers who had no taste for the task in hand. As details of the massacre leaked out from the lips of those who had got away, including the brutal murder of MacIain as he tried to pull on his trews, the story spread so fiercely that the government was forced to set up a commission of inquiry. Like all such postponing manoeuvres in our own time, this apportioned little blame to those most guilty. Stair was edged out of his official position but was consoled with a royal grant of lands. The Campbells were condemned for their treachery by every other clan in the land; yet this did nothing to lessen their power.

Today a small folk museum in a cruck-framed cottage displays clan and Jacobite souvenirs and information about the massacre, and there is a tall stone cross in memory of Alasdair MacIain; but most of the region is garnished with chair-lifts and ski tows.

A year before the Jacobite rising of 1745, a major transformation of the Campbell estate on Loch Fyne was put in hand. The old castle and town of Inveraray were dismantled and a palatial new castle set in landscaped parkland half a mile away, with a model township neatly and respectfully assembled on the edge of Loch Fyne. Today it is the home of the twelfth Duke of Argyll, chief (*MacCailein Mor*) of Clan Campbell.

In both Jacobite risings the Campbells prudently sided with the Hanoverians. Others wavered. In 1714 the sixth Earl of Mar, who had represented his country during discussions of the 1707 Act of Union and had served Queen Anne as Secretary of State for Scotland, wrote obsequiously to her successor, George I, offering the same devotion (and clearly expecting the same perks). Rebuffed, he at once became a fervent Jacobite. Not for nothing was he known to his contemporaries as 'Bobbing John'. He now espoused the backing of all true Scotsmen for James Edward Stuart, son of the discarded King James II of England, James VII of Scotland, and in their view legitimate King James III of the recently united kingdom. Widespread opposition to that Act of Union gave Stuart loyalists the chance to urge the Pretender's return, backed by French forces. In September 1715 the Earl of Mar raised King James's standard at Braemar.

Clansmen hastened to join his army on its way from the Highlands across Fife and Perthshire, until he could count on a force of more than 6,500. His opposing Hanoverian general had hastily mustered fewer than 2,000; but that general was the skilled chieftain of Clan Campbell, the second Duke of Argyll. Instead of marching on briskly into England, where he hoped to win support from those also suspicious of the Germanic accession, Mar hesitated, and released only a token detachment to join Lowland sympathizers already gathering along the Border. This task force showed more dash than Bobbing John himself. On their southward progress they decided to try and seize Edinburgh. Argyll intercepted them, whereupon they hurried on to join the Lowlanders, and in their company got as far south as Preston in England. There, after two brief battles, they found that supporters were not rallying to the cause and that they might as well surrender.

Mar at last bestirred himself and, after one mistaken foray towards Stirling, set off for England. Again Argyll was alerted, and hurried through the old cathedral city of Dunblane to cut across the rebels' route. An inconclusive conflict on the moorland of Sheriffmuir sent some of Argyll's men back in disarray to Stirling, and some of the Jacobites back across the Allan Water. The site of the encounter is marked by the Gathering Stone at which the clans assembled.

The rebels began to lose all sense of purpose and direction. After the death of Louis XIV the French seemed to have decided on a different political game, and no reinforcements were sent. The only significant arrival was that of James Edward Stuart himself at Peterhead early in December. He was too late, and cut a far from inspiring figure: he had hardly set foot in his kingdom before he began complaining that he had been stricken by 'three Fits of an Ague'. With the remorseless approach of Argyll's forces it was clear that the rebellion was at an end. On 4 February 1716 James and the Earl of Mar left Montrose on a ship bound for France.

Retribution was swift, though perversely the main dispossessions and executions fell upon Lowlanders and northern English rather than the Highland chiefs. One significant move was, however, made against the clansmen: an act was passed forbidding them to carry arms, and Independent Companies were set up to police the unruly regions as an adjunct to the regular army, watching for breaches of the Disarming Act and for cattle thieves, always the plague of the land. These companies eventually amalgamated into the Royal Highland Regiment, known as the Black Watch because it wore dark tartan uniform instead of the usual red. Among the clans from which these governmental contingents were drawn was, inevitably, that of the Campbells.

The man appointed commander-in-chief to implement the new regulations and ensure there was no resurgence of Jacobitism was no Scot but a member of the Anglo-Irish gentry. General George Wade is remembered less for his military prowess than for his simplification of troop movements to trouble spots. The Romans had always recognized the value of well-laid roads for this sort of containment. Almost any old track or road in the Highlands is today casually identified as a 'Wade road', even though many of them were built by his successors.

Oliver Cromwell had established fortifications at Inverness and Inverlochy, the latter being later expanded and named Fort William in honour of William III. Now Wade set about linking the garrisons in order to keep an eye on the Jacobite heartland of the Great Glen, and introduced another at Kilchumen, which he renamed Fort Augustus after William Augustus, Duke of Cumberland, who was to play a much reviled part in subsequent events. A road from Inverness to Perth took in Ruthven barracks, which Wade extended on its hilltop where the Wolf of Badenoch had once had a fortress. (An inn established for the benefit of the Ruthven garrison and the roadbuilders was the forerunner of the present tourist centre of Aviemore.) Wade's five-arched bridge over the river Tay at Aberfeldy is an impressive survivor of his 40 bridges, and the modern A9 pays tribute by following fairly closely his road from Inverness to Dunkeld. He combined military strategic planning with the economical use of military resources, obtaining extra pay for his soldiers so that they could lay the roads which they themselves might need to use.

In spite of much local resentment, there were some Highlanders shrewd enough to see the value of what was being created for them and, as Wade reported, 'from the ease and conveniency of transporting their merchandise begin to approve and applaud what they had first repined at and submitted to with reluctancy'. One of the toughest challenges and achievements among the 250 miles he had completed by 1739 was the conquering of the twists and gradients of Corrieyairack Pass between Dalwhinnie and Fort Augustus – which, ironically, was to prove valuable to Jacobite forces in the 1745 uprising, and later to be appreciated mainly by sheep and cattle drovers.

Rebel hopes stirred again when Spain and England fell out, and the Spanish offered to provide an invasion army of 5,000 in support of a Jacobite restoration. The main force would land in England; a smaller one, under George Keith, the Earl Marischal, in Scotland. In March 1719 Keith and his 300 Spanish soldiers sailed to Stornoway on the isle of Lewis in the Outer Hebrides, where the Earl Marischal learned to his indignation that the Jacobite court in Paris had vested command in the Marquis of Tullibardine. The two men effected an uneasy compromise, and after arguments about tactics it was decided to head for the mainland and march on Inverness. Battered by gales, their two frigates found shelter in Loch Alsh, where the Mackenzie castle of Eilean Donan was taken over as headquarters and magazine.

Eilean Donan, surely one of the most photographed and most familiar views on calendars and tourist guides, is now linked to the shore by a bridge but was originally accessible only by boat. It is known to have been the site of a prehistoric fort, and the tower built for the earls of Ross in the fourteenth century must on its rocky islet have been well-nigh impregnable to anything but a protracted starvation siege. It was not, however, capable of withstanding cannon fire. Keith and Tullibardine, having sent the frigates away so that there should be no turning back for their diminutive army, received first the news that the larger fleet had been scattered by a gale and so had called off their part of the operation, and then the unwelcome attentions of an English naval squadron. While they made a belated attempt to raise the clans in their support, the castle was bombarded and then attacked by a landing party. The remaining garrison of 45 Spaniards surrendered without a fight and without losing a life. After 200 years in ruin, the castle was restored in this century and now houses a war memorial to the Clan Macrae, who from the sixteenth century held it as hereditary constables on behalf of the Mackenzies.

Although surrounded, with no hope now of escape by sea, Tullibardine persuaded some clansmen to help his expeditionary force fight their way out. At Glenshiel, in hillside conditions favouring the Highlanders rather than General Wightman's advancing troops, he was in the end betrayed by clansmen who ran away, leaving only the bewildered Spaniards in what to them must have been an utterly alien land. They surrendered, were treated with considerable sympathy, and eventually shipped back home. A corrie above Glenshiel is still known as *Bealach na Spainnteach* – the Spaniards' Pass.

The year after this abortive 1719 rising, James Edward Stuart's wife, the Polish princess Clementina Sobieska, gave birth to a son. Charles Edward Stuart was brought up in Rome in an atmosphere of scheming and squabbling, both political and domestic. As he grew into a tall, comely young man with liquid brown eyes and that pale skin which so often goes with auburn hair, he cut a fine if foppish figure when dancing at fashionable gatherings. Yet at some stage he must have had a vision of his melancholic father in a nobler light: or, rather, a regal one. Prince Charles Edward turned from dancing to physical exertion and tough training to fit himself for a stern task which lay ahead. It became in his view his destiny to restore the rightful king to his throne.

In 1739 war broke out between England and Spain, and three years later there was trouble with France. Such a situation could not help but reawaken Jacobite yearnings. It was agreed that France would back another attempt at restoration: the Earl Marischal would take 3,000 French troops to the Highlands, while 12,000 were to land within marching distance of London, where Prince Charles Edward would be installed as Regent until his father could be brought over. Not for the first time, the winds of heaven seemed to favour England. The

French fleet set sail in February 1744 but was blown back by a gale which wrecked a large proportion of the transports. Yet another campaign had to be abandoned.

The Prince, whose full, pouting lips in portraits suggest the impatience and nervous energy commented on by those nearest to him, fretted the summer and autumn away. Then he impetuously let his Scottish contacts know that he intended to get to Scotland the following summer, French support or no French support. Jacobites in both countries were horrified and warned him against such a rash notion. One of their most lucid warnings in 1745 failed to reach Charles, and at the end of July he arrived with nine companions on the isle of Eriskay. His welcome was a cold one. Various clan chiefs assured him of undying loyalty but hastened to dissociate themselves from the present enterprise. Calling for patriotic support from others, 'Bonnie Prince Charlie' left for the mainland and Loch nan Uamh (Bay of Whales), north-west of Moidart, in the company of a handful of followers who became admiringly known thereafter as the Seven Men of Moidart. There were in fact rather more than seven – four of them Irish – but the romantic concept of that ever mystical number has lived on.

One of the most devoted of the pro-Stuart faction was 'Gentle Lochiel', chief of Clan Cameron. He was planting a line of seven beech trees on his Achnacarry estate when news was brought of the Prince's summons for his followers to assemble at Glenfinnan, at the head of Loch Shiel. Lochiel rode off at once to warn against any such ill-timed campaign. Charles convinced him that French money and troops would be forthcoming and that they should press on without delay. Lochiel's trees lay in the trench where they had been dropped until later rescued, becoming known symbolically as the Seven Men of Moidart, though today only five remain.

A tall monument set up at Glenfinnan in 1815 and topped 20 years later by the figure of a Highlander (not, as some suppose, of Prince Charles Edward himself), marks the point where King James's silken flag was reputedly unfurled. In fact it was reported by eye witnesses that the standard was raised on a knoll above the present road, and this was confirmed in 1976 when a hill fire exposed a rock slab with a Latin inscription identifying the spot.

From there the march to the south proceeded very well at first, since the wars with Spain and France had denuded the country of government troops. Such as remained were elderly or untrained. Their commander, Lieutenant-General Sir John Cope, decided that a swift response to the still vague threat would soon finish the whole matter and that the majority of clansmen would join him rather than the Prince. He was soon disillusioned. Even Clan Campbell, which had helped to enforce the Disarming Act, declined to issue weapons for the 'well-affected' (that is, pro-Hanoverian) clans on the neatly evasive grounds that this would be a breach of regulations.

Cope headed unhappily for Fort Augustus, on the fringe of the perennially disaffected area. At least he could comfort himself with the backing of two companies of the Black Watch. As they approached his goal, however, word came that the Jacobites already held Corrieyairack Pass on the hillside road which Wade had so obligingly created for them some years earlier. Cope veered off towards Inverness to replenish supplies and acquire more troops. Volunteers were scarce. While he was trying to organize things more efficiently, word reached him that the Highlanders had taken the opportunity to head south via Blair Atholl and Dunkeld to Perth. Obviously they had their eyes on the Lowlands and what lay beyond.

In Perth the Prince appeared to be having better luck than his antagonist. The Duke of Perth and Lord George Murray joined him and were appointed joint Lieutenant-Generals. Historians have since argued over the merits of Murray: to some he was a gifted strategist and loyal supporter, to others a vain and inconsistent man whose bad advice was mainly responsible for wrong decisions and ultimate defeat. The Young Pretender himself later declared 'Ld G's vilany proved out of all dispute'. At the outset, though, the future seemed bright. On went the army, crossing the Forth and marching to Falkirk, and then daringly demanding the capitulation of

Edinburgh. Although the castle held out for King George and lobbed an occasional cannonball down the hill, the lower regions of the Canongate were taken by Lochiel's men with no resistance, and Bonnie Prince Charlie danced in Holyroodhouse.

Further triumphs included victory at the battle of Prestonpans against Cope's troops brought by ship from Aberdeen; the capture of Carlisle across the Border; and an unopposed march to Manchester and Derby. There the tide began to turn.

The whole campaign had been based on the belief that once things started moving the English would gladly throw off the Hanoverian yoke, and the French would fulfil their earlier promises. No such alliances had been forthcoming. The Scots were far from home, and government troops including Dutch and Hessian contingents were closing in under the commands of Cope, Wade, and George II's son William Augustus, Duke of Cumberland. They outnumbered the rebels six to one. In spite of Charles Edward's pleas, his advisers were resolved that it was time to head back to Scotland.

Towns which had granted them a wary welcome on the way south now abused them on their way north. At Carlisle it was decided to abandon all save a few pieces of artillery and to speed on via Longtown and ultimately to Glasgow. Also left at Carlisle was a garrison of men from Manchester who had joined and stayed loyal to the Prince but who were reluctant to accompany him into Scotland. When they finally surrendered to Cumberland, he treated them with ferocious cruelty, and nearly all the officers were taken to London to be publicly hanged and disembowelled.

For a time it seemed that on Scottish soil the Jacobite cause might be regenerated. At Falkirk a pursuing army was routed, and some Jacobite officers even suggested a return across the Border and a march on London. But while they argued, and Lord George Murray in particular warned of desertions and the need to retreat, the Duke of Cumberland came hurrying towards them. He took over Edinburgh, and the Prince's disorganized troops wandered about aimlessly until it was decided to direct the clan regiments to Crieff, the remainder to Perth. A council of war in Crieff was torn by 'heats and animosities', but

> after a great deal of wrangling and altercation, it was determined that the horse and low country regiments should march towards Inverness, along the coast, while the Prince with the clans, took the Highland road thither.

In spite of heavy snow the two columns managed to reach their goal by the separate routes. From Inverness a few successful sorties were launched, resulting in the ejection of government troops from Fort Augustus and the surrender of several Campbell garrisons. While all this went on, however, Charles Edward seemed alternately sunk in gloom and impulsively eager to dance or go off fishing. Cumberland used the time more rationally, and, after being foolishly allowed to cross the Spey without any opposition, began to move in on Inverness.

One group of the Prince's officers recommended setting up a defence over broken, boggy ground near Dalcross castle where the English gunners would have difficulty in manoeuvring and the Highlanders could make use of the steep slopes for their favourite tactic – a musketry barrage followed by a terrifying downhill rush with all their weight behind their broadswords. Instead, the arrogant Irish captain John William O'Sullivan, whom Charles Edward had misguidedly promoted to Quartermaster-General, prevailed with the suggestion that they should form up on Culloden Moor between the Moray Firth and the river Nairn, about 5 miles east of Inverness. The Prince's headquarters had already been established in Culloden House nearby after its pro-Hanoverian laird, Duncan Forbes, had fled north. Apart from that the choice was an inexplicable one: the low ridge of what locals called Drumossie Moor was exposed on all sides, offering ideal conditions for Cumberland's artillery and cavalry.

In addition to such drawbacks, on the morning of the battle,

16 April 1746, the Jacobite forces were in poor shape after several days with very little food, and a night misguidedly spent trying to launch a surprise attack on Cumberland's camp, during which they got hopelessly lost in the dark. The actual battle took little more than forty minutes. All the advantage was on Cumberland's side. The Highlanders fought fiercely, but were shot down or bayoneted. At the end the Jacobites had lost at least 1,200 men, against about 300 of the enemy.

A tall cairn of heavy boulders was erected in 1881 on the battlefield, with a memorial plaque set into it. Communal burial places known as the Graves of the Clans are marked by headstones with the names of individual clans beside the road which an early nineteenth-century landowner drove across the site, now closed off. One legend has it that the grass refuses to grow on these patches; but in the 1790s a local witness, minister of the parish, was to aver just the opposite – that the graves were 'discerned by their green surface while the rest of the ground is covered with black heath'. Fewer distinctions were made on behalf of the opponents. Beside the Well of the Dead is a stone with the curt inscription:

FIELD

OF THE ENGLISH

THEY WERE BURIED

HERE

From a larger stone the Duke of Cumberland is supposed to have surveyed the progress of the battle. One old farm cottage thatched with heather, which escaped demolition during the years of agricultural 'improvement', has been preserved as part of the Culloden museum.

The rest of the story is one of brutal repression for the Prince's supporters, and a protracted flight through the heather and the glens by the Prince himself.

There is still controversy as to whether Charles Edward, shattered by the collapse of his most cherished beliefs and believing that Lord George Murray had wantonly contributed to this destruction, fled the battlefield or stayed on until forced to leave. Lord Elcho, commander of his bodyguard, cried after him: 'There you go for a damned cowardly Italian.' The record of the fugitive's subsequent progress owes a great deal to notes written up soon after the events by one of his attendants, Captain Felix O'Neil. O'Neil, an Irishman who had been in French service, was firm in his assertions that the Prince remained on the field 'Untill there were no more Hopes left, and then Could Scarce Be persuaded to Retire'. He had decreed that in case of defeat the Highlanders should make what escape they could from the moor and reassemble at Fort Augustus, where he would join them. Certainly he reached Fort Augustus, and waited; but many men had made their way to Ruthven barracks where they, too, waited. It was here that they received the final despondent message, 'Let every man seek his own safety the best way he can.' Before leaving they blew up the barracks.

Entrusted with French funds, a group of Jacobites hastily buried them beyond the Dark Mile on the shores of Loch Arkaig, giving rise to many long-lived tales of money and valuables still unaccounted for.

Even the hardiest mountaineer or fell-walker would find it no easy task to tread in the steps of Bonnie Prince Charlie during the months of pursuit. Shelter in the houses of various lairds was loyally or grudgingly accorded, but always in the knowledge that he must move on after the briefest respite. The first to hide him were the Grants of Glenmoriston, a family still living today on their estate after thirteen generations. In that same glen, where trees cluster protectively below stern ridges and hillsides littered with boulders, the Prince won a head start thanks to the gallantry of a young supporter. Roderick Mackenzie, who bore a remarkable physical resemblance to him, was shot by Cumberland's men, but before dying managed to gasp out, 'You have murdered your prince.' The hunt was called off until closer examination revealed the truth. Mackenzie is buried beside the road, and opposite his grave stands a commemorative cairn.

Persuaded at last by O'Neil and O'Sullivan to quit the

mainland for an island until he could be taken off by a French ship which had been appealed for, the fugitive reluctantly agreed to set sail in an open fishing boat around eight o'clock one dark night. In O'Neil's words,

> About one hour after we Parted a Violent Hurricane Arose, which Drove us Ninty Miles from our Intended Port, and next Day Running for Shelter, into the Iseland of North Wist [Uist], Struck upon a Rock and Stove to Pieces, and with great Difficulty Sav'd our Lives. At our Landing we were in the most Mellancholy Situation, knowing no Body, and wanting the Common Necessarys of Life.

In spite of the dismal conditions they struggled on, until on South Uist they found themselves more fortunate. The Clanranald chieftain concealed the Prince in a turf house in the glen of Coradale, and invited him into his home to drink heavily with the local gentry. Then word reached them of the approach of search parties under the command of Major-General John Campbell; and it was off across the water once more.

On Benbecula, between North and South Uist, they encountered a young lady of Jacobite persuasion, Flora Mac-Donald, whose father was captain of an Independent Company and could 'Accord her a pass for herself and a Servant to go visit her Mother' on the isle of Skye. Dressed as a serving maid, 'Betty Bourk', Charles Edward accompanied Flora to Skye – thereby missing a rescue party from France which reached South Uist three days later. Even on Skye he was not safe, in spite of the protection of the Mackinnons, and after further trudgings through rain and any number of alarms, he was taken back to the mainland. Desperate quarry in what one of his pursuers called 'The Summer's Hunting', he wandered through Knoydart and, sadly, the once optimistic region of Moidart, joined by a loyal new septet, the 'Seven Men of Glenmoriston': two Macdonalds, three Chisholms, a Mac-gregor and a Grant. Further French rescue attempts were mounted until at last the Prince, Lochiel and a handful of endangered supporters were picked up from the very loch where he had so eagerly landed the year before – Loch nan Uamh.

'And so he left us,' wrote John MacDonald of Borodale bitterly, 'and he left us all in a worse state than he found us.' Laments and love songs linger on, asking if he will 'no come back again' and assuring him that 'better luved he canna be'. But he did not come back. After a succession of rebuffs in France and elsewhere he settled in Rome, contracted an unhappy and childless marriage, took to the bottle, and lived dismally on until 1788. Some followers had hastened to disown him: his own secretary, John Murray of Broughton, turned King's Evidence and betrayed, among others, the 80-year-old Lord Lovat, the last peer of the realm to be beheaded. Others who could not hide their love for the 'king over the water', and even those who had happened to be innocently in the neighbourhood of Culloden, were hacked to death, hanged, or thrown into the hulks, their cattle sequestered and their wives ravished, in token of which the Hanoverian composer Handel acclaimed 'Butcher' Cumberland with a resounding anthem, 'See the Conqu'ring Hero Comes'.

To guard against any future insurrection, a vast artillery fortress was built to accommodate a complement of 70 guns on a promontory in the Moray Firth 11 miles east of Inverness. In honour of the monarch it was named Fort George. Today its smartly regular lawns give it the air of a vast college rather than a military centre, but it still maintains a garrison, the regimental museum of the Queen's Own Highlanders, and two rooms fitted out as rank-and-file barrack rooms of 1780 and 1868, together with an officer's sparsely furnished quarters.

Most demoralizing of all for the Highlanders was the order that from now on it was forbidden not merely to carry arms but for them to wear the tartan or the kilt.

The national dress we have come to associate with the warrior families of the glens had in fact not been so distinctive in its patterns or so defiantly associated with specific clans in pre-Union days. Then the most usual dress had derived from the Irish combination of linen shirt, woollen mantle, and chequered hose which developed as 'trews'. Colours tended to be of a muted, heathery mixture, or a dull brown so that 'when lying upon the heather in the day, they may not be discovered by the appearance of their clothes'. In the fifteenth century John Major observed that

> From the mid-leg to the foot they go uncovered. Their dress is, for an over-garment, a loose plaid and a shirt saffron-dyed . . . The common folk among the Wild Scots go out to battle with the whole body clad in a linen garment sewed together in patchwork, well daubed with wax or pitch, and with an overcoat of deerskin. But the common people among our domestic Scots and the English fight in a woollen garment.

The loose plaid referred to was for centuries the most characteristically Scottish garment. This long, belted *feileadh-mor* (a 'large fold') was wrapped round the body and pinned over one shoulder. The 'small fold' of the *feileadh-beag* or philibeg, a short kilt, did not appear until the early eighteenth century, followed by the addition of a goatskin purse or *spleuchan* – the sporran. Tartan designs woven into the plaid became brighter and more assertive during the rise of nationalism which led to the Jacobite rebellions, an association which was undoubtedly the main reason for the official proscription. Yet even at Culloden the clans had been distinguished not by individual tartans but by their cockades.

In addition to the assault on their family identity, the lands of all known rebels and of many others whose sympathies were even vaguely suspect were confiscated and their revenues administered by a Crown Commission for the Forfeited Estates. Of all the draconian measures taken, this last was to be the one which proved paradoxically beneficial in the long run.

A town such as Crieff, on the Highland Line where Highlanders and Lowlanders met for a huge annual tryst or cattle fair, was in a splendid trading position on one of the major drove roads, but a vulnerable one when different elements fell out with one another. During the rising of 1715, the town was burned. By 1722 it had recovered and a Hanoverian agent reported of the great Highland Tryst on Michaelmas Day that over 30,000 guineas was paid over in ready money, after which 'poor creatures hir'd themselves out for a Shilling a Day to drive the Cattle to England to return home at their own Charge'. In 1731 a large linen factory was built, but then in 1746 was destroyed by Jacobite militia, occupying the town during their retreat, while Prince Charles Edward stayed at neighbouring Drummond castle – itself soon to be largely dismantled. There was also a threat of burning the whole town once more because of its pro-governmental stance. After the collapse of the rising, properties taken from such Jacobite loyalists as the lairds of Strathearn were divided up among local inhabitants with a view to stifling unrest and improving social and economic conditions. Among feus granted to those in Crieff were premises to house more than 90 master weavers, one of whose workshops has been restored as a Highland Tryst Museum displaying traditional handloom tartan weaving.

The calculated dismembering of the clan system went hand in hand with farming improvements in the Highlands, which had hitherto lagged far behind the Lowlands. A long-standing functionary was thus doomed to disappear. The tacksman had reaped his middleman's benefits largely by overseeing the military obligations of his sub-tenants to the landowner. Now the whole concept of ward tenure, the granting of land in return for military service, was banned. Improvements were initiated to ensure fairer division between owner and tenant, offering secure tenancies to those willing to take responsibility for ditching, fencing, and introducing more scientific stock and crop handling. Run-rig strips gave way to larger, economically viable fields. An official road-building programme, incorporating Wade's military roads where feasible, simplified transport to more distant markets.

Those markets had always been supplied in one way or

another in spite of the financial and physical hazards. Cattle bred in northern Scotland had for long been driven down every autumn to the Crieff and Falkirk trysts, and when bought were sent south in droves which could amount to a thousand at a time. By the middle of the eighteenth century as many as 80,000 cattle and – significantly – growing quantities of sheep could be seen plodding their way towards the satisfaction of southern stomachs. The company rep of today, entering up his expense sheet in a cosy hotel, might prefer not to contemplate the conditions under which drovers travelled with their merchandise along drove roads softer to the hoof but less stable than the new thoroughfares, bedding down with the cattle at night, drowsing uneasily in fear of pouncing rustlers, with little more to eat than what they themselves could provide – oatmeal, whisky from a horn flask, and the occasional supplement of black pudding made from bleeding the cattle in their charge. The cattle made up such blood loss from the rich grazing spread out before them when they reached the more luxuriant English pastures.

In trying to ease (or enforce) the passage from a fiercely regional past to a national future, inevitable errors were made and clashes were provoked between traditionalists and entrepreneurs. Then, as now, London speculators made haste to buy up whatever they could – in this case, forfeited lands going cheap. Lairds who had stayed clear of the Jacobite fever were also in a position to acquire the lands of disgraced rivals and exploit new business practices. Most far-ranging of all in its influence, the raising of sheep was seen as less troublesome and more swiftly profitable than the time-honoured raising and droving of cattle. So, after what had promised for a time to be beneficial development for all, began the ill-famed Highland Clearances.

In relation to its resources that could be utilized, the region had by the eighteenth century become overpopulated. When families were resigned to living in the rural squalor of clachans (small rural hamlets) and bleak crofts, it had been possible to scrape a bare living, and the heads of the clans had counted their assets in potential fighting men rather than in output of saleable produce. Now the day of the fighting man was over and the lairds began to see themselves at a serious disadvantage in comparison with their prosperous Lowland counterparts. Instead of looking after the 'children' of their clan, the leaders began to impose crippling burdens, demanding cash for their tenancies at ever-increasing rates, until whole communities of peasant smallholders emigrated to America, and other groups and individuals went to seek work in the factories of the Lowlands and England. Those still imbued with the fighting spirit found employment in regiments formed to fight Britain's foreign wars and enforce Britain's colonial authority, carrying the formidable reputation of the Scottish warrior to the far corners of the earth.

The lairds themselves had moved to the cities, especially to London, and needed money to support their expensive emulation of the grandees of English society. Profits from cattle droving to southern markets had to some extent subsidized their conceits in less demanding days in spite of its rather speculative nature; but now such income was far from sufficient. Sheep farming was cheaper to run, more profitable, and required fewer men. Villages fell into dereliction, cattle trysts were forgotten, and sheep – the 'four-footed clansmen' – grazed through the glens and over the moors. Absentee landlords grew rich with little effort: there were many graziers from the south willing to lease the land at favourable rates and do all the work.

In a sad majority of cases the callousness of the Scottish landowner to his own kin was cumulatively worse than what had been inflicted by political oppressors in London. There were only a few who, though anxious to make large profits in keeping with the spirit of the age, still felt constrained to put up a pretence of watching over the welfare of families who had for generations lived on their lands. One such was Elizabeth, Countess of Sutherland, whose English husband Lord Stafford had inherited a fortune from the Bridgewater canals. Exploitation of their assets was reflected in an extravagant status symbol, the rebuilt Dunrobin castle; but humbler, less glamorous memorials remain in the company of the prehistoric stones of Sutherland and Caithness.

In Helmsdale, one of the coastal villages planned for evicted tenants, is the splendid Timespan visitor centre. It is no museum of mere historical record, but in its displays of the Clearances, murders at Helmsdale castle, and the burning of the last witch in Britain, has a quite frightening immediacy. The last remains of the castle were demolished in 1970 to make way for a new bridge carrying the A9 across the river. Fortunately Telford's original graceful bridge has been preserved, close beside the Timespan building and its garden of herbs traditionally used in cooking, dyeing and home medicine. The exhibitions in the Centre include life-size tableaux and all too convincing sound-tracks of villagers with their crofts being set on fire about them, and of the arch-villain of the region, the factor Patrick Sellar.

The idea in Sutherland was that tenants and sub-tenants should be not simply removed but resettled. While it had become accepted by the owners that the Strath of Kildonan should be given over to extensive sheep runs, there was also profit to be made from mining and fishing: so why not build a whole new range of facilities and provide the dispossessed with new employment? Some farms could be subdivided to sustain the reduced number of agricultural workers who would still be needed, a cluster of them around Bettyhill. It has long been claimed that this little coastal settlement on the north coast of Sutherland was affectionately named after the countess, Elizabeth, but local lore prefers to associate it with a certain Betty 'Cnocan' who ran an inn at the top of the *cnoc* (hill). The eastern coastal village of Brora, a little way north of the Sutherlands' grandiose family seat, was expanded with a brickworks, the Highlands' only coal mine, a fishing harbour, and a whisky distillery which would provide a reliable market for local tenants' grain 'without their being obliged to dispose of it to illegal distillers'. The distillery, modernized in the late 1960s, still functions under the name Clynelish.

Further north the Helmsdale settlement, bright and wel-coming as it may look today, failed to live up to the founders' expectations. A fishing harbour designed by John Rennie included a fish-curing plant; streets were laid out in a smart grid pattern; and there was talk of attracting woollen and leather industries into the little community. The Strath of Kildonan tenants, however, were reluctant to move, especially when they discovered that plots of land supposedly allocated to them had either not been completed in time or were inadequate. When forced into resettling, they found it difficult to adjust to an utterly different way of life. Other banishment areas were even less congenial. One of the most distressing scenes to this day is the lonely slope of Badbea, five miles north of Helmsdale, where a handful of evicted families struggled for decades to scratch a bare living above cliffs so dangerous that children and animals had to be tethered to prevent them falling over or being blown over. Many bore the Sutherland surname, including a John Sutherland usually known as John Badbea because of his work on behalf of the whole community. The last tenant of the perilous settlement, John Gunn, survived there until 1911.

Serious original mistakes were compounded. Agricultural experts who had been appointed to administer the transition adopted such ruthless methods that one was brought to trial in Inverness. In what became known as the Year of the Burning, the factor Patrick Sellar was accused of driving families out of their houses, setting fire to their roofs, and in one case of murdering an old woman in her own home. In a blatantly rigged trial he was acquitted of 'culpable homicide', but his reputation had already, according to one of his more enlight-ened colleagues, done irreparable damage by 'disposing the minds of the people against all reasonable change'. The dis-tinction between reasonable and unreasonable change was perhaps not easily comprehended by those taking the full impact of resettlement or exile.

An exploration of Strathnaver and the Strath of Kildonan today presents evocative parallels between abandoned settlements of the nineteenth century and those of prehistoric times. In a Forestry Commission clearing off the B871 near Syre are juxtaposed remains of an Iron Age souterrain and the longhouses, barns and corn-drying kilns of Rosal village, once administered by that very Patrick Sellar whose own comfortable house still stands nearby. Before 1815 there were 39 'townships' along the east side of the river Naver, inhabited by 212 families. Along the west bank, 126 families farmed over 600 acres of arable land. One man who saw what happened to them is commemorated in a memorial cairn by the riverside: Donald MacLeod's *Gloomy Memories* was written as an eye-witness's account of brutalities to set against the rose-tinted rhapsodies of Harriet Beecher Stowe's *Sunny Memories*, which lauded the Duchess of Sutherland's lavish hospitality in London and at Dunrobin.

In an idyllic setting near Bettyhill, stony fragments of Achanlochy village on a mound above its gleaming lochan (a small loch) are all too symbolically covered with sheep droppings. It was emptied during the third great Strathnaver clearance by the factor Francis Suther, a worthy (if that is the correct description) successor to Patrick Sellar. An informative plaque and numbered markers have been installed to identify various parts of the settlement, and there is further explanatory material in the little Strathnaver museum east of Bettyhill. Achanlochy, too, has ancient neighbours: beside the by-road between the A836 and Skelpick is an impressive sequence of ruined brochs and chambered cairns.

Near the bridge over Kilphedir burn in Kildonan, two abandoned clachans with livestock enclosures and cultivation ridges share the landscape with an ancient ruined broch, hut circles, cairns and a souterrain. Incongruously there is also the site of a gold-rush town. In 1868 a native of the region returned from the Australian goldfields, panned for gold in the river, and struck lucky. After a brief boom, when a shanty town grew up beside the burn, profits were not enough for the Duke of Sutherland to resist his neighbours' complaints about damage to salmon fishing and deer stalking, and the prospectors were driven off. In 1989 fresh traces renewed interest in the region, and there have since been further speculations about a rich vein of Scottish gold.

Australia had been only one destination of those driven from their homes. Many found their way to Canada. A group from Kildonan founded a settlement on Hudson Bay, but when it proved unworkable they trekked over 800 miles to the Red River and started all over again on a site they named Kildonan, which grew to become Winnipeg.

Pitiful memories remain at Croick's old parish church, at the end of a meandering road from Bonar Bridge. During the century after Culloden more than 40 'Parliamentary churches' were built throughout the Highlands to designs by Thomas Telford, in an effort to woo Papist Jacobites finally to Protestantism. When the clearing of Glen Calvie residents began in order to make way for sheep in 1845, many of the dispossessed tried to fight off banishment by setting up improvised shacks in Croick churchyard. Their sad messages can still be seen scratched into the glass of the east window. Gillanders, the estate factor who drove them out, was buried in due course near the churchyard gate, but descendants of the evicted families visiting the tragic scene threw such quantities of stone and rubbish on it that the desecrated grave is no longer identifiable.

A famine caused by potato blight in 1846 did nothing to alleviate the anguish of those still struggling to eke out a living on the few remaining farmsteads. The better landlords and a church appeal fund raised money for the relief of the starving. Labour on 'destitution roads' in the glens and barely accessible wilds such as Torridon provided work and a pittance for some. Below Benn Eighe's glistening grey quartzite face, Kinlochewe bridge, nicknamed the Hunger Bridge, was paid for by Mary Hanbury Mackenzie as part of local famine relief. But few of even the more benevolent landlords had sufficient income to cope with an unproductive tenantry, and those estates in impersonal, commercial trusteeship were administered without any concern for human suffering. Less sympathetic churchmen, holding their livings by favour of their lairds, prophesied damnation for wretches who resisted eviction. Food riots provoked the use of Highland regiments against their own people. In 1851 the chairman of the Scottish Poor Law Board announced that no more funds were available and, along with the Highlands and Islands Emigration Society, advised people to emigrate. When one recruiting campaign appealed to Scots to offer their services in the Crimean War, the answer was hardly surprising: 'Since you have preferred sheep to men, let sheep defend you.'

The depopulation of the Highlands continued until well into our own century, in spite of belated acts to protect crofters, and the development of fisheries around Ullapool, Oban, Wick and other coastal settlements thrown the lifeline of the railways. Light industries offered a precarious living in some areas, but not in sufficient quantity to revivify a whole region. A remote town such as Thurso, though not reached by the railway until comparatively late on, achieved sudden prosperity in the 1830s with the quarrying and shaping of Caithness flags, exported by sea down the British coast and across the world for paving city streets. Then the invention of concrete, produced at a third of the cost, virtually destroyed the trade.

Landowners who had acquired wealth from exploitation of family lands found that extension of their sporting estates brought social and political advantages – and, as the Highlands grew more accessible by means of public and private transport, also ensured an inflow of more money. Still there were few attempts to deal comprehensively with the region's special characteristics until the Highlands and Islands Development Board was set up in 1965, followed ten years later by the Scottish Development Agency. Agricultural co-operatives have been encouraged; foreign firms have been coaxed into Scotland; fish and deer farming have been built up as an alternative to individual fishing and hunting. Salmon hatcheries were by the late 1980s heading for a production worth some £200 million a year. North Sea oil promised a period of widespread benefits, but now provides problems of retrenchment: seen from the northern waterside road of the Black Isle, the Cromarty Firth has become a vast parking lot for senile drilling rigs. The nuclear power station at Dounreay provoked argument and gloomy forebodings before and after it came on stream. Yet when there is talk of running it down for safety and environmental reasons, local inhabitants protest about the possible disappearance of the only major employer in their district. The balance is, as ever, a delicate one and there are, as ever, many shifts and clashes between swings and roundabouts. One man trained at Dounreay launched out in 1975 on a venture in electronics at Wick which has become a major provider of underwater television cameras for surveillance and control of unmanned submarines. Suppose such things had been available to Bonnie Prince Charlie . . . ?

New political pressures already weigh more heavily on parts of Scotland than on the rest of Britain. The controversial community charge or 'poll tax' was first imposed in Scotland, and within a few months was having a dismaying effect. One farming family in remote, hill-girt Knoydart, in a rate-free tied house without any council provision of mains electricity, sewage or refuse collection, and without even a proper road to their holding, was reported in September 1988 to be facing an annual charge of £1,500. The Highland and Islands Development Board foresaw the devastating effect the arbitrary tax would have for others in similar situation across the region, and made earnest representations to the government. No notice was taken. When the history of our own times comes to be written, there seems every likelihood of it repeating the earlier conflicts and resentments in the Highlands.

SELECTED SITES OF INTEREST

Antiquities

APPLECROSS   Church on an unclassified, magnificently scenic road following the coast of Wester Ross, looking out towards the islands of Rona, Raasay and Skye and then turning inland towards the precipitous Pass of the Cattle. A slab almost 10 feet high beside the gate of the old churchyard carries an engraving of a large ringed cross. Inside the church are fragments of other cross-slabs ornamented with intricate spirals and birds' heads. This is thought to be the site of a small monastery founded in the seventh century by St Maelrubba from Bangor in Ireland.

BALLYMEANOCH   Off the A816 about 5 miles north-west of Lochgilphead. A cairn within ditch and bank of a henge; and, nearby, three groups of standing stones with cup-and-ring-markings.

CAIRN OF GET   Beside a minor road from the A9 about 7 miles south of Wick. A whole family of cairns, together with an Iron Age fort, stone rows and a number of identifiable hut circles. The burial chamber of the Cairn of Get itself is open to the sky. When excavated in 1866, bones of people and animals were found together with pottery and flint arrowheads.

CARN LIATH   About $2\frac{1}{2}$ miles north of Golspie on the A9, the lower courses of a broch dating from perhaps the first century BC, with part of an inner staircase still intact, stand on an impressive knoll whose earthen ramparts may once have supported outer stone walls. Identifiable traces of a number of houses huddle within its protection.

FORRES   Sueno's Stone, a 20-foot high stone elaborately carved, within a railed enclosure beside the town's bypass, best reached from the B9011.

STRATHPEFFER   The Eagle Stone, in a field above the old railway station, is a Pictish symbol stone whose deeply incised horseshoe and eagle figures have in recent times been coloured, as they probably were originally.

(*For a general study of the foregoing see also Chapter 1.*)

Historic Buildings

AUCHINDRAIN   Beside the A83 about 5 miles south-west of Inveraray. A reconstructed West Highland township, visited by Queen Victoria in 1875 and still preserving family long-houses and cottages complete with original domestic equipment and box beds, barns, wash-house and characteristic field pattern. A Museum Centre displays West Highland life in bygone days.

BERNERA BARRACKS   A minor road from the A87 near the seaward end of Glenelg leads to substantial ruins of barracks similar in design to those at Ruthven. The buildings were set up about 1722 to watch over the narrow channel between Skye and the mainland, in case of attempted Jacobite incursions from that quarter, and not finally abandoned until 1800. There are sketchy traces of the old military road linking Bernera with Fort Augustus.

CARNASSERIE   Set on a slope high above the A816 about 9 miles north of Lochgilphead. A tower house overlooking the historic cairns, carved stones and strongholds of the Kilmartin valley, this was built on an earlier castle site by John Carswell, first Protestant Superintendent of Argyll and the Isles in the sixteenth century. He translated Knox's Liturgy into Gaelic, the first book to be printed in that language. The Gaelic inscription above the door, *Dia le ua nduibhne*, pays homage to his Argyll patrons: 'God be with the Chief of the Campbells.'

CROMARTY   Hugh Miller's Cottage, an eighteenth-century white-harled building in Church Street, birthplace of a local stonemason who became a famous geologist and wrote a classic study of *The Old Red Sandstone*.

SINCLAIR/GIRNIGOE CASTLE   A spectacular coastal fortress $4\frac{1}{2}$

miles north-east of Wick, originally the seat of the Sinclair earls of Caithness, and for 200 years from the fifteenth century the governmental seat of the region. When a debt-ridden earl handed it over to a Campbell of Glenorchy, the rightful heir besieged the castle, using cannon for the first time in Caithness. He regained the castle, but it was never lived in again.

TARBERT In a key position between the south-west end of Loch Fyne and Tarbert West Loch leading out towards the islands of Jura and Islay, the compact fishing village has been a fortified spot since the Iron Age. The first Christian king of Kintyre built a castle in the sixth century; the Norse king Magnus Barelegs claimed the region for his own; Robert the Bruce rebuilt the fortification as a royal castle, once on a par with Edinburgh and Stirling. Now only its ivy-choked keep still stands above the harbour.

Museums

COMRIE (Tayside) Scottish Tartans Museum displays the largest existing collection of Highland dress in general, tartans in particular, and historical background material. There is also a garden of the main plants which provided the original dyes.

FORT WILLIAM West Highland Museum with displays of local history and customs, a tartan section, and a secret anamorphic portrait of Bonnie Prince Charlie.

GAIRLOCH Heritage Museum has displays covering main features of West Highland life from prehistoric times to the present, including a Pictish symbol stone and a croft reconstruction (*see also Chapter 9 for crofting*).

LHAIDHAY A mile north of Dunbeath beside the A9, the Lhaidhay Caithness Croft Museum is built around an early eighteenth-century croft with dwelling, stable and byre under one roof, furnished in the style of the time, with a cruck barn adjoining (*see also Chapter 9 for crofting*).

THURSO Heritage Museum in Thurso High Street has Pictish and Norse stones, and exhibitions on the local flagstone and fishing industries.

TORRIDON In a wild mountain setting, the National Trust for Scotland has a Visitor Centre with audio-visual display on the wild life of the region; and at Torridon Mains nearby is a museum devoted to the life of the red deer.

8

Grampian and the Great Glen

IN THE vast time scale of the region's ancient granite rocks, the name bestowed on it is a comparatively recent solecism. In his biography of Agricola, Tacitus wrote of the Roman victory at Mons Graupius in the north-east. A fifteenth-century Dundee historian, Hector Boece or Boethius, who was partly responsible for the misconceptions on which Holinshed and Shakespeare based their slanders on Macbeth, spawned another error in mis-spelling this name as Mons Grampius. The error persisted through later printings until the mountains lying between the two fault lines of the Great Glen and the Highland Line became irrevocably known as the Grampians. The once separate shires of Moray, Banff, Aberdeen and Kincardine are now described overall as Grampian. The ranges, overlapping into the Highland region, include peaks such as Ben Nevis – the highest point in the British Isles – Ben Lomond and the Cairngorm ski slopes, and are equally entitled to be called Highlands, though their smoothed-off shoulders, corries, and coastal headlands are geologically different from, and much more ancient than, the heights west of the Great Glen.

Granite is the substance not merely of the countryside but of its royal burgh and port, Aberdeen, steely and forbidding on a rainy day but sparkling with embedded shreds of mica when the sun is out. The name of Scotland's third largest city is taken from one of its rivers, the Don, making it first Aberdon (whence 'Aberdonians') and then Aberdeen. The oldest part of the town, its streets compressed between high buildings, is near the waterfront and the 'Auld Brig' of Don, some 600 years old. The other river is the Dee, whose bridge is a century and a half younger.

The city was given its royal charter by William the Lion in 1179. Its civic motto, *Bon Accord*, derives from the rallying cry of the Bruces: Robert had one of his clashes with the rival Comyns here. Burnt by Edward III in 1336, Aberdeen was soon rebuilt on a grander scale. In that same century its cathedral of St Machar was founded, to be graced with two spires added by Bishop Dunbar in the early sixteenth century. The transepts are now picturesque ruins around the altar tomb of the bishop, but the nave and towers are still in use as a church.

Aberdeen University was originally two separate establishments. King's College was founded in 1494, its first patron being James IV, in whose honour the crown spire was erected. In 1593 Marischal College was built on the site of an old monastery, and functioned as a separate university until 1826, when the two were amalgamated. The two oldest surviving houses in the city date from the sixteenth century, but the more sumptuous of them carries the name of a seventeenth-century Provost (or Chief Magistrate), Sir George Skene. Its near neighbour was the home of Provost Ross who, like Skene, was a prosperous businessman dealing in the Baltic trade. Skene's House was occupied for some weeks by the Duke of Cumberland and his entourage when pursuing Princes Charles Edward's forces northwards in 1746, and it is recorded that when they finally moved on not only did they offer no payment for their stay but also General Hawley helped himself to several hundred pounds' worth of his hostess's valuables. Today its rooms, some with fine painted ceilings, are furnished in period style as a background to local history displays.

The 'Granite City' had suffered far worse losses during the excesses of Covenanting times, when it had the misfortune to be attacked and occupied three times by a Royalist general over whose beliefs and policies there is still profound disagreement. Some regard him as a man of honour cruelly betrayed by those he sought to protect, especially his king. Others call him a turncoat and a murderer.

Born in 1612, James Graham, fifth Earl and later first Marquis of Montrose, was from his youthful years a strict Presbyterian, though still endeavouring to balance this against allegiance to the Crown. Gradually alienated by Charles I's insensitive and high-handed policy towards the Scottish church, he eventually committed himself to the cause of the most fervent nationalists, and in 1638 assisted at the signing of the Covenant.

Throughout his campaigns and troubled changes of opinion Montrose had as a colleague, rival, and ultimately bitter enemy Archibald Campbell, eighth Earl of Argyll. This powerful chieftain acquired a reputation for vacillation and deviousness, yet affirmed the most staunch Calvinist views. He refused to become a member of the Standing Committee formed by Covenanters after Charles I had prorogued the Scots Parliament, but was brutally eager to 'root out of the country' recalcitrant objectors to an unqualified acceptance of the Covenant. Among those who suffered from his policy of fire and sword was Lord Ogilvy, whose 'Bonny House of Airlie' was burned and whose cattle were driven away into Campbell country in spite of (or perhaps because of) the attempted intercession of Ogilvy's neighbour, Montrose. Flushed with success and ambition, Argyll showed every sign of wishing to become dictator of Scotland. When Montrose tried to mount a protest in 1641, he was imprisoned and kept out of the way while Charles I was in Edinburgh parleying with Argyll, creating him a Marquis, and apparently giving in to all his demands; but hardly had Charles turned his back before the Covenanters were promising support to the English Parliamentarians in return for a guarantee that Presbyterianism would be established throughout England.

The excesses of the worst Covenanters sickened Montrose. After vainly attempting to persuade his co-religionists to moderation, and disapproving of their sly willingness to do business with the English rebels, he went over to Charles on the grounds that the very wording of the Covenant bound its adherents to defend their king.

In 1644, with the rank of Lieutenant-General and the title of Marquis, Montrose raised an army of Highland clansmen and a number of their Irish relatives, and defeated Covenanting forces at Tippermuir near Perth. He then marched his men northwards towards Aberdeen; and made a decision which was to haunt his reputation long after his death. Although an enlightened disciplinarian throughout most of his career, on this occasion he allowed his troops to run wild through the city, looting and indulging in indiscriminate slaughter, raping women and taking some off as virtual slaves. The hideous day was known in Aberdeen thereafter as 'Black Friday'.

Now Argyll came on the scene with a force of some 4,000 in the hope of putting an end to his erstwhile associate's betrayal of the Covenant. Montrose headed through Strathbogie to Speyside, and began a game of hide-and-seek through the eastern glens and moors, awaiting reinforcements from the west. While these were on their way he turned his men south through Badenoch to Atholl before wheeling eastwards through Angus to approach Aberdeen again. With the onset of winter it was generally assumed on both sides that the armies would be disbanded for the season. But Montrose's right-hand man, Alasdair Macdonald, had by now brought more clan chiefs and their followers to join Montrose, and proposed a daring plan to march through the snow and take the hated Argyll unawares in his home at Inveraray. The flamboyant, impetuous Macdonald had Irish blood in him. His father had been known as *Coll Ciotach* ('left-handed'), a name which descended to Alasdair as 'Colkitto'. His kinsmen, the Macdonalds of Glencoe, had long been at feud with the Campbells and gladly provided guides for the venture. It proved so successful that Argyll himself had to flee down Loch Fyne from his burning stronghold before he could muster enough forces to turn back against the invaders.

Well satisfied with their achievement, Montrose's men retired up the Great Glen, only to learn that Covenanting troops had set out from Inverness to intercept them. They turned cunningly back through the hills south of Loch Ness and took Argyll by surprise once more. The two armies met at Inverlochy castle in Lochaber, a square fortress once belonging to the Comyn family, with heavy drum towers which even in ruin present to this day a staunchly defiant appearance. Those walls looked down now on the slaughter of 1,500 Campbells, and another flight across the water by their chieftain.

Montrose and his inspired Colkitto rampaged through the eastern Highlands and the Grampians. In the north they scored another triumph at the battle of Auldearn and repeated this at Alford, where the hapless Argyll was almost killed by a Macdonald. Then they headed south to yet another victory at Kilsyth near Glasgow. Montrose felt the time had come to march into England in King Charles's cause and back the Royalists fighting there; but found himself with little support in the Lowlands, and watched bitterly as the Highlanders decided to go back home rather than continue into alien country. A pitiful handful of remaining troops, largely Irish, were routed at Philiphaugh outside Selkirk. Here the Covenanters took savage revenge on the Irish in return for the butchery in Aberdeen.

After vain attempts to raise another army Montrose fled to the Continent, where he was later to learn of the execution of Charles I. Transferring his devotion to Charles II, who appointed him Lieutenant-Governor and Captain-General in Scotland, he raised a force of mercenaries and landed in Caithness via Orkney. By now despondently aware of Charles's readiness to sign the Covenant in order to win Scottish backing, and knowing what little chance he himself stood in the middle of such politicking, Montrose and his small force were easily defeated at Carbisdale, near Invershin in Sutherland. On the run, he was taken by MacLeod clansmen to their chief at Ardvrech castle on the shore of Loch Assynt. Neil MacLeod promptly put him in the dungeon and notified the Parliamentarians. He was rewarded, but did not enjoy the spoils for long. The MacKenzies, outraged by this breach of Highland hospitality, sacked Assynt and at the Restoration seized all MacLeod's lands. The ruins of their own Calda house beside the loch stand not far from those of Ardvrech.

Under the gloating gaze of his old enemy Argyll, Montrose was hauled on a cart through Edinburgh to be hanged in the Grassmarket. His head was displayed on the Canongate Tolbooth; but ten years later Argyll's head, too, was set up on the spike. Charles II, restored to his throne, had learned just how deeply Argyll had plotted with the Cromwellians.

During Cromwell's campaigns in the Highlands and Grampian he had been determined to get his hands on the Honours of Scotland – the Scottish regalia – rather as if, like Edward I and the Stone of Scone, he felt this would give him moral power over the country. In 1651 the crown, sceptre and sword were sent for safety to Dunnottar castle, a clifftop fortress of the Earls Marischal of Scotland from the fourteenth century, south of Stonehaven. On its rocky height it still looks fearsome; but Cromwell battered it into submission with cannon-fire, only to find that the crown jewels had gone. The wife of the minister of Kinneff church had smuggled them out in a linen basket, and for nine years they lay beneath the floor of the Old Kirk until the Restoration and their return to Edinburgh castle. Grainger, the minister, is commemorated within the little building:

> He who his country's honour saved below,
> Now wields a sceptre in the realms of bliss.

The interpretation of the concept of honour seems in many cases to have been less noble than Mr Grainger's and very much a matter of personal appetite. John Graham, 'Bluidy Clavers', whom we have already seen in action in Galloway, was to leave just as horrific an imprint on the east. A kinsman of that other Graham, Montrose, his harassment of Covenanters was fired by fervent episcopalian convictions which had certainly not been shared by the Marquis. In 1679 he miscalculated the strength of the conventiclers, and was defeated at the battle of Drumclog; but made up for this, in company with the Duke of Monmouth, at Bothwell Bridge, after which rebels or supposed rebels all across the country were fined, dispossessed, tortured, or deported in their hundreds to the American colonies.

With the coming of William III, Claverhouse stirred up further strife by espousing the cause of the banished King James, who had created him Viscount Dundee, and rallying clan chiefs to him at Dundee. His main opponent was General Hugh Mackay of Scourie in Sutherland, who after some inconclusive manoeuvrings confronted 'Bonnie Dundee' in the pass of Killiecrankie, below Blair Atholl, whose castle the Jacobites had already seized. Today the steep flanks of the pass shine golden with gorse and broom in summer sunshine, one of the loveliest stretches of the A9 on its way towards crowded Aviemore. It may have been just as picturesque, but certainly less conducive to contemplation, on the July day in 1689 when Claverhouse encouraged his outnumbered clansmen to launch one of their terrifying Highland downhill charges from the heights of the gorge. The effect was devastating: the enemy were swept into the turbulent waters of the river Garry, and Mackay fled with the remainder of his force towards Stirling. What he did not know at the time, and what put paid to Jacobite hopes for many years to come, was that during the battle Claverhouse himself had been killed by a musket ball in his side. A National Trust visitors' centre at Killiecrankie displays the whole story of the battle, along with details of local natural history; and there are a Claverhouse memorial stone and the 'Soldier's Leap' across the river.

Aberdeen has from its earliest days been one in a string of ports, large and small, serving North Sea trade routes and the fishing industry. Wool, leather and coal were shipped out; timber from the Baltic and manufactured goods from France and the Low Countries were imported. Many erstwhile customers came as immigrants or at least visited often enough to leave their mark on the place: Flemish influence is clear in the little harbours of north-east Fife. Some of the more exposed ports all around the coast, such as Avoch in the Black Isle, have houses built end-on to the sea, not only to shelter the main frontages but so that fishing boats could be drawn up between them in stormy weather.

As trade declined, fishing grew more important; but this, too, inexorably became the province of larger vessels and larger companies, and while the little boats of Crail and Pittenweem eked out an inshore living, the fleets of Aberdeen expanded. Until World War II, Anstruther was the most important of all the herring fishery centres. Today the strict international controls on catches and the need for conservation of breeding grounds have caused headaches all the way up the coast.

There have always been international headaches of one kind and another. In the fifteenth century James III offered bounties and concessions to east coast fishermen in order to compete with Dutch and German boats scouring Scottish waters. Aberdeen became famous for its cod, exporting so much that in Flanders the fish became known colloquially as *abberdaan*. By the eighteenth century, trade was brisk enough for some fishermen to keep two boats – one for inshore fishing, one for wider-ranging operations. It was in that century that the great herring boom began. In order to move fish in large enough quantities and get it to market in good condition, merchants and curers on the Caithness coast arranged regular contracts with the fishermen, setting up curing and pickling facilities which made it possible to distribute herring not only throughout Britain but also as far away as the West Indies. In a good season there might be 200 boats landing more than 10,000 barrels. By the middle of the nineteenth century two-thirds of the catch from under the sea was being transported back across the sea to Germany, eastern Europe and Russia. In 1907 it was recorded that some two and a half million barrels of herring had been cured that year.

The first steam drifter was built in Aberdeen in 1868, but the expense was such that local fishermen did not really begin investing in steam-powered vessels until the turn of the century. This went hand in hand with the development of trawling for white fish, which led to Aberdeen becoming, during the thirty years after 1880, the fastest growing town in Scotland. In spite of restrictions it remains one of the three major fishing harbours, along with Peterhead and Fraserburgh. Their rivals on the west coast, including Ullapool, have switched by necessity from herring to mackerel, a great deal of it for export to the Soviet Union.

Fishermen have always been, by nature, grumblers; but in the 1980s they have been given good reason for worry. Quite apart from curbs on herring fishing, heavy cuts in North Sea cod and haddock quotas were recommended by marine scientists and introduced under Common Market regulations in 1988. The number of men in Grampian managing to make a living out of fishing dropped from 11,000 to 9,000 in six years, and by early 1989 seemed likely to lose another couple of thousand. Many men who had taken out mortgages on expensive new boats and equipment were faced with high interest charges in an industry less able to offer them an adequate income.

South of Aberdeen, Stonehaven had a herring fleet of over a hundred in the 1880s. Today there are more pleasure craft than fishing boats within the arms of its harbour, and the historic Tolbooth in the Old Town is now occupied by a small local museum and tea shop. An annual fair is held, not for its original purpose but for the entertainment of participants in period costume – the Feeing Market, recalling the common practice of 'feeing' or hiring farm and other employees for a year.

North of Aberdeen, Fraserburgh and Peterhead face the sea from an exposed coast whose cliffs match the defensive aspect of Kinnaird and Inverallochy castles, though Kinnaird's ruins are now less important than the lighthouse rising from them. Fraserburgh, original seat of Clan Fraser, for ten years had its own university, established in 1595 but closed after its principal quarrelled with James VI. Within Peterhead's wave-lashed harbour, one of whose granite breakwaters was built by convict labour from stone hewn out of the headland of nearby Buchan

Ness, the scene is still colourful enough, but may not be so within another decade. Its Arbuthnot Museum nostalgically tells the story of a busier past in whaling and seal fishing, together with displays of Arctic wildlife.

A grimmer, if very proud, memorial is that of the Fraserburgh life-boat shed, still alive with the spirits of a crew who perished in 1970. On the evening of 20 January a Danish fishing vessel, the *Opal*, had set out from Buckie in Banffshire for the Fladden fishing grounds, to find later that night that its engine-room was flooding and the pumps had packed up. It made radio contact with Skagen in Denmark, and Wick and Peterhead coastguards were also alerted to the situation. Although it proved impossible to find a substitute pump in the time available, the Fraserburgh life-boat, the *Duchess of Kent*, decided to set off in the teeth of a gale at 6.30 a.m. to ensure that at any rate the crew of the *Opal* should be saved. At the same time, without the RNLI being informed, two Russian vessels and two others had converged on the stricken boat to offer assistance, a helicopter had taken off one of the Danish crew, and by the time the life-boat got there a Russian trawler had the *Opal* in tow. Without warning a large wave broke over the port bow of the *Duchess of Kent* and capsized her. One of the Russian ships moved in to right the boat and save the only one of its crew who had been able to swim free. The life-boat and the trapped corpses were taken by the Russians to Buckie.

An official enquiry at the Sheriff Court House, Aberdeen, concluded that life-boat rescue operations must, by their very nature, be extremely hazardous, and that no blame could be attached to those who decided to launch the boat or to the coxswain and crew.

In the same year as the building of its first steam drifter, Aberdeen had launched a vessel of a very different kind. Thomas Glover, a Scottish shipowner and trader in Nagasaki, was influential in placing a contract for three warships for the newly emergent Japanese navy. The first of these, the 1,500-ton *Ho Sho Moru*, was launched from Alexander Hall's shipyard in 1868, to be followed by two more and, in the same period, five merchant vessels. Hall's also built a dock and sent it in sections for reassembly at Kosuge, laying the foundation of what was to become the vast Mitsubishi shipbuilding concern. Glover grew wealthy as consultant to the firm, and married a Japanese wife. Their son survived the Nagasaki atomic bomb, but hanged himself a few days later, leaving all his money towards the city's rebuilding.

The deployment of British warships in home waters had presented some problems towards the end of the eighteenth century. The threat of war with France, always uppermost in military minds and especially so as the shadow of Napoleon fell across the Channel, caused concern to both naval and merchant ship operators. From time to time plans had been implemented for canals through various parts of Britain so that goods could be shipped in safer conditions than those faced by coastal traffic. Around Scotland there were also natural hazards to be faced: the currents and storms of the Pentland Firth, Cape Wrath and the Atlantic coast. For defence purposes, for an easier flow of freight, and for 'civilizing and improving the Highlands of Scotland and securing the peace and loyalty of its inhabitants', there had for years been a growing demand for a canalization of the Great Glen to provide a continuous waterway right across the country.

The fault-line of this trench, cutting a south-westerly diagonal from the Moray Firth to the Firth of Lorn, appeared during the birth of the Caledonian mountains, when there must have been a mighty lateral shift of rocks, tearing open a rent in the earth's crust. The gap can never have presented a great physical impediment to anyone wishing to cross; yet the granite rocks of the Cairngorms and eastern highlands are different from those to the west, and the glen itself somehow became a symbolic dividing line between clans to either side.

Within the cleft lie four lochs: the Firth of Inverness feeds down the River Ness into Loch Ness, most celebrated for its mythical monster and the tourist trade which colourful legend has created; Loch Oich and Loch Lochy are pinched into the narrower central section; and from Fort William onwards Loch

Linnhe broadens towards the Atlantic and its fringe of islands. If the lochs could be linked, stormy round trips could be eliminated and warships, supply ships and men could be shifted in sheltered conditions. Money for such a project could be made available from the Forfeited Estates Fund. There was every incentive to proceed.

The feasibility of such a short-cut sea-to-sea ship canal had been surveyed by James Watt in 1773, and John Rennie prepared a second scheme in consultation with Watt in 1793. It was not, however, until the turn of the century that construction from Fort William to Inverness began under the supervision of Thomas Telford, with the assistance of an eccentric engineer. Matthew Davison had started his working life with Telford as a mason in Langholm, Dumfriesshire. After assisting his master on projects in the south, such as the superb Welsh aqueduct of Pontcysyllte, he seems not to have relished the return to his own country as resident engineer on the Inverness end of what was to be the Caledonian Canal. The poet Southey, who took a keen interest in progress on the waterway, heard any number of tales about Davison when he visited Inverness, and summed up:

> He was a Lowlander who had lived long enough in England to acquire a taste for its comforts, and a great contempt for the people among whom he was stationed here; which was not a little increased by the sense of his own superiority in knowledge and talents ... He used to say, of Inverness, that if justice were done to the inhabitants there would be nobody left there in the course of twenty years but the Provost and the Hangman.

One of his colleagues reported in a letter that, despite his own Scottish birth and background,

> Mr Davison declares he would not accept a seat in Heaven if there were a Scotsman admitted into it.

Nevertheless Telford had great faith in his assistant's technical abilities. Other abilities were also called for, above and beyond mere engineering matters. To get the job done on time there was need of a regular, reliable labour force. This seemed forthcoming, drawn from men of Caithness and other Highland regions where the land enclosures of 'improvement' had driven many from their traditional occupations. But even these labourers would wander back to more familiar part-time work during the harvest or the best fishing season; and during the winter no Highlander was accustomed to doing any work anyway. On top of all this, obtaining supplies of oatmeal to feed the workers was often difficult, and provided another excuse for men to quit the arduous job and go in search of subsistence elsewhere. Accommodation had to be built for them; but materials and skilled craftsmen were rare, and often the promised funds for successive stages of the project did not arrive on time. Still the houses were built somehow, and solidly enough to withstand the passage of the years. At Muirtown basin, planned as a second harbour for Inverness, Clachnaharry village consists largely of single-storey dwellings for the canal workers, smart in whitewashed walls with black doors and black shutters, matching the maintenance workshops and black and white lock gates. Close to the impressive sea lock is the swing bridge carrying the Highland Railway on its scenic route to Kyle of Lochalsh (damaged in a gale in 1989).

In spite of technical and human setbacks, the canal was opened in 1822, partly reconstructed in the 1840s, and reopened in 1847. As a bonus, traffic between its western end and the Clyde was greatly assisted by completion of the Crinan Canal across the Mull of Kintyre from Ardrishaig to Loch Crinan. But much of the original purpose of offering a passage to sailing warships and coastal traders between the east and west coasts was by now irrelevant: by the time it was finished, the war with France had long been over, privateers no longer preyed on merchant shipping, and before the waterway could prove its purely commercial worth, steam had begun to replace sail. Still, passengers on smaller vessels found the route an enjoyable one, and MacBrayne's excursion steamers plied a busy trade through the Crinan and Caledonian canals in the late nineteenth century.

Certainly the canal was and remains one of the most noteworthy engineering achievements in all Britain. The great summit cutting at Laggan between Loch Oichy and Loch Lochy and the flight of eight locks at Banavie known as 'Neptune's Staircase' still merit unstinted admiration, not just for their practicality but for the beauty of their design. Unlike Wade's roads, little restoration needed to be done by successors. Apart from about two hours before and after low water, boats may enter the eastern end of the Caledonian canal at any state of the tide, a result achieved by thrusting two parallel embankments a good 400 yards out into Beauly firth from Clachnaharry and its deeply muddy shore, with locks at each end of the channel thus enclosed.

Gates of the sea locks were built of Welsh oak to resist the action of sea water, but those of the freshwater locks were of cast-iron sheathed with pine from Memel on the Baltic. The ironwork on the western side of the summit also came from Wales, shipped from Chester.

In 1822, the year of the canal's opening, another great boon was offered to Scotland. King George IV arrived in Edinburgh, the first Hanoverian monarch to set foot in this part of his kingdom; and, flamboyant as ever, he displayed himself in full Highland rig.

Proscription of wearing the kilt, tartan and other nationalistic costume had been lifted in the 1780s when it became apparent that there was little further danger from the once lawless clans. At its worst the ban had, in any case, been strictly applied only in Scotland itself. The growing numbers of Scottish regiments raised to tame the savagery not of their own folk but of natives in distant parts of the British Empire were allowed to make a feature of such distinctive dress. Officers stationed in London formed a Highland Society, wore the kilt, sang old ballads and bawdy songs, and were reputed to drink inordinate quantities of whisky. One of the founding members was James Macpherson, self-proclaimed translator of the poetic fragments of Ossian – a supposedly third-century Celtic bard – most of them actually contrived by Macpherson himself while employed as a tutor in the household of the Earl of Hopetoun at Moffat. In fact he could not speak a word of Gaelic, but these spurious echoes from a world of heroic daydream suited the mood of the day, and contributed to a romantic reassessment of the Highland image. From being intolerable barbarians, the clansmen had become noble savages. Instead of being persecuted, they must be regarded as a unique, endangered species whose customs and clothing should be preserved at all cost.

Some of the dress was, in fact, as dubious in its authenticity as the verses of Ossian. The much admired kilt was itself an invention of the 1720s. The belted plaid had for centuries been the most characteristic everyday wear. It is ironic that the 'traditional' garment romantically associated with the Highlander should in fact have been a product of the industrial age, and probably the invention of an Englishman, at that! Thomas Rawlinson, a Quaker ironmonger from Lancashire, set up a forge in Glengarry and engaged local labour to work in it and to supply timber from the Macdonald chieftain's estates around Loch Ness. A full swathe of plaid was a hot thing to wear in a forge, so Rawlinson is said to have sent for a regimental tailor from Inverness and, with his help, devised a new garment suitable for the workers: cutting off the top of the belted plaid, they created the short pleated kilt as we know it today. The story is indignantly repudiated by many patriotic wearers of the garment, but it is interesting to note that the very word is not of even remotely Gaelic origin: 'kilt' derives from Scandinavia, as in the Danish *kilte op*, to tuck up.

The savage grandeur of that other contemporary creation, the Celtic Homeric 'Ossian', appealed to devotees of 'the sublime' all over Europe. An even more influential figure was Sir Walter Scott, with his chivalric tales and mystical landscapes. Musicians were to seize on his fictions as plots for their operas and dramatic overtures. Painters were lured by his florid scenic descriptions to visit the places he depicted, and set about their own interpretations. And when George IV arrived in Scotland, Scott was ready to give of his best.

As master of ceremonies, the novelist devised glittering pageantry, masques, theatrical performances, receptions and publicity worthy of the most skilled modern advertising agency. When 'our Fat Friend' (as Scott referred privately to his monarch) arrived at Leith in the *Royal George*, towed by the steam tug *James Watt*, crowds thronged the quayside, and there were cheering crowds all along his route into the centre of Edinburgh. He wore a kilt, though prudently added pink tights underneath. Kilt, sporran and tartan trimmings proved a godsend to local tailors: not merely was such dress permissible now, but it had the seal of royal approval, and manufacturers hurried to devise different patterns and persuade the gentry that each family should have its own special tartan.

Scott's lingering influence was to affect – or infect – another monarch, Queen Victoria. After a couple of visits to Scotland she set her heart on finding a home there, and used Scott's works much as an estate agent's list. Her royal physician praised the fine air of Deeside, and steered her towards Balmoral castle, which she described as 'a pretty little castle in the old Scottish style'. She and her beloved Albert first took it on lease from the Earl of Aberdeen, but within a few years coveted it as their own. Once it had been acquired, Albert set about transforming it into something grander. In September 1853 he laid the foundation stone for a new castle, built of bluish granite quarried from the estate, and two years later they formally moved into the new building with its Germanic machicolations, pepper-pot turrets and peaked gables. It became a favourite setting for escape from the cares of state in London, a focus for private picnics, the hunting and shooting of which Albert was so fond, and for quiet domestic evenings, less quiet when they indulged in the dancing of Scottish reels.

Later generations of the Royal Family have enjoyed regular holidays in the castle, though it is not as remote and secluded as it used to be. The public are allowed to visit and wander through the grounds during May, June and July, and there are such modern features as souvenir shops, a refreshment room and pony-trekking.

What has come to be slightingly called 'Balmorality' affected other buildings throughout the country. Gothic shooting lodges sprang up in every glen, sporting estates became the haunt not merely of the aristocracy but of the *nouveau riche*, and Highland costume was all the rage. Victoria had been disappointed on her first visit to Crathie church that not everyone was wearing kilts. She ordered her household to set an example by always wearing kilts in a special Balmoral tartan which she and Albert designed.

Albert condescendingly approved of the simplicity of 'our people in the Highlands' who, he wrote, were 'altogether primitive, true-hearted, and without guile'. Referring to a passing encounter with the Forbeses of Strathdon, he recorded:

> When they came to the Dee, our people offered to carry them across the river, and did so, whereupon they drank to the health of Victoria and the inmates of Balmoral in whisky, but as there was no cup to be had, their chief, Captain Forbes, pulled off his shoe, and he and his fifty men drank out of it.

Whether such producers of whisky as, say, the Macallan distillery, which matures its spirit in the most carefully chosen sherry-impregnated casks, would approve of such a lovingly tended product being tippled from a none too fragrant shoe is open to question.

Whisky is a product so much associated with Scotland that any good Scot might glower at the suggestion that it originated in Ireland, where there is a legend of St Patrick having been the first to disseminate the art. The word comes from the Gaelic *uisge beatha* or *usquebaugh* – 'water of life'. In spite of much mysticism attached to the process by devotees and shrewd manufacturers, the basic method is fairly straightforward and has altered little from the earliest private stills to modern commercial distilleries. In domestic and farmhouse production, malted barley was mixed with water and yeast in a pot still over a fire, the smoke from the peat adding a distinctive flavour. The quality depended to a large extent, as it still does, on the quality of the water: it has become almost an article of religious faith that only Highland water from a stream running swiftly down from the glens is suitable. Once the vapour has been condensed, it is diluted to about 110 per cent proof before being matured in oak casks. The maturation period must by law be at least three years, but the finest malt whiskies are allowed to lie much longer.

Although a so-called 'straight malt' or 'single malt' is the joy of the real connoisseur, far larger quantities of blended whisky are sold throughout Britain and abroad. These blends are brought about by mixing different malted spirits with grain (largely maize) spirit produced in a still process patented at the beginning of the nineteenth century.

The history of whisky distilling has had its ups and downs. Always anxious to slap taxes on anything that breathes, successive governments tightened regulation of private production. Some tenant farmers in the remoter hills set up illicit distilleries as the only method of 'converting our victual into cash for the payment of rent and servants'. After a bad harvest in 1644 the authorities restricted distillation to the nobility and the gentry for their own use, and when matters improved and production was more general again, imposed varying duties. Excise officers or 'gaugers' were sent around to check on quantities and strength of the product. Local operators had to set lookouts to watch for them and for robbers keen to smuggle barrels into England to avoid duty. Secret 'whisky roads' became as important as the drovers' roads, if rather less respectable. Gaugers and robbers were not the only dangers. One of General Wade's assistants recorded that of three English officers drinking raw spirit, one was smitten with gout, another with a fever, and the third lost all his hair.

The Highland remoteness of a region such as Glen Affric encouraged secret distilling and discouraged interference. On one occasion Customs officers who had broken up illicit stills were besieged in an inn by indignant residents, and in 1835 a

Revenue group which had been landed from the cutter *Atalanta* were set upon and chased all the way to Beauly.

More legitimately, a large export trade was later built up with the United States of America. The coming of Prohibition there struck a mortal blow to many distilleries. Small companies went out of business. One example, Glenturret outside Crieff, which at its peak had exported 90 per cent of its output to the USA, was not reopened until long after World War II. The Prohibition period is referred to throughout the whisky trade as 'the wasted years'.

One of the most remarkable concentrations of individual malt distilleries (though some of them operate under the umbrella of larger concerns and supply a proportion of their product for blending) is along a stretch of the swift-flowing river Spey, which rises some ten miles from Fort Augustus and runs past Kingussie, Aviemore and a string of little towns and villages each of whose names is familiar from different bottle labels. All the Spey valley was once the property of a family which gave its name not merely to one of the whiskies, Glen Grant, but to the sparkling main town of the region, Grantown-on-Spey. There is a Clan Grant Association, and the family mausoleum is in Duthill church on a bend of the road leading to so many distilleries. But the elegant Grant house of 1700 is now in the hands of Macallan, who have commendably restored it as a dignified office block and reception area.

Production in the region began, as elsewhere, in homes and farm buildings for personal use or for illicit sale to drovers and other travellers. One of the most famous names was established when a certain George Smith abandoned secret manufacture and legally registered his Glenlivet distillery. It was such a success that other firms appropriated the name, sometimes linking it to their own by means of a hyphen. In 1880 a lawsuit ended with the ruling that only the Smith distillery was entitled to use the name of 'The Glenlivet' unqualified.

Most single malt distilleries such as Glenlivet, Cardhu, Glengoyne and Tomatin are named after their situations rather than founders or proprietors. One of the smoothest Speyside whiskies may seem to carry a family name but it, too, derives from its actual place of origin: registered many years ago as Macallan-Glenlivet, it now stands confidently on its own merits as the aforementioned Macallan.

The hamlet of Macallan near Craigellachie stood above a ford across the Spey much used by cattle drovers. A local farmer profited from supplying them with his home-produced whisky until eventually he was persuaded that it would pay him to make the distillery legal. It has remained in the hands of the same family ever since, and has continued its tradition of distilling in small copper stills rather than acquiring the larger vessels installed by most competitors. Until comparatively recent times it followed the old practice of cleaning out vessels with brooms made of heather collected from the surrounding countryside. Also it retains a hallowed method of maturing the spirit which gives it a distinctive flavour. Whisky has always lain most satisfactorily in oak casks which previously contained sherry. Because of changing procedures in the shipment of sherry and the gradual elimination of wooden casks, most distilleries have abandoned the practice. The Macallan, however, insist on maintaining it: they go so far as to pay for the manufacture of such casks in Spain, leasing them out to bodegas to be filled with the best Oloroso, and after a few years reclaiming them to be filled with maturing whisky. This gives the resultant drink its bouquet and unmistakable flavour.

Many distilleries now offer travellers conducted tours, an explanatory visitor centre and tastings. A 'Whisky Trail' encompassing several major sites is advertised by tourist boards, but is best followed by coach passengers rather than the individual driver who can too easily imbibe more than is advisable. One other word of advice might be proffered: do not grow too enthusiastic on Speyside about the joys of other delectable whiskies waiting at the far end of the Road to the Isles.

SELECTED SITES OF INTEREST

Antiquities

CHAPEL OF GARIOCH   A red granite pillar beside a by-road 1 mile north-west of the village. Wonderfully preserved Pictish stone carved with figures of a man, fish, cross, strange beasts, and the familiar Z-rod and mirror-and-comb symbols.

CULLERLIE   13 miles west of Aberdeen, a tidy, compact stone circle enclosing some tiny cremation cairns.

CULSH   13 miles north-east of Ballater, an Iron Age 'earth-house' or souterrain strengthened with heavy boulder walls and roofed with large slabs.

LOANHEAD OF DAVIOT   About 4 miles north-west of Old Meldrum, a ring cairn at the centre of a ring of recumbent stones, with neighbouring cremation pits and cairns.

MEMSIE   3 miles south-west of Fraserburgh, a huge cairn about 25 yards in diameter, which may owe its impressive size and height to the addition of stones from two other cairns which once formed part of a group.

(*For a general study of the foregoing see also Chapter 1.*)

Historic Buildings

ABERDEEN   The massive single-arched 1320 bridge, Auld Brig o' Don, repaired early in the seventeenth century. Compare with seven-arched Bridge of Dee, built in 1500, decorated with heraldic carvings.

CRATHES   Castle and gardens. The original seventeenth-century building is a striking example of a Scottish tower house with richly painted ceilings in the Chamber of the Nine Nobles, the Chamber of the Nine Muses, and the Green Lady's Room. Eight gardens neatly enclosed by early eighteenth-century yew hedges.

ELGIN   Cathedral founded 1224, known as the Lantern of the

North. Burned 1390 by the Wolf of Badenoch, and allowed to fall further into ruin after the Reformation.

PLUSCARDEN Abbey 6 miles south-west of Elgin, founded 1230 and burned by the Wolf of Badenoch at about the same time as his burning of Elgin cathedral. In 1948 it was restored to monastic use by monks from Prinknash abbey in Gloucestershire.

TUGNET On Spey Bay, 5 miles west of Buckie, a large early nineteenth-century ice house accommodates an exhibition of Speyside history, fishing and wildlife.

TYNET St Ninian's chapel, 3 miles east of Fochabers, was built in 1755 by the local laird, supposedly as a sheep-cote but in fact as a centre for secret celebration of the Mass. It now claims to be the oldest post-Reformation Catholic church still in use.

Museums

ABERDEEN Gordon Highlanders Regimental Museum in regimental HQ, Viewfield Road, displays collections of uniforms, campaign medals, colours and banners, with a special Victoria Cross exhibition.

ALFORD Grampian Transport Museum, with collection of road vehicles, and railway souvenirs in Alford's old railway station.

ELGIN Elgin Museum has displays of local natural history, and a celebrated collection of geological specimens and fossils, especially of the Old Red Sandstone.

PITMEDDEN Garden and Museum of Farming Life on the outskirts of the village, built around an elaborate garden laid out in the seventeenth century with pavilions and fountains. Agricultural and domestic implements are housed in the museum, and there are woodland walks and a Visitor Centre with explanatory material and garden exhibitions.

9

· The Isles

THOSE WHO may have ventured along the 'Whisky Trail'
organized for tourists by a string of Speyside distilleries
can undertake another such pilgrimage in the Western Isles,
though more informal and involving a number of ferries to
mix the waters with the spirit. Connoisseurs are only too happy
to hold forth on the relative merits of Highland and Island
single malts, and no two are ever likely to agree; but in general
it may be said that Speyside whiskies are smoother, while the
island whiskies – especially those of Islay – are quite fiery.
Otherwise the story is much the same: domestic pot stills,
illicit production, smugglers and gaugers, and ultimately the
respectability of open commercial manufacture and the open
discussion and fervent advertising of subtle variations in water
and peat flavours. Even as far north as Orkney there is a
distillery which has been operating since 1798.

In the early 1970s an English composer, fascinated by
the historical, mystical and musical resonances of the Orkney
islands, restored a tumbledown croft on Hoy, founded the
annual St Magnus Festival of music and drama, and became
the latest in a long, long line of settlers contributing to the
development and variety of the northern outliers. Peter
Maxwell Davies (now Sir Peter) was very conscious of the
traditions of the place, and most vividly expressed this awareness in his *Stone Litany* and *Solstice of Light*.

The first sequence is an evocation of Maes Howe, a great
chambered cairn on a rocky knoll about 4 miles north-east of

Stromness. This is one of the most skilfully designed Neolithic tombs known in Europe, with a large central chamber and side cells sturdily and even elegantly made of rock beams so well shaped and balanced that they look almost like neatly cut timber. Alterations were made over the centuries; and at some stage, or probably at more than one stage, grave robbers removed the buried chieftains and their grave goods. Quite late on in its existence, after some 3,000 years or more, the Vikings broke in, boasted of having acquired a great gold treasure, and gouged a number of runic inscriptions into the walls. Maxwell Davies used five of these as the basis for his composition, with a wordless voice invoking the eerie, timeless quality of the site. He finished, perhaps with his tongue in his cheek, by altering one piece of ancient graffiti – 'Hermund of the hard axe carved these runes' – to 'Max the Mighty carved these runes'.

The *Solstice of Light* is an even wider-ranging conjuration of the past. To a text by the Orcadian poet and novelist George Mackay Brown, the composer chronicles successive waves of incomers, beginning with rovers who 'rowed blindly north and north'. Melting of the primeval ice is depicted in a clamorous organ solo; the 'earth breakers, hewers of mighty stone' who built Maes Howe and the stone circles are recalled once more; and then comes a procession of Pictish farmers, fishermen, priests, Vikings, and at last St Magnus, whose protection against new threats such as the oil and uranium industries is sought in a final prayer.

A great deal of early history survives in stone in both the Nordreys and the Sudreys – the Viking names for the Northern Isles (Orkney and Shetland) and the Southern Isles (Man and the Hebrides). The ceremonial circle at Callanish on Lewis incorporates a chambered cairn which must have been of great regal or priestly significance to have been placed so close to the tall central pillar. The Ring of Brodgar on Orkney has lost some of its original 60 monoliths, but the remaining stones and their encircling ditch are still awe-inspiring, raising a score of questions about the everyday life and beliefs of folk who left such enduring memorials. At Skara Brae by the edge of the bay of Skaill, on Orkney Mainland, a Neolithic village from about 3000 BC has been preserved in wonderful condition thanks to its having been virtually buried by blown sand. Its houses are all of much the same pattern, with one main room surrounded by cupboards and cubicles in the solid walls. Remains of stone beds with high corner posts suggest that hides might have been stretched over them as a canopy. There were even kitchen dressers of stone, with shelves of the Old Red Sandstone flags which underlie most of Orkney's gently undulating landscape. The villagers had every advantage for leading a well-organized and fruitful life: this group of islands, for all its exposure to ocean gales, has a fairly mild climate and (with the exception of bleak Hoy) a fertile soil, so that such a settlement could rely on agriculture, stock-rearing, collecting shellfish along the shore, and fishing.

It is said of the two northern groups that an Orcadian is a farmer with a boat, a Shetlander a fisherman with a croft. Separated by 50 miles of sea, these archipelagos differ both geologically and in character. Shetland retains far more Norse influences, in its dialect as in its customs and even its inhabitants' facial characteristics. It is shaped by some of the oldest rocks in the world, fissured by faults of which one is probably the northern end of the Scottish Great Glen. On this lies a thin soil, heathery moorland and peat beds. Fishing was always more profitable than tackling such unpromising land, and attracted both rivalry and profitable trade from other European countries. This in turn helped the Orkney–Shetland relationship: in 1701, in *A Brief Description of Orkney, Zetland, Pightland Firth and Caithness*, the Rev John Brand wrote of

the Advantage that these Isles do reap by their Neighbourly Commerce with one another, for as Zetland could not well live without Orkney's Corns, so neither could Orkney be so well without Zetland's Money.

That spelling of the name derives through several stages from the Norse *Hjaltland*, which appeared also as Hetland and Yetland and then, since in early Scots the letter Y was written as Z, as Zetland. The county council and other bodies still use that form rather than Shetland.

The coasts of Shetland, close to Scandinavia and threatened by pirates of several nationalities, bristle with ancient defences. Forts and brochs sprang up on rocky promontories to watch over the waters. Ness of Burgi has a stone fort on a headland which, with its great rampart and gatehouse, would have excited the envy of even the builders of Tantallon in Lothian. The isle of Mousa, 12 miles south of Lerwick, has the mightiest of surviving brochs, over 40 feet high and with a stairway still accessible within its walls. Facing it across a narrow strip of water is the more ruinous broch of Burraland, as if the two of them had been set up to control traffic through that channel.

Brochs were once referred to as 'Pict houses', but archaeological research has shown that they pre-date the Picts by many centuries. Nevertheless it has been fairly well established that both Orkney and Shetland did belong to the Pictish empire in its heyday. The name of the Pentland Firth between Orkney and the Scottish mainland derives from a Norse formation defining it as the Pictland Firth. They were still in control when Christian missionaries began to venture into the region. Raiding Norsemen reported on two distinct kinds of people on the islands: Picts the size of pygmies who hid away underground for a large part of the day but 'did marvels in the morning and the evening, in building towns'; and white-clad *Papae* (missionaries sent by St Columba), who gave their name to a number of isles and places such as Papa Westray, Papa Stronsay and Papa Little.

A Shetland settlement offering a remarkable palimpsest of successive cultures is Jarlshof, where archaeologists have established an almost unbroken occupation from prehistoric days until the seventeenth century. Over 60 Neolithic round or oval dwellings have been exposed since the end of World War II, including evidence of some of the earliest cattle stalls in Britain.

In the wall of one house was set a whale's vertebra for use as a tethering post. At some period an Irish metal-worker took over a room in one house, and 2,000 years later his sand-filled casting pit and a number of broken moulds were found, showing clearly the kinds of axes, knives and Irish-style pins he fashioned. Pictish farmers continued working the land and fishing. Then Norse settlers took over and built longhouses, including one 30 yards long, with two substantial rooms: a living-room with a central hearth, and a kitchen with an oven and fireplace. This lasted a couple of centuries and then was superseded by another building of much the same character. A final phase was that of a seventeenth-century laird who built his house above remains of the buried settlement, on which Sir Walter Scott was to bestow the romantic name of Jarlshof.

It is clear that the Picts were unable to withstand the invasions of the Norsemen. Sporadic raids might be fought off; steady infiltration of settlers with entire families was to swamp them. Excavations in Orkney and North Uist show a continuation of many local farms, lands and customs, but under Norse rather than Pictish rule, suggesting that those of the earlier population who had not been wiped out were forced into subservience and possibly slavery.

The first use the Norsemen made of Orkney and Shetland was as bases for raids on Ireland and then on England. Towards the end of the ninth century, chiefs rebelling against King Harald Fairhair of Norway went so far as to launch attacks from here on their native land. Harald struck back with a major campaign against the Nordreys and pressed it on down the Hebrides and as far as the Isle of Man. The sequence of dates and actual events, as opposed to those dramatically embroidered in the Norse sagas, is confusing; but certainly at some stage Harald appointed a trusted follower, Rognvald of Møre, as first Earl of Orkney. This included Shetland, though the earldom rarely deigned to incorporate that name. Having extensive estates to cope with in Norway itself, Rognvald handed over responsibility to his brother Sigurd.

Norwegian kings, like English or Scottish kings, could rarely

rely on the loyalty of the men they had ennobled. Lords of the 'Old Earldom' began to dabble with the notion of acquiring more territory on the not too distant mainland or 'southern land' – hence Sutherland. Playing a familiar dynastic game, one Orcadian earl, Sigurd the Stout, married the daughter of King Malcolm II of Scotland. He was still, however, under the thumb of his own king, Olaf Tryggvason. A few years before this marriage Olaf, an assertive convert to Christianity, had offered the earl a choice between immediate baptism in Scapa Flow or immediate drowning in the same waters. Sigurd was not stout-hearted enough to argue. Earl Thorfinn the Mighty by the time of his death controlled Orkney, Shetland, and much of Caithness, Sutherland, and Ross and Cromarty; and after his death his widow Ingibjorg (surely 'Ingibjorg the fair widow' commemorated in one of the Maes Howe runic inscriptions) married Malcolm III – Malcolm Canmore. It took some time before cultural ties with Scotland became so much obviously stronger than those with remoter Norway that Scottish rulers debated means of shaking off Norse influences on islands so close to their own realm.

It was from Orkney that Harald Hardrada launched his fateful attack on England in September 1066, with some aid from Scotland. The Saxons under Harold Godwinsson defeated the invaders and killed Harald Hardrada himself; but then had to make a forced march back south to meet the threat of William of Normandy, which less exhausted troops might have been able to repel.

Still the Norwegian kings clung to their possessions. The very name of Dingwall recalls its function as the southern outpost of Norse rule: the *thing* or *ting* was a general council, and 'wall' is a corruption of *vollr*, meaning a field or meadow. Anxious to add more territory to his southern islands, Magnus Barelegs reached an agreement with King Edgar of Scotland in 1098 that Norway should be given all the Western Isles around which a ship could sail; and had his ship dragged across the narrow isthmus between West Loch Tarbert and Loch Fyne in order to claim the entire Kintyre peninsula as an island.

It was this same Magnus Barelegs whose voracity led to the emergence of the region's most celebrated native saint.

A gentler exponent of Christianity than Tryggvason was Magnus, joint heir to the earldom of Orkney. As a youth he was in the service of his royal namesake, Magnus Barelegs, but during a pointless battle which the king waged in the Menai Strait against two Welsh earls the younger man declared that he had no quarrel with anyone in that land and, instead of fighting, opened a psalter and occupied himself singing psalms. Later jumping ship, he found his way to the court of Edgar, King of Scots, son of that devout Margaret who had become second wife of Malcolm Canmore. Edgar took after his mother, and his piety must have strengthened Magnus in his convictions.

In 1106 Magnus reappeared in Orkney to claim his half-share in the earldom from his cousin Haakon, who had been favoured by Magnus Barelegs. He married a Scottish girl of noble descent, but both of them were so committed to religious austerity that the union was never consummated. He and Haakon managed their joint administration tolerantly enough until Magnus decided for some reason to make a protracted visit to London, where his friend Edgar's sister was now the wife of Henry I. In his absence Haakon reassumed absolute power; and was greatly displeased when eventually his cousin showed up again, this time with five armed ships. After some discussion it was arranged that the two men should meet on the small island of Egilsay in Easter week 1117, each backed up by two ships, to thrash out the problems of future administration.

It was obvious from the moment that Haakon arrived with eight ships what his intentions were. Magnus, instead of giving battle, surrendered and offered to go into retirement, to go on pilgrimage to the Holy Land, or to be blinded and confined in a dungeon for the rest of his life. The island council, the Althing, impatiently declared that they did not care which it was to be, but one of the cousins must die: they had had enough of two earls at a time.

Haakon had no intention of yielding. Magnus knelt, forgave his enemies, and asked the executioner to stand in front of him while cleaving his head open with an axe. His mother was given permission to bury the corpse in Christ's Kirk in Birsay, which soon became a place of pilgrimage in spite of the antagonism of Haakon and his subservient bishop to such practices. Later the bones were removed to a church in Kirkwall around which a cathedral was begun in 1137 by the martyr's nephew Earl Rognvald, the year after Magnus was canonized. The authenticity of the account of his last wish was verified in 1919, when an oak coffin discovered in one of the massive central pillars of the cathedral was found to contain the bones of a man whose skull had been cleft in precisely the way described. Ruins of a contemporary church on Egilsay, with a round tower in Irish style, also bear the name of St Magnus. In 1150 another church, the first of three towered churches on Shetland, was built with the same dedication at Tingwall, the administrative centre of Shetland and residence of the Archdeacon. This survived until the end of the eighteenth century, but was then demolished to supply stones for some drab Presbyterian kirks. Yet again inspired by a local theme, Peter Maxwell Davies composed a *Hymn to St Magnus* and his second opera, *The Martyrdom of St Magnus*, performed in the cathedral at Kirkwall during the 1976 and 1987 festivals.

In 1194 an attempt was launched from Shetland to depose King Sverre of Norway. The army of islanders taken to Norway were, however, soundly beaten, and Sverre decided to separate Shetland from the earldom. For almost two centuries it came under direct Norwegian rule. The Norwegians themselves undertook various retaliatory or acquisitive measures from time to time. Worried about increasing Scottish influence in the Western Isles and their blatant disregard of his own suzerainty, King Haakon was partly amused and partly angered by an offer from Alexander III of Scotland in 1263 to buy the Hebrides from him. Determined to teach the young upstart a lesson, he equipped a fleet and set out from Kirkwall towards the mainland. A storm drove some of his ships aground on the

Ayrshire coast. Near Largs those of his men who managed to get ashore were met by Alexander's army, and scattered in some confusion. It may not have been the magnificent feat of arms lauded by subsequent patriotic poets, but it was enough to send the Norwegians off to regroup on Orkney. They did not return. Haakon died at Kirkwall in the Bishop's Palace, a thirteenth-century building rebuilt in the sixteenth century and joined to a sumptuous Renaissance building next door by the despotic Earl Patrick, who was finally ousted and executed in Edinburgh after being allowed a few days in which to learn the Lord's Prayer.

By the 1264 Treaty of Perth, Norway kept Orkney and Shetland but renounced all claims to the Western Isles and the Isle of Man on condition that Alexander made a down payment of 4,000 marks compensation and a yearly tribute of 100 marks – the 'Annual of Norway' – in St Magnus cathedral, Kirkwall. In the following century Shetland was rejoined with Orkney, but the prevailing influences and the appointment of officials were increasingly Scottish rather than Nordic.

Some two centuries later King Christian I of the now joint kingdom of Denmark and Norway realized that the yearly instalments had been allowed to lapse and that an enormous debt had accrued. He demanded payment in full from James II of Scotland, who not only rejected any such liability but actually asked for Orkney and Shetland to be handed over to the Scottish crown. Arguments were still proceeding when James died. In September 1468 a marriage treaty was drawn up between his son James III and King Christian's only daughter Margaret, with some crucial financial clauses. The princess's dowry was agreed at 60,000 florins, of which 10,000 were to be paid within the year, the Danish-Norwegian crown lands of Orkney standing guarantee for the balance. Only 2,000 florins were forthcoming by the due date. In May 1469 the crown lands of Shetland were pledged for the outstanding amount. The following year Earl William St Clair yielded to James III all title to the earldom, and in 1471 the northern isles were annexed to the Scottish crown. Norse influences remained stronger for some time in Shetland than in Orkney, in long-house building style and several aspects of the legal system. The distinctive variant of Norse language known as Norn, however, succumbed gradually to the Scots tongue, though even today there are many local dialect words and pronunciations with ancient echoes.

Freed from the Danish king's nominal control of trade, the Shetlanders expanded their fishing trade. Each year during the summer, fleets of boats from the Hanseatic ports would come trading in the extensive markets set up by local merchants. The islanders operated their own salting and drying sheds to prepare fish for export to Germany. Even more numerous were the Dutch herring fishermen, whose trade at a market outside Scalloway was so great that its site is still called Hollanders' Knowe. Scalloway was then the islands' capital, but a rival market grew round the bay known as Ler Wick, and in due course a new capital was established at Lerwick.

A sturdy surviving example of a merchant's stone *bød* or booth can be found at Symbister on Whalsay, a Shetland isle which still supports a secluded little fishing community and provided a haven for the poet Hugh MacDiarmid between 1933 and 1942 while he wrote pungent attacks on profiteering absentee lairds who exploited crofters and fisherfolk alike.

One immigrant Dutchman has left his name firmly on the map. Jan de Groot settled on the north-eastern tip of Scotland at the end of the fifteenth century, and his descendants operated the first regular ferry service between the mainland and Orkney. Their Caithness base has become John o' Groats. Jan and other members of the family are buried in the medieval white-harled church at nearby Canisbay.

The Western Isles retain fewer traces of Norse rule than Orkney and Shetland, but are still commonly referred to in a description bestowed on them by those rulers. The name of the Hebrides comes from the Norse *havbredey*, meaning 'isles on the edge of the sea'. There are some 500 in all, of which about 100 are inhabited, divided into two groups with the North Minch, the Little Minch and the Sea of the Hebrides between them. The Outer Hebrides form a region designated the Western Isles, while administration of the Inner Hebrides is divided between Highland and Strathclyde. The principal outer islands, last stronghold of the Gaelic language, are Lewis, Harris, North and South Uist, Benbecula, Barra and remote St Kilda. The largest, harbouring 80 per cent of the population, are Lewis and Harris. The inner islands are Skye, Rhum, Eigg, Coll, Tiree, Mull, Staffa, Jura, Islay and Iona.

Iona has always had an importance out of all proportion to its size since St Columba's arrival at the Bay of the Coracle in AD 563. Missionaries went out from it throughout Scotland, northern England and the Continent. After a long period when Viking raids made it uninhabitable, a Benedictine abbey was built in the thirteenth century around traces of Columba's early settlement. Allowed to fall into ruin after the Reformation, it was restored in our present century. Two free-standing crosses have survived, the best preserved being St Martin's, with serpents and bosses of obviously Pictish origin, and figures on the reverse of David, Abraham and Isaac, and the Virgin and Child. A replica of a third cross stands before St Columba's shrine at the west door of the abbey. Nearly 50 kings of the Scots are said to lie buried on Iona, along with kings of Ireland and Norway, and several Lords of the Isles.

The designation of Lord of the Isles was one which vexed many of the mainland monarchs. The first significant, lasting name to emerge from the shadowy quarrels and conflicts of history is that of Somerled Macgillebride – Somerled meaning a 'summer wanderer' or Viking, though both his father and grandfather were named after Celtic saints, and he and his descendants were passionate upholders of 'the Gael' resistance to rulers in the faraway Lowlands. Somerled himself began as thane or self-styled 'Regulus' of Argyll, but then did battle with his brother-in-law in order to add a large portion of the Isles to his domain. Having signed a treaty with Malcolm IV with all the grand assumptions of equal regality, he soon broke it and launched an invasion of ships up the Clyde, only to be killed in the attempt. His lands were divided among his sons, and from one of his grandsons, Donald, descended the great MacDonald clan whose chiefs were to be Lords of the Isles for centuries and speak proudly of themselves as 'the sons of Somerled'.

One of the most influential of the family was Angus Og of Islay, who at the time of Bannockburn brought the clansmen of the west to form the strongest of Robert the Bruce's contingents. As a result the MacDonalds were granted lands and royal approval for their domination of the Isles. By the time of his death in 1387 John, son of Angus Og, was lord of all the Western Isles save for Skye. Unfortunately for the MacDonalds, Bruce had also bestowed sweeping powers on the Campbell clan on the mainland. When the MacDonalds grew arrogant and from their offshore territories caused trouble to successive kings of Scotland, the Campbells benefited.

In 1411 the then Lord of the Isles, Donald MacDonald, set out with an army estimated as being over 10,000 Highlanders and Islesmen to enforce his wife's claim to the earldom of Ross. There was even talk of his wishing to overthrow the Regent Albany and claim the throne of all Scotland for himself. After some early victories he was defeated some miles from Aberdeen by a Lowland army under the Earl of Mar, bastard son of the Wolf of Badenoch, in an encounter so bloody that the site was known ever after as Red Harlaw. Nevertheless he had achieved his aim in that his wife's title to the earldom was confirmed. It took his grandson John to lose all that his ancestors had acquired. When he succeeded in 1449 he could well say that he was monarch of all he surveyed; but, not content with this, he intrigued with Edward IV of England for a division of the Scottish kingdom and, on discovery by James III, forfeited a large part of his lands. His own son, another Angus Og, assembled enraged clan leaders and defeated him in a sea battle fought at Bloody Bay, north-west of Tobermory on Mull. Attempts to revive the old MacDonald hegemony failed, and James IV was to include in his denunciations of the detested, turbulent Highlands 'the wicked blood of the Isles'. In 1493 the lordship was declared forfeit to the Crown. The title is today automatically granted to the heir to the throne, in the present case Charles, Prince of Wales.

For most of the time Skye had managed to keep apart under a separate lordship. Its essential character is summed up in both Norse and Gaelic names: *skuy* ('cloud') and *Eilean a Cheo* ('Isle of Mist'). Even Skye, however, came eventually into the hands of John MacDonald when he had secured the earldom of Ross, and remained there after James III had seized the rest. Yet at the full height of their authority the Lords of the Isles were still not entirely masters of Skye. The other powerful family on the island, the MacLeods, was continually at odds with the MacDonalds, and the slopes and glens are dotted with scenes of their battles. Dunvegan castle above its loch has been the seat of Clan MacLeod since the early thirteenth century: the longest occupation of a castle in Scotland. Family relics on display include Rory Mor's drinking horn, the fif-teenth-century Dunvegan Cup, and a miracle-working 'Fairy Flag' of yellow silk which has supposedly twice come to the aid of the MacLeods and now has only one saving boon left. In grimmer mood is a 16-foot deep oubliette within the tower, into which shackled prisoners were dropped and left to rot.

A fairy element creeps into another celebrated feature of Skye. Generations of the MacCrimmon family were hereditary pipers to the MacLeods of Dunvegan, so skilled in the fashion-ing of complex variations on a set theme in the form known as a pibroch (from the Gaelic *piobaireachd*, a pipe tune) that they established what might almost be described as a classical tradition, and disheartened their rivals by attributing their genius to a magic chanter given to an ancestor by a fairy. In property granted by the laird across the loch from Dunvegan, the family duly established a college of piping at Boreraig. Today a small museum of family and musical history is over-looked by the MacCrimmon Memorial Cairn, to which descendants from all over the world make an annual pilgrimage.

One visitor to Dunvegan was to provide the world with much better-known music than that of the MacCrimmons, if rather less authentic after being watered down. In 1905

Marjory Kennedy-Fraser, a music teacher and lecturer from Perth, began visiting Barra, Eriskay and eventually Skye in search of original Gaelic songs which she set about adapting for drawing-room performance. Sincere and dedicated as she undoubtedly was, she did not speak Gaelic. The translations of original verse which filtered through helpful friends 'with the Gaelic' and then through her own tidying-up propensities were as prettified as the music whose awkward rhythms and melodic eccentricities she smoothed out to suit the ear of the average European listener.

Nevertheless she had conscientiously recorded cylinders of the original words and music sung by the local people, and so drew the attention of researchers not merely to the folk-songs but to social history and the wealth of tradition linked with everyday life and work. The sentimental ballads which so appealed to the Edwardian public were of less significance than the 'waulking songs' which were such an essential accompaniment to one staple craft of the Isles: the weaving and finishing of cloth. Teams of women would sit opposite each other across a long board on which cloth was spread, moistened with hot urine as a fulling agent whose chemical reaction removed natural greases and lanolin. They rhythmically kneaded the material with their hands or, when tired, their feet. Such a monotonous and skin-searing task demanded the equivalent of a sea shanty, steady and numbing until the job was finished.

The sheep which drove so many workers from their homes provided others with a livelihood. Spinning, weaving and knitting of wool by the island women contributed to the mixed economy of farming, fishing and any added part-time occupation which would help make ends meet. It is believed that the patterns so well known from Fair Isle knitters in the Shetlands came in a distant past from Spaniards who had learned them from Arab traders. The isle of Harris had its own distinctive tweeds, looked down upon as inferior to smoother fabrics until in the nineteenth century they became all the rage with the landed gentry and romantic tourists. Even remote St

Kilda could devote itself almost exclusively to the production of tweed. This had to be a domestic industry based on small individual production runs, integrated with other family routines; and each island jealously protected its trade name against imitators. Today, though, outworkers have dwindled in this as in every other craft. Harris tweed, its description and manufacturing area still delimited by law, is now dyed, spun, washed and packaged on an industrial estate just outside Stornoway on Lewis.

Such work had remained an essential standby after the eviction of families from Highland and Island farmsteads to make way for expanded sheep ranges, inexorably encroaching on the old steadings which had once raised basic food for those families and reasonably profitable cattle for export. The Hebrides, and Skye in particular, had been among the first to build up a healthy business in beef stock to the trysts of southern Scotland for sales onwards into English markets. To add to the normal hazards of moving a herd, the drovers from the island to the mainland had to face the crossing of a waterway which, narrow as it might be, was lashed by strong currents. Skye cattle were driven to the channel of Kylerhea to head for a landing a few miles north-west of Glenelg. There each beast was haltered and led into the water until, out of its depth, it was forced to swim. A string of seven or eight would be roped together, each fastened to the tail of its predecessor, with the leader's rope held by a man in a rowing-boat. Once they were ready, the boat was rowed across the unpredictable water to the mainland.

Islanders who had been forced to abandon the old ways of life in favour of sheep were, if lucky, rehoused in crofts along the coasts. Here, as well as striving to pay rents by working at home, both men and women were expected to provide their landlords with cheap labour, especially in the then busy kelping industry. Plentiful supplies of seaweed were collected, dried in the sun, and burned in shallow pits to produce potash for use in soap and glass manufacture, and other salts rich in iodine. Like so many rural industries, this waned when scientific advances produced cheaper and more efficient substitutes, leaving the crofters yet again in near poverty.

Living was hard at the best of times. A bad season or a change of attitude by speculative and often absentee landlords could threaten immediate starvation or a gradual recession in the demand for local crafts or produce. In 1882 a potato famine and savage gales left hundreds of families hungry and jobless, without food and without the wherewithal to pay their rents, which in spite of the obvious hardship and the general conditions of slump the landlords continued to demand. There were widespread demonstrations and a mounting taste for violence. Police forces were strengthened, and shiploads of Marines cruised in readiness for intervention around the Isles and along the coastal fringes of the Highlands. In 1882 some 600 crofters confronted a detachment of Marines who were attempting to arrest so-called ring-leaders at Glendale on the isle of Skye. One of these leaders, John MacPherson, died in the scuffle and became known as the Glendale Martyr. A monument in his memory, with a tribute also to the Glendale Land Leaguers who banded together against exploitation of crofters, stands a mile and a half east of the village.

In response not merely to local protest but to the indignation of a wider public aroused by newspaper reports, the Crofters Holdings (Scotland) Act was passed in 1886 to guarantee security of tenure. It took time to enforce, and some landlords still sought loopholes through which to drive tenants off the land, preferably on to emigré ships. Towards the end of 1887 one landowner decided to turn the whole of his Eishken estate into a deer park, provoking an invasion of crofters who killed several deer before being forced to withdraw by police and Marines. Demonstrations grew so menacing that the Riot Act had to be read in crofts near Stornoway.

By the middle of the 1920s the flight from the land and the appalling conditions upon it stimulated government intervention. Crofters were settled with government assistance on sheep farms in the Hebrides and Highlands. Although the part-time, diversified character of crofting resulted in some of these holdings remaining uneconomic for many years, a traditional way of life was doggedly preserved. Adjustments made after World War II and the gradual increase in population of the Western Isles' crofting 'townships' has saved whole areas from complete dereliction, in spite of condemnation by some sceptics of 'so-called crofters living on social security and tinned milk'.

Traces still remain of the most characteristic of crofters' dwellings, the 'black houses', particularly common on Barra, Eriskay and Lewis. The description of 'black house' could well apply to either the dark stone exterior, contrasting with later whitewashed cottages, or the interior blackened by peat smoke. Thick double layers of drystone walls were lined inside with peat or earth to keep out wind and rain. The roof, thatched with turf and heather, or sometimes straw, was supported on whatever wooden beams were available – often a con-glomeration of driftwood. Windows were usually small ones in the roof thatch. A hearth in the centre of the main room sent smoke wreathing up through a hole in the roof, helping to warm not only the family but also the animals, kept at the lower end of the same Norse-style longhouse, with one entrance shared by man and beast.

Dwellings like this were occupied until well into our present century. One can still find traces of whole townships, as at Centangaval on Barra, and a now ruined group at Garenin on Lewis which was abandoned only in the 1970s in favour of modern council houses nearby. A more solid survivor is one at Arnol which has been preserved as a black house museum. Another typical example has been reassembled at the Highland Folk Museum in mainland Kingussie.

There are less tangible and rather incongruous mementoes in Lewis and Harris of a very grand venture which came to nothing. In 1918 and 1919 Lord Leverhulme, the soap millionaire, became the largest landowner in Scotland when he bought both islands. Fired by some magnanimous dream he set about revivifying his new possessions by modernization of the crofting and fishing communities. One little port was renamed Leverhulme, and he planned busy fishing fleets which would supply a major cannery and the chain of shops famous as MacFisheries. He had a vision of Stornoway as a civilized centre not just for trade but for the arts and gracious living; not to mention provision of a cinema and the publication of a local daily newspaper. Distinguished friends were invited to his new home in Lews castle (today a school), and any member of the populace was welcome at his garden parties. Unhappily the islands had lost many of their young able-bodied men during World War I; many more were drowned at the entrance to Stornoway harbour when on their way home; the fishing industry was in decline; and a much less welcome incomer, the disease of tuberculosis, was one against which the islanders proved to have no ingrained resistance. By 1923 Leverhulme had decided to wrap up all his enterprises, and generously offered the islands back to their people, with free ownership of their crofts. Some critics say that it was the crofters themselves who, by sticking sullenly to their old ways and refusing to work in his well-meant factories, destroyed their best hopes for the future and at the same time destroyed Leverhulme's dream.

But when it comes to dreams, the most moving are those not of well-meaning incomers but of those forced to move out. For all the successes that Scotsmen have achieved abroad, and the enduring marks they have left on their adopted countries, there is always a note of yearning when they look back through the mists of the past and implore their lost world to become real and solid again and take them back. Most of the clan museums owe their existence to large endowments from the descendants of those clans now in Australia, New Zealand and especially in the 'New Scotland' of Nova Scotia and other tracts of Canada. Robert Louis Stevenson, seeking a warmer clime in which to fight off his lifelong weakness of the lungs, grew homesick for the debilitating smoke of Edinburgh and 'that dirty Water of Leith', though he realized full well that change, and the masons, and the pruning-knife, have been busy; and if I could hope to repeat a cherished experience, it must be on many and impossible conditions. I must choose, as well as the point of view, a certain moment in my growth, so that the scale may be exaggerated, and the trees on the steep opposite side may seem to climb to heaven, and the sand by the water-door, where I am standing, seem as low as the Styx. And I must choose the season also, so that the valley may be brimmed like a cup with sunshine and the songs of birds; – and the year of grace, so that when I turn to leave the riverside I may find the old manse and its inhabitants unchanged. It was a place in that time like no other.

After World War II a Crofters' Commission worked to make the crofting system viable in a competitive age. A vigorous Scottish Crofters Union was founded in 1986. Efficient ferry services between the islands and between them and the mainland made business and supply contacts easier. Some islands experienced a dangerous new prosperity in other fields – especially oil fields. In Shetland the local authorities were wise enough to ensure that revenues from the land leased for a huge terminal at Sullom Voe (*voe* meaning an inlet) should be invested in schools, libraries, community services and other amenities which would survive after the industrial complex is abandoned. Any nostalgic exile revisiting such scenes might not find them so rurally romantic as cherished visions had coloured them. But one must hope that there will be no cruelties or catastrophic slumps in the future to match those of the past, and no more emigrations of those condemned like their predecessors, in spite of healthier and more rewarding conditions elsewhere, to feel themselves forever 'exiles from our fathers' land':

> From the lone shieling of the misty island
> Mountains divide us, and the waste of seas –
> Yet still the blood is strong, the heart is Highland,
> And we in dreams behold the Hebrides.

SELECTED SITES OF INTEREST

Antiquities

BRIDGEND (Islay)   Dun Nosebridge, about half a mile south-east of Bridgend, a hilltop walled fort with lower ramparts and ditches, commanding wide views across the island.

CALLANISH (Lewis)   Chambered cairn and standing stones on a ridge 13 miles west of Stornoway. The roofless remains of the cairn lie beside a tall pillar at the centre of a circle, from whose rim run lines of megaliths to north, south, east and west.

CARLOWAY (Lewis)   Dun Carloway broch, 15 miles west of Stornoway, though much robbed of stones by later builders, still humps up imposingly with one side reaching about 30 feet. The internal structure, with its galleries and chambers, is clearly visible. Norsemen almost certainly used it at one period of its history, and there are tales of cattle raiders in medieval times taking advantage of its thick, sheltering walls.

CLICKHIMIN (Shetland)   A blockhouse fort with thick walls and massive gatehouse replaced a farmstead near Lerwick in about 700 BC. Later it was supplemented by a broch acting as a sort of castle keep, centuries later reverting to domestic use.

HOY (Orkney)   The Dwarfie Stane, about a mile and a half south of the Bay of Quoys, is a long sandstone block into which a passage and two burial chambers were carved, with a large square stone to seal the entrance. The name derives from Hoy legend in which it was the home of a local dwarf.

(*For a general study of the foregoing see also Chapter 1.*)

Historic Buildings

ARMADALE (Skye)   So-called castle, in fact basically an eighteenth century mansion largely burnt out in 1925 and replaced by a building which in its turn became dangerous and had to be partially demolished. At present its stable block houses an exhibition of Clan Donald, for long Lords of the Isles and rivals of the MacLeods at Dunvegan.

DOUNBY (Orkney) In working order, the click mill is the last survivor in Orkney of the horizontal watermills once common throughout the isles.

DUART (Mull) Duart castle, rearing above the Sound of Mull, grew from a simple thirteenth-century fortification into an imposing tower house with a well-protected courtyard. It became the property of the MacLeans, who lost it in the mid-seventeenth century; but a twentieth-century Fitzroy MacLean restored it. One room has an exhibition on the Boy Scout movement, Lord MacLean having been Chief Scout during the 1960s.

KIRKWALL (Orkney) The hall-house of the twelfth-century Bishop's Palace had a massive round tower added in the sixteenth century, and was linked in 1607 with Earl Patrick's Palace, built by an arrogant Earl of Orkney whose equally tyrannical father had already set up an Earl's Palace at Birsay. The newer building is one of the finest remaining examples of Renaissance architecture in Scotland, today housing an introductory exhibition to much earlier Orkney monuments.

SCALLOWAY (Shetland) Scalloway castle was built in 1600 by Patrick Stewart, the Earl of Orkney who harassed his own islanders, rebelled against his monarch, and was executed in 1615.

Museums

DERVAIG (Mull) Old Byre Heritage Centre is a crofting museum with re-creations of house interiors at the time of the Clearances, and an audio-visual programme of life at that time.

DUNROSSNESS (Shetland) Croft House Museum is set within a preserved mid-nineteenth-century thatched croft house, adjoined by original outbuildings and a working watermill.

KIRKWALL (Orkney)   Tankerness House, a sixteenth-century merchant's town house, has been laid out as a museum of Orkney life throughout the ages, including Norse influences, with frequent visiting specialized exhibitions.

LERWICK (Shetland)   Shetland Museum tells the story of man in the islands throughout the ages, including colourful displays of art and textiles, folklore, fishing and shipping.

LIONEL (Lewis)   The Ness Historical Society maintains a permanent display of photographs, documents, slides and videos on local subjects, with relics of crofting and fishing, in the Old School. About 20 miles south-west, the Shawbost School Museum also has exhibits devoted to crofting, fishing and weaving, and nearby a Norse watermill has been restored.

PORT CHARLOTTE (Islay)   Museum of Islay Life tells the island story from prehistoric times until our own century.

Chronology of Scottish and English Monarchs

From the Norman Conquest to the Act of Union

Scotland		England	
Malcolm III ('Canmore')	1057–1093	William I	1066–1087
Donald Bane	1093–1094	William II	1087–1100
Duncan II	1094		
Donald Bane	1094–1097		
Edgar	1097–1107	Henry I	1100–1135
Alexander I ('the Fierce')	1107–1124		
David I	1124–1153	Stephen	1135–1154
Malcolm IV ('the Maiden')	1153–1165	Henry II	1154–1189
William I ('the Lion')	1165–1214	Richard I	1189–1199
Alexander II	1214–1249	John	1199–1216
Alexander III	1249–1286	Henry III	1216–1272
Margaret ('Maid of Norway')	1286–1290	Edward I	1272–1307
Interregnum	1290–1292		
John Balliol	1292–1296		
Interregnum	1296–1306		
Robert I ('the Bruce')	1306–1329	Edward II	1307–1327
David II	1329–1371	Edward III	1327–1377
Robert II	1371–1390	Richard II	1377–1399
Robert III	1390–1406	Henry IV	1399–1413
James I	1406–1437	Henry V	1413–1422
James II	1437–1460	Henry VI	1422–1461
James III	1460–1488	Edward IV	1461–1470
		Henry VI	1470–1471
		Edward IV	1471–1483
		Edward V	1483
		Richard III	1483–1485
James IV	1488–1513	Henry VII	1485–1509
James V	1513–1542	Henry VIII	1509–1547
Mary	1542–1567	Edward VI	1547–1553
		Mary I	1553–1558
		Elizabeth I	1558–1603
James VI	1567–1625		

·CHRONOLOGY·

From 1603 onwards the two countries shared a ruler but their royal designations were kept distinct, as follows:

James VI of Scotland, James I of England	1603–1625
Charles I of Scotland, Charles I of England	1625–1649
Commonwealth	1649–1660
Charles II of Scotland, Charles II of England (Crowned at Scone on New Year's Day 1651)	1660–1685
James VII of Scotland, James II of England	1685–1688
William II of Scotland, William III of England, and Queen Mary II of Scotland, Queen Mary II of England	1688–1702
Anne	1702–1714

Act of Union combining the two countries and crowns, 1707.

Select Bibliography

Essential reading for anyone interested in the relationship between Scotland's historical sites and their present appearance and lasting significance are the splendid illustrated volumes of *Exploring Scotland's Heritage* produced by HMSO, Edinburgh, under the editorship of Anna Ritchie. Titles in the series are:

> *Argyll and the Western Isles*
> *Lothian and the Borders*
> *Orkney and Shetland*
> *The Clyde Estuary and Central Region*
> *Dumfries and Galloway*
> *Grampian*
> *Fife and Tayside*

Other books listed below are recommended as being eminently readable in their own right and not merely as works of reference.

Ashley, Maurice, *The House of Stuart*. Dent, 1980.
Bain, J. (ed.), *Calendar of Border Papers*, 2 vols. H.M. General Register House, Edinburgh, 1984.
Bailey, Patrick, *Orkney*. David & Charles, 1971.
Brander, Michael, *The Making of the Highlands*. Constable, 1980.
Brown, Keith M., *Bloodfeud in Scotland*. Donald, 1986.
Cameron, Archibald, *Escape of Prince Charles Edward*. Luttrell Society, 1951.
Campbell, R. H., *Scotland since 1707*. Blackwell, 1965.

·SELECT BIBLIOGRAPHY·

Donaldson, Gordon, *Scottish Kings*. Batsford, 1977.
Donnachie, I. L. and MacLeod, I., *Old Galloway*. David & Charles, 1974.
Fraser, George M., *The Steel Bonnets*. Barrie & Jenkins, 1971.
Graham, Cuthbert, *Aberdeen and Deeside*. Hale, 1972.
Grant, James Shaw, *Highland Villages*. Hale, 1977.
Jackson, Anthony, *The Pictish Trail*. Orkney Press, 1989.
Lindsay, Maurice, *The Lowlands of Scotland*. Hale, 1977.
Linklater, Eric, *Orkney and Shetland*. Hale, 1965.
Mack, James Logan, *The Border Line*. Oliver & Boyd, 1926.
Macnab, P. A., *The Isle of Mull*. David & Charles, 1970.
Millman, R. N., *The Making of the Scottish Landscape*. Batsford, 1975.
Mitchison, Rosalind, *A History of Scotland*. Methuen, 1970.
—— *Life in Scotland*. Batsford, 1978.
Moody, David, *Scottish Local History*. Batsford, 1986.
Nicolaisen, W. F. H., *Scottish Place-names*. Batsford, 1976.
Nicolson, James R., *Beyond the Great Glen*. David & Charles, 1975.
—— *Shetland*. David & Charles, 1984.
O'Neil, Capt., *A Narrative of the Wanderings of Prince Charles Edward after the Battle of Culloden*. Privately printed, 1983.
Peck, Edward, *North-east Scotland*. Bartholomew, 1871.
Prebble, John, *Mutiny*. Penguin, 1985.
—— *The Lion in the North*. Penguin, 1988.
Ritchie, Anne, *Scotland* BC. HMSO Edinburgh, 1988.
Schei, L. V., and Moberg, G., *The Shetland Story*. Batsford, 1988.
Scott-Moncrieff, George, *The Lowlands of Scotland*. Batsford, 1939.
Stevenson, David, *The Scottish Revolution 1637–44*. David & Charles, 1973.
Tabraham, Christopher, *Scottish Castles and Fortifications*. HMSO, Edinburgh, 1986.
Tomasson, K., and Buist, F., *Battles of the '45*. Batsford, 1962.
Tough, D. L. W., *The Last Years of a Frontier*. Sandhill, 1987.
Tranter, Nigel, *The Fortified House in Scotland*, 5 vols. Oliver & Boyd, 1962–70.
Wason, Roly, *Rebel Scotland*. Exposition Press, 1976.
White, John Talbot, *The Scottish Border and Northumberland*. Eyre Methuen, 1973.
Whyte, I. and K., *Exploring Scotland's Historic Landscapes*. Donald, 1987.

Index

Illustration numbers are shown in italics

·INDEX·

Port William, 109, 130
Portpatrick, 109
Preston, 47
Preston (England), 164
Prestonpans, 170
Prestwick, 145
Pringle family, 91, 96

Queensferry, 67, 70
Queen's Own Highlanders, 175

Raigmore, 4
Railways, 70, 93, 136, 143–4, 202, 211
Ramsay, Sir Alexander, 81
Ramsay, Allan, 137
Ratho, 68
Rawlinson, Thomas, 205
Redeswire, 76
Reformation, 15, 21, 22, 222
Reivers, Border, 74ff., 112, 133
Renfrewshire, 134
Rennie, John, 47, 181, 201
Renwick, James, 122, 125
Rhum, 222
Richard I, King of England, 25
Richard III, King of England, 51
Ri Cruin, 154
Rizzio, David, 64
Robert I (Robert the Bruce), 31ff., 48, 51, 54, 105ff., 110, 145, 159, 188, 191
Robert II, 38
Robert III, 38, 48
Rognvald, Earls of Orkney, 216, 219

Roman sites and influence, 3, 4, 5, 7, 8, 40, 68, 74, 98, 134, 143, 145
Rosemarkie, 13–14
Ross and Cromarty, 153
'Rough Wooing', the, 59, 61, 69
Roxburgh (and shire), 6, 33, 50, 71, 92
Russell, Lord Francis, 76, 77
Ruthven barracks, 165, 173, 187
  castle, 86
  family, 64
  raid of, 42, 87
Ruthwell, 114–15, 130

St Andrews, 13, 17, 22–3, 42, 43, 49, 53, 60, 63, 87, 116, 145, 146
St Clair, William, Earl of Orkney, 220
St Kilda, 222, 225–6
St Mary's Loch, 74
St Vigeans, 13
Saltoun, 46
Sanquhar, 112, 122–3
Sauchieburn, 51
Scalloway, 221, 232
Scapa Flow, 217
Scone, 18, 21, 26, 28, 32, 38, 49, 51, 105
  Stone of, 14–15, 18, 32, 36–7, 195
Scots language and dialects, 9, 10
Scots tribes, 8ff.
Scott, Sir Walter, 39, 57, 70, 75, 77, 91–2, 96, 98, 101, 111, 124, 205–6, 216

Scott (*cont.*)
Sir Walter, of Buccleuch, 78
Sir Walter, of Harden, 91
Scottish Development Agency,
  184
Seafield, James Ogilvy, 1st Earl
  of, 97–8
Selgovae tribe, 4
Selkirk (and shire), 71, 75, 92,
  94, 96, 101, 121, 194
Earl of, 128
Selkirk Grace, 128
Sellar, Patrick, 180, 181, 182
Severus, Emperor, 7
Shambellie House, 133
Shebster, 11
Sheriffmuir, 164
Shetland Islands, 4, 11, 66,
  156, 214ff., *1*
Shipbuilding, 17–18, 138ff.,
  197–200
Sidlaw Hills, 16
Sigurd, Earl of Orkney, 216
  the Stout, 217
Sinclair/Ginigoe castle, 187–8
Skara Brae, 214
Skelpick, 182
Skeoch Hill, 125
Skye, 13, 174, 222, 224ff.
Smailholm tower, 91–2
Solway, firth and river, 7, 67,
  128, 130, 131
  Moss, 39, 58, 102
Soulis, Lord, 81
Souterrains, 4, 40, 182
Southey, Robert, 201
Spey, river, 171, 193, 208–9
Staffa, 222
Stair, Master of, 162
Standard, battle of the, 25

Stenton, 46
Stephen, King of England, 25
Stephenson, Robert, 143
Stevenson, Robert, 42
Stevenson, Robert Louis, xi,
  70, 146–7, 148, 229–30
Steward, Walter the, 37
Stewart family, 28–9, 48, 159
Sir James, 49
Robert, 38
Sir Walter, 49
Stewartry of Kirkcudbright,
  102–3
Stirling, x, 2, 16, 29–31, 34ff.,
  40, 42, 47, 49, 50, 51,
  55–6, 65, 87, 105, 108,
  134, 139, 164
Stone circles and standing
  stones, 1ff., 41, 81, 103,
  131, 149, 186, 210, 213–
  14, 231, *2*
Stonehaven, 108
Stornoway, 166, 227, 229
Stranraer, 102, 109, 131
Strathbogie, 193
Strathclyde, 9, 18, 134ff.
Strathearn, 177
Strathmore, 16
Strathnaver, 181
Strathpeffer, 5, 186
Strontian, 126
Stuart, Charles Edward ('The
  Young Pretender',
  'Bonnie Prince Charlie'),
  x, 56, 100, 123, 167ff.,
  188, 191, *10*
Esme (Duke of Lennox), 86
James Edward ('The Old
  Pretender'), 163ff.
Sueno's Stone, 186, *2*